D0933696

MONEY TALKS

ERICA R. GOULD

Money Talks

The International Monetary Fund,
Conditionality, and Supplementary Financiers

STANFORD UNIVERSITY PRESS

STANFORD, CALIFORNIA 2006

Stanford University Press
Stanford, California

Printed in the United States of America on acid-free,
archival-quality paper

Library of Congress Cataloging-in-Publication Data

Gould, Erica R.
    Money talks : the international monetary fund,
conditionality, and supplementary financiers /
Erica R. Gould.
        p. cm.
    Includes bibliographical references and index.
    ISBN 0-8047-5279-6 (cloth : alk. paper)
    1. International Monetary Fund.   I. Title.

HG3881.5.I58G68 2006
332.1'52—dc22   2006010489

Typeset by G & S Typesetters, Inc. in 10/14 Janson

For Tim and Henry

Contents

Acknowledgments

Over the past seven years, I have learned that a research endeavor such as this one is not only an intellectual challenge, but also a personal one. Many individuals and institutions have provided intellectual, personal, and practical support to help me complete this project.

First and foremost, I am incredibly lucky to have had Judy Goldstein as an advisor from this project's inception to its completion. Judy's mind works in original and wonderful ways, and I feel truly privileged to have been able to mull over my research questions so frequently with her. Judy has an uncanny knack for approaching the same problem (or chapter) with a fresh eye and consistently providing that incisive comment which sends you scurrying back to your notes to unravel the logic that you have constructed and rebuild it on a sturdier foundation. Although Judy's intellectual mark is apparent throughout this book, her biggest contribution has been much more personal. Over the years, she has been not only a wonderful mentor, but also a close friend and inspiring role model.

Both Judy and Stephen Krasner, my other principal advisor, taught me the important lesson that your harshest critics are often your greatest allies. Steve offered this wonderful, dichotomous mix of penetrating, relentless criticism, and calming support and encouragement. He taught me to think big when generating an original idea, to have fun while thrashing that idea into a testable, coherent argument, and to be practical in creating a feasible research design.

Stanford is intellectually exciting and vigorous, yet relaxed and friendly; it was an ideal place to be trained and socialized as a political scientist. Numerous other Stanford faculty members provided extremely valuable feedback and support in the early stages of this book project, including Steve Haber, Peter Henry, Nick Hope, Simon Jackman, Mike McFaul, and Paul Sniderman.

In addition, there have been many individuals from Stanford University Libraries and the International Monetary Fund archives without whom I could have never completed my empirical research. From the Stanford University Libraries, thanks go to Chuck Eckman, Judy Esenwein, and Ron Nakao. The IMF archives staff were extremely generous with their time in retrieving and vetting over 20 boxes of documents, copying the documents I requested, and allowing me to visit the archives for several two-week stretches. In particular, I thank Michelle Dolbec, Madonna Gaudette, Deloris Hermanstein, Beibei Li, Jean Marcouyeux, Kehinde Mbanefo, Norma Samson, and Craig Sevy. Numerous individuals throughout the International Monetary Fund agreed to speak with me about my research; their assistance and generosity contributed significantly to this project.

Since leaving Stanford, I have benefited from a warm, generous, and incisive intellectual community at the University of Virginia and in the broader academy. My colleagues at the University of Virginia, particularly Lawrie Balfour, Jeff Legro, John Owen, and Herman Schwartz, have helped create a welcoming and supportive new intellectual home. Tom Willett has followed this project since we first met at the American Political Science Association's Annual Meeting in 2000, always expressing excitement and interest in the development of the project, raising new questions at each iteration, and sharing contacts at the IMF. Jim Boughton, Marty Finnemore, Jeff Frieden, Miles Kahler, Lisa Martin, Helen Milner, Ashok Mody, Randy Stone, Michael Tierney, and Jim Vreeland have all offered unusually useful feedback at various stages in this project. In addition, this project has been presented in various incarnations at numerous seminars and conferences over the years. Many other participants at these seminars and conferences have influenced my thinking and contributed to this book's improvement.

Both Stanford University and the University of Virginia provided the financial support necessary to complete both the research and writing stages of this project. I could not have completed this project without the generous financial support from the following Stanford University sources: the Department of Political Science, the Graduate School of Business, the Graduate Research Opportunity program, the Admiral and Mrs. John E. Lee Fund of the Social Science History Institute, the Littlefield International Graduate Fellowship from the Institute for International Studies, and the O'Bie Schultz Fellowship in International Studies from the Institute for International Studies. The University of Virginia's generous support enabled me to revise the dissertation into a final manuscript and complete additional research through my research leave, Sesquicentennial Fellowship, and summer funding.

Many thanks go to Amanda Moran, my editor at Stanford University Press, who has been enthusiastic and supportive of this project since we met, and a calm guide through the review and production process. Thanks also go to Jared Smith, my editorial assistant, and the two anonymous reviewers for Stanford University Press.

On a more personal note, my family has been a continuous source of encouragement and stimulation. My parents, Jerry and Barbara Gould, instilled the bug of intellectual curiosity in me at a young age, and I still have some of my most stimulating conversations sitting around a dinner table with them. My sister Juliet's love and support have been invaluable. Gloria Schonwald and Gerald E. Gould were constant sources of inspiration, and continue to be. My son Henry has put everything in perspective and made me realize what pure joy really is. Finally, my deepest thanks go to my husband, Tim Bei. Without Tim's humor, support, patience, and love, I truly could never have completed such a daunting task.

MONEY TALKS

CHAPTER ONE

The Puzzle of International Monetary Fund Conditionality

Introduction

Over the last several decades, the activities of international organizations—including the United Nations, the International Monetary Fund (IMF or Fund), the World Bank, and the General Agreement on Tariffs and Trade (GATT), now the World Trade Organizations (WTO)—have expanded dramatically, landing these organizations with increasing frequency on the covers of our newspapers and drawing crowds of protesters to their meetings each year. One of the most influential and puzzling expansions in international organizational activity—the change in Fund conditionality—is the focus of this book.

Today's International Monetary Fund appears to be more of a master of states than a servant to them. When state representatives established the IMF at the Bretton Woods Conference in 1944, they did not even design it to wield power over states' policies through the conditionality arrangement, a special loan agreement that requires borrowers to meet certain targets or implement certain policies in order to receive timely installments of their Fund loan. The IMF was originally created to serve the broad, collective goal of international monetary stability by monitoring and maintaining the Bretton Woods par value exchange rate system, and it loaned resources on a revolving basis to help members offset short-term payments imbalances and thereby defend their exchange rates. In 1952, the Fund first attached conditions to its loans, and since then, Fund conditionality has changed dramatically. The number of conditions that a borrowing member must meet has increased. The types of conditions have evolved, from broad macroeconomic targets in the 1950s and 1960s to "microconditionality" today, which specifies conditions pertaining to policy implementation in great detail. The Fund's loans are now generally larger, longer term, and tackle new problems. Today the Fund offers advice and sets conditions not only on policies from areas of long-standing focus like exchange rates and credit expansion, but also new areas of concentration, including governance and enterprise reform.

These changes in the terms of Fund conditional loan arrangement influence the policies and the political and economic trajectories of states and individuals all over the world. In the 2001–2002 fiscal year alone, 69 countries participated in Fund conditionality agreements.[1] According to one congressionally mandated report released in 2000, Fund conditionality in its current form "has given the IMF a degree of influence over member countries' policy making that is unprecedented for a multilateral organization . . . and has undermined national sovereignty."[2] In response to these conditionality agreements that reverse government policies and arguably eat away at citizen control of their governments, citizens in borrowing countries around the world—Egyptians in 1977, Moroccans in 1981, Sudanese in 1982, Dominicans in 1984, Koreans and Indonesians in 1998, to name just a few— have protested and often rioted.[3] More recently (and for less coherent reasons), citizens from developed countries have joined the protests, marching in Washington, DC, Prague, and elsewhere, against the expansion of Fund conditionality.

What makes these changes in Fund conditionality so puzzling is that, despite this great influence over the policies of countries around the world, the Fund appears to be exercising power over member states in a way not only that its founders did not intend, but even more disconcertingly, in a way that the international consensus opposes. The key changes in the terms of conditional loan arrangements—the increase in the number of conditions, the change in the types of conditions, the structure of the agreements, and the goals of the recommended programs—have long been the subject of perennial debate and dissent. In fact, the Fund's governing body of state representatives, the Executive Board, has repeatedly passed "conditionality guidelines" to rein in the number of conditions and limit the inclusion of intrusive, policy-oriented conditions. But recently these changes have provoked a more vocal and coherent opposition.[4]

In the wake of the Asian financial crisis, a broad coalition—from esteemed economists and top IMF officials to powerful state representatives and nongovernmental activists—has argued that these expansions in conditionality, particularly the increase in long-term conditional loan agreements with numerous conditions—were misguided and should be reversed.[5] Some critics have argued that Fund conditionality has expanded far beyond the Fund's original mandate of low or no conditionality lending for short-term payments imbalances and that the Fund should return, at least in part, to this original mandate. For instance, when Lawrence Summers was secretary of the Treasury under President Bill Clinton, he called for a return to the Fund's core mandate of short-term emergency financing, rather than longer-term development lending with numerous structural conditions. The Fund's managing director from 2000 to 2004, Horst Köhler, had also argued that Fund conditionality had expanded excessively and that the Fund must "reduce the conditions it attaches to its lending."[6] Other critics contend that original mandate aside, the current forms of Fund conditionality are ineffective, even harmful, to borrowing countries and need to change. For instance, Joseph Stiglitz has focused on the economic costs, arguing that the IMF uses outdated, inappropriate economic models and simplistically applies a "'one-size-fits-all' approach" to designing policy programs that have actually depressed growth and disproportionately hurt the poor.[7] Others focus on the political costs associated with the expansion of Fund conditionality, arguing that these changes in conditionality have deepened the Fund's intrusion on the domestic sovereignty of borrowing member states and worsened the "democratic deficit" inherent in international level domestic policy making.[8] A report written by a group of academic economists, each of whom had spent time working at the Fund, urged the Fund to limit the use of structural conditions that "are often interfering with sovereignty."[9] The IFIAC (or Meltzer Commission), established by the Republican U.S. Congress in 1998, unanimously recommended that "the International Monetary Fund should restrict its lending to the provision of short-term liquidity," and that "the current practice of extending longer-term loans for poverty reduction and other purposes should end."[10] The Fund's conditional loan arrangements, they argued, "have not ensured economic progress" and "have undermined national sovereignty and often hindered the development of responsible, democratic institutions that correct their own mistakes and respond to changes in external conditions."

Today, seemingly everyone, from economists to activists, from politicians to Fund staff, and from the left and the right, seems to agree that Fund conditionality has expanded beyond the Fund's original mandate and that, for various reasons, this expansion is bad. These critics make strange bedfellows. Their overwhelming consensus about the inappropriateness of Fund conditionality raises the question: why are Fund conditional loan agreements designed this way? What has driven these changes in Fund conditionality over time? How did the Fund move from being circumscribed in its activities and interactions with states to being a powerful player regularly accused of dictating policies, altering domestic political debates, and violating state sovereignty? This puzzle is particularly intriguing because the conventional wisdoms about IMF conditionality and the drivers of international organizational activity (to the extent that those conventional wisdoms exist) appear inadequate in explaining the changes we observe when rich empirical work is undertaken.

Unraveling the puzzle of Fund conditionality is important not only to assess the immediate normative implications and to further our understanding of how the *content* of "second-image reversed" international influence is constructed and defined.[11] Unpacking this puzzle may also help us better understand international organizational activity and the degree to which states control international organizations. Moreover, it may speak to broader debates in the field of political science about the compatibility of democracy and development, the role of states in the international system today, and, more broadly, what the drivers of institutional and organizational change are.

Conventional Wisdoms

For many, the changes in Fund conditionality may not appear puzzling at all. Two general explanations of Fund activity and Fund conditionality already dominate the scholarly and nonscholarly literature.[12] Pundits, practitioners, and academics alike tend to argue that increases in Fund conditionality are either being driven by the Fund's most powerful shareholder, the United States, or that Fund bureaucrats themselves have defined the contours of Fund conditionality change. A third explanation, considered here but less frequently articulated to explain Fund conditionality change over time, suggests that the changes have been driven by the borrowing states themselves—by their demands and their needs. In this section, I briefly introduce each of these arguments and suggest why they initially appear inadequate in explaining the increasing stringency of Fund conditionality. Later chapters address the two main alternative explanations—the realist and bureaucratic arguments—more systematically. Chapter 4 considers the observable implications of these arguments; Chapters 5 through 7 use proxy variables to "test" these arguments quantitatively using the Conditionality Data Set (Appendix 1) and qualitative analyses.

The most common explanation is that changes in Fund activity, including the design of Fund conditionality agreements, have been externally driven by powerful states. Realist scholars have argued that powerful states, most often the United States, use international organizations like the Fund as tools to achieve their own foreign policy goals. For realists, international institutions (IIs) and international organizations (IOs) are themselves epiphenomenal, reflecting and acting according to the interests and preferences of powerful states.[13] By this logic, changes in IO activity, like the particular changes in Fund conditionality, should presumably have been pushed by powerful states—either because of a change in powerful state preferences or a change in the distribution of power.

The conventional wisdom is that the United States dictates Fund activities, and therefore the shifts in Fund conditionality reflect U.S. preferences. Examples of this argument abound in the mainstream media and academic literature.[14] Many realists assume that the state is a unitary actor, and thus powerful state preferences over IMF activity derive from broad state interests.

For instance, Strom Thacker, using Fund lending data as a proxy for Fund behavior, argues that the United States' political preferences and the international balance of power are the "underlying causes of the IMF's behavior."[15]
He argues that during the Cold War, the United States used IMF loans as car-
rots to entice countries to become more closely aligned with the United
States, as measured by certain key United Nations votes. After the Cold War
and the collapse of bipolarity, both a country's initial voting position relative
to the United States' (at time $t - 2$) and its subsequent movement (from $t - 2$
to $t - 1$) are important in determining whether or not a country is granted a
Fund loan at time t. Similarly, Barro and Lee find that a country's "political
proximity to the United States," as measured by its UN voting record,
influences the country's probability of receiving a Fund loan.[16] With respect
to Fund conditionality in particular, Dreher and Jensen also use UN voting
patterns as a measure of alliance with the United States and find that "closer
U.S. allies . . . receive IMF loans with fewer conditions" by using a sample of
agreements from 1997 to 2003.[17] Miles Kahler has argued that the United
States under the Reagan administration successfully pushed for increases in
the stringency of Fund conditionality.[18] Others also argue that the United
States (and other powerful states) dictate Fund activities but consider the domestic sources of their preferences. Joseph Stiglitz contends that the terms of
Fund conditionality reflect the preferences of the U.S. Treasury in particular.[19] Thomas Oatley argues that the IMF's lending decisions are influenced
by several powerful states, and that their preferences are defined by domestic
constituents, particularly their commercial banks' interests.[20] Other U.S. domestic institutions and groups (such as labor and environmental groups) have
expressed preferences about IMF activity and could similarly influence U.S.
preferences over Fund conditionality, according to this logic.

These types of arguments not only have a good deal of theoretical and intellectual support, but they also seem particularly plausible given the design
and structure of the Fund itself. The Fund was established by states at the
1944 Bretton Woods conference in New Hampshire in order to serve state
interests.[21] The IMF is funded by states. Larger economies provide most of
the Fund's lifeblood through the Fund's quota system, with the United States
providing the largest share of the Fund's resources (about 17.5% today, and
nearly 38% at the Fund's founding). State representatives sit on the Fund's
two main governing bodies, the Board of Governors and the Executive Board;

for many of their decisions, state representatives vote according to a weighted voting system, whereby an individual state's quota contribution share corresponds to their voting power. In other words, powerful states' greater influence over the Fund's activities is institutionalized through the weighted voting system in the Fund's governing bodies (although actually this weighted voting rule does *not* govern the decisions to approve individual conditionality agreements or make conditionality policy). Moreover, the Executive Board, which approves most day-to-day activities, including the approval of conditionality agreements, functions according to a "consensus method," by which decisions are rarely voted upon explicitly, but instead the secretary and managing director "surmise" the consensus decision.[22] Some argue that this consensus method further empowers the more powerful states, which are able to define the terms of the consensus.

However, even a quick glance at the evidence suggests that this argument may not be very convincing at explaining the changes in Fund conditionality, most immediately because the United States (and other powerful states, although I will focus here on the United States for argument's sake) has been arguing since the late 1960s that the Fund should stick to short-term lending with less conditionality, rather than long-term lending with more conditionality. In other words, the United States and other powerful state representatives have fought against what they have perceived as an increase in the stringency of Fund conditionality and attempted to rein in Fund conditionality. Starting in the late 1960s, the United States (and the Executive Board more generally) vocally criticized the Fund's "proliferation of conditions" and passed the first Conditionality Guidelines in 1968, which directed the Fund staff to minimize the number of conditions required.[23] Since then, although there has been some natural ebb and flow in U.S. policy, U.S. and Executive Board criticism of the Fund expansion of conditionality has continued. Later, in 1979 and most recently in 2002, the Fund's Executive Board revised the Conditionality Guidelines a second and third time. Both times, Fund conditionality had increased in the interim, and both times, the Executive Board sternly instructed the Fund's staff and management to limit the number of conditions required by its programs and require fewer of the intrusive, policy-oriented conditions.[24] The Reagan administration opposed the IMF's "drift" into "longer-term adjustment programs," rather than its mandated short-term balance of payments loans.[25] More recently, the Clinton administration has criticized the IMF's expansion of conditionality and increase in longer-term adjustment loans. In December 1999, as mentioned earlier, Treasury Secretary Larry Summers presented a reform program that included fundamental changes in Fund practices, including returning to the Fund's core mandate of short-term emergency financing, rather than the current practice of longer-term development lending with numerous structural conditions.[26] Similarly, President George W. Bush's Treasury Secretary John Snow also argued that the Fund needed to "refocus on its core area of expertise," noting that "when it comes to lending, the United States favors conditions focused on the core macroeconomic challenges."[27]

At first glance, then, the changes in Fund conditionality do not seem to reflect U.S. preferences (whether they were initially determined by broad state interests or domestic pressures), and therefore the United States does not appear to be the main driving force behind these changes. If anything, the United States and the Executive Board more broadly have appeared to be trying to reverse the increasing stringency and intrusiveness of Fund conditionality. These impressions are admittedly preliminary. Chapters 4 through 7 deal more explicitly and systematically with assessing the explanatory power of the realist argument by considering several of its observable implications, through large-N quantitative and small-N qualitative work. They too find that this conventional wisdom does not appear to be a powerful explanation for the changes in Fund conditionality.

Another common argument is that changes in Fund conditionality have been driven by the Fund's bureaucracy. Scholars employ either a more rationalist logic or a more sociological logic to argue that the IMF should be understood as an actor in itself, not just a conduit for state preferences, with autonomy to pursue its own interests or goals. The two camps differ both in how they conceive of the source of organizational autonomy and in the purposes to which this autonomy is put.[28] However, they both point to the organization's bureaucracy—either its interests or its culture—as the driving force behind organizational activity. Any changes in Fund activity must then be understood as a product of the Fund's bureaucracy, either its interests or its culture.

Those from the rationalist school tend to argue that IOs achieve a degree of autonomy as a result of principal-agent issues of informational asymmetry and incomplete monitoring.[29] IOs use their autonomy to pursue "power, prestige and amenities," often operationalized as budget or task expansion. For instance, in a series of articles Roland Vaubel focuses on the Fund bureaucracy's efforts to "maximize their budget, their staff and their independence."[30] Vaubel views Fund conditionality—and the expansion of Fund conditionality—as a mechanism to pursue those interests. Similarly, George Shultz has argued that this is a classic case of mission creep. In his words, "In the tradition of skilled bureaucrats, the IMF has turned to new areas and has managed to expand substantially its financial resources and, in the process, its influence."[31]

By contrast, those from the sociological school emphasize that the international organization is a product of its institutional environment, not actor interests per se, and achieves its independence from states as a result of its expertise and externally derived legitimacy.[32] As Barnett and Finnemore have written, "IOs can become autonomous sites of authority, independent from the state 'principals' who may have created them, because of power flowing from at least two sources: (1) the legitimacy of the rational-legal authority they embody, and (2) control over technical expertise and information."[33] IOs use that autonomy to pursue activities determined by their specific bureaucratic culture, defined, for instance, by their professional training or other particularlistic factors.[34] Organizations can use that autonomy to impact our social understanding of the world around us, by classifying and defining actors, and by developing and spreading norms.[35] For instance, in their 2004 book on international organizational "dysfunction," Michael Barnett and Martha Finnemore address the puzzle of Fund conditionality directly. They argue that the Fund staff's expertise has given them a great deal of latitude to develop and adjust certain intellectual models, which in turn justify the expansion of Fund conditionality. Mimicking Kuhn's scientists, Fund economists include new conditions outside their area of expertise when existing models and methods fail.[36]

Initially, both the rationalist and sociological variants of the bureaucratic argument appear to be plausible explanations for the expansion of Fund conditionality. The Fund staff certainly have a good deal of expertise and specialized knowledge that, according to both variants, may contribute to organizational autonomy. The Fund's historic opacity protects its staff by insulating them from intensive lobbying by domestic interest groups and subsequently depressing state activism in controlling their activities.[37] Finally, the Fund staff have agenda-setting powers; they design preliminary versions of the loan agreements, negotiate them with borrowers during staff mission trips to the prospective borrowing country, and then present the Executive Board with the negotiated agreement, which can be voted up or down.[38] The Executive Board rarely votes down or even modifies staff proposals, particularly concerning loan arrangements. This suggests that the Fund staff have an overwhelming amount of discretion in choosing its actual activity outcome (within the acceptable range defined by states).[39] In other words, the IMF appears to be a particularly apt example of an organization that may be able to exercise some autonomy—whether due to bureaucratic interests or culture—over its own activities.

However, I also found these explanations initially unconvincing in explaining the changes in Fund conditionality and the design of these agreements. For one, evidence from the Fund archives indicated that staff actually opposed many of the changes in conditionality because they felt that these areas were outside of their core expertise and not easily measurable, among other things. In addition, both variants provide plausible explanations for why organizational activities may change—because bureaucrats want to increase their power or because of their bureaucratic culture—but they do not provide clear explanations of why international organizational activities changed in these particular ways. For instance, the rationalist variant suggests that Fund bureaucrats pushed for more stringent conditionality to increase their power and prestige. Similarly, the sociological variant suggests that Fund conditionality changed because the bureaucratic culture impelled the Fund economists to seek out new intellectual, causal models as their old models fail. However, the particular pattern of Fund conditionality change matters to borrowers, to politicians, and to citizens around the world. The Fund has been advising countries and monitoring programs for years, but not until the late 1980s were countries required to implement Fund-designed investment programs and Fund-approved tax reforms as a condition of the program; and not until the early 1990s was the taboo on advising countries about the redistributive consequences of certain policies lifted. Why did the Fund condition use of its resources on those policies in the late 1980s and early 1990s but not sooner, or later? Neither of the bureaucratic variants provides a clear explanation of the particular changes in the content of Fund conditionality. In this book, I advance an argument that attempts to explain not only why change occurs, but why we observe particular changes in the design of Fund conditionality agreements. Chapters 4 through 7 include more systematic testing of these bureaucratic variants. Chapter 4 considers the observable implications of both variants, whereas chapters 5 through 7 "test" the rationalist variant by using the Conditionality Data Set (Appendix 1) and quantitative and qualitative analyses.

A third alternative argument suggests that changes in Fund conditionality have ultimately been driven by the borrowing states themselves. The general insight is that domestic politicians use international organizations or institutions to help them fight their own domestic battles (or tie their own hands).[40] For instance, with respect to the IMF in particular, James Vreeland has argued that domestic politicians use Fund conditional loan agreements as political cover to implement their preferred policies and mute domestic opposition.[41] This type of domestic political argument has been more frequently used to explain cross-national variation in Fund programs or to explain why borrowers enter into Fund programs, rather than over-time change.

In order to explain change over time, one would have to argue that there has been a systematic, longitudinal change in the Fund's clientele (or their preferences) that has led to different demands regarding the terms of Fund conditionality agreements over time. For instance, Devesh Kapur has argued that changes in Fund activities have been driven at least in part by a change in the Fund's clientele.[42] As the more developed and powerful countries stopped borrowing from the IMF, they tightened the terms of Fund conditionality agreements for the less powerful, developing countries. The Fund itself has also articulated a version of this argument: Fund conditionality has changed to respond to the changing economic needs of borrowers.[43] The official position is that borrowers with excessive foreign debt or structural impediments to growth have increasingly turned to the Fund for assistance, requiring more detailed and intensive Fund programs. The Fund has argued that Fund program design has changed to meet the objective needs of borrowers facing increasingly severe payments imbalances and economic crises.[44] The Fund has also argued that less developed countries require different Fund conditionality—including more or different binding conditions—than more developed countries, and has responded by developing different lending vehicles that required more detailed conditionality.[45] As the economic needs or attributes of borrowing member states change, so do the activities of the Fund including the terms of Fund conditional loan arrangements. One could imagine other versions of the domestic argument. For instance, democracies may interact differently with the Fund. Politicians in countries with democratic institutions and viable, active oppositions may be more likely to try to tie their own hands by means of international agreements and similarly demand more stringent, encompassing Fund conditionality agreements.[46] As a result, it may have been global shifts in domestic-level institutions that drove the longitudinal changes in Fund conditionality. As the third wave of democratization spread, the mix of borrowing countries became more democratic; they demanded more constraining agreements from the Fund to tie their hands; hence, Fund conditionality changed.

This type of domestic-level argument is articulated less frequently as an explanation of Fund conditionality change than the realist or bureaucratic arguments, but it also seems quite plausible. One would certainly hope that the Fund tailors the terms of its agreements to the specific needs and demands of Fund borrowers, rather than applying a "cookie-cutter" program, as has been suggested by Joseph Stiglitz.[47] It is indisputable that over time the Fund's clientele has shifted in a variety of different ways—less "developed," more severe balance of payments problems, greater poverty, more democratic institutions—that may have affected the terms of Fund conditionality agreements. In the hopes that Fund programs are tailored to the particular needs and demands of borrowers, this alternative explanation is also addressed more systematically in the empirical chapters. However, initial indicators suggest that this type of domestic-level explanation may not account for many of the broad changes in Fund conditionality that we observe. First, if Fund conditionality agreements are responsive to borrower demands, then one should presumably observe broad cross-national variation in the terms of Fund conditionality agreements. If the terms of Fund conditional loan arrangements are reflected the domestic political needs of borrower governments, one would see greater variation in the design of programs and more particularistic policies that served individual borrower government domestic needs, such as side payments to constituency groups. The Conditionality Data Set reveals that programs are not the simple "cookie-cutter" models that Stiglitz describes; however, they also do not exhibit as much variation as a domestic political argument would imply. Second, if Fund conditionality agreements are not responsive to borrower government demands, but instead borrower's economic needs (which is the Fund's argument), then we are still missing the political link. Why is the Fund empowered to expand its power and activities in the face of a changing functional environment? Why is the Fund able to fill the vacuum created by these new needs? Even in the face of new needs and problems, a political actor, whether it be the borrowers, the powerful states, or the organization itself, would need to assign or approve this expansion of Fund activity. The agent is missing from this explanation, and thus the puzzle remains.

Argument and Roadmap

Why has International Monetary Fund conditionality changed in particular ways over the last 50 years? What drives changes in international organizational activity broadly? Contrary to conventional explanations, I argue that the changes in the terms of Fund conditionality agreements are best explained by shifts in the sources of borrowing state financing.[48] The Fund regularly relies on external financing to supplement its loans to countries facing payments imbalances. As a result, these supplementary financiers are able to exercise leverage over the Fund and the design of its conditionality programs. The supplementary financiers may exercise their influence either directly, by actively communicating their preferences to IMF staffers, management, or borrowing state representatives, or indirectly, by having the Fund staffers anticipate supplementary financier preferences and adjust the design of a particular Fund program to those anticipated preferences in order to encourage an inflow of supplementary financing. The different types of supplementary financiers—including creditor states, private financial institutions, and multilateral organizations—have systematically different preferences over the terms of Fund conditionality arrangements. Thus, many of the changes in Fund conditionality can be explained by the shifting mix of supplementary financing over the past 50 years. As the sources of state financing have changed from being dominated by creditor states to a more diverse mix of creditor states, private financial institutions, and multilateral organizations, so have the demands on the Fund and the Fund's subsequent activity.

The book will proceed as follows. Chapter 2 will present the book's central argument—the theory of supplementary financier influence—in greater detail. The theory itself has two main parts. First, the static part of the argument concerns why supplementary financiers exercise leverage over the Fund. The second, dynamic part of the argument concerns the shift in the sources of supplementary financing, which has contributed to a change in the content of Fund conditionality. The book's conclusions are supported by rich empirical material gathered directly from the IMF archives, including descriptive statistics and statistical analyses using an original data set, the Conditionality Data Set described in Appendix 1, as well as case studies substantiated with archival and interview evidence.

Chapter 3 focuses on the dependent variable. It rewrites the history of Fund conditionality. I use previously published secondary sources, as well as original archival research from the IMF archives and the Conditionality Data Set, which is the first (and, to my knowledge, currently the only) data set coding the terms of 249 Fund conditionality agreements from 1952, when Fund conditionality began, to 1995. It includes extensive descriptive statistics, which clarify how Fund conditionality has changed both longitudinally and cross-sectionally.

Chapters 4 through 7 provide several different empirical assessments of the supplementary financier argument versus the alternative arguments. Chapter 4 compares the broad observable implications of the realist and bureaucratic alternative arguments with the actual record of Fund conditionality change, as elucidated by the Conditionality Data Set. Chapters 5 through 7 each focus on a different type of supplementary financier: creditor states, private financial institutions, and multilateral organizations, respectively. Each chapter discusses that supplementary financier's interests in providing financing to other states, and subsequent preferences over the design of Fund conditionality agreement in detail. Three types of evidence are employed in order to establish a causal relationship between the supplementary financier and particular changes in Fund conditionality. First, the pattern of supplementary financing is compared to the predicted changes in Fund conditionality. Second, statistical tests are performed, utilizing the original Conditionality Data Set, to determine whether this type of supplementary financier seems to have influenced Fund conditionality arrangements in predicted ways, controlling for other significant variables. Once the relationship between the supplementary financier and a change in Fund conditionality is established, the third section of evidence evaluates one or more case studies of a Fund conditionality agreement to uncover the causal mechanisms by which this type of supplementary financier influences the terms of Fund conditionality agreements.

The final chapter reviews the central findings of the book and discusses how these findings relate both to the current debate on the appropriateness of Fund activity and to the general literature on international organizations.

CHAPTER TWO

The Theory of Supplementary Financier Influence

Argument

International Monetary Fund conditionality is influenced by supplementary financiers. The Fund often provides only a fraction of the amount of money that a country needs in order to balance its payments that year and implement the Fund's recommended program. Supplementary financiers provide financing that supplements the Fund's loans to borrowing member states. The Fund relies on this supplementary, external financing to ensure the success and feasibility of its programs. This reliance gives the supplementary financiers some leverage over the design of Fund programs. The financiers are able to make demands on the Fund, stipulating which conditions must be included in a particular Fund program in order for their financing to be forthcoming.

Supplementary financiers are a different kind of international actor. They are defined not by ascriptive characteristics or legal status, like states or even multilateral organizations, but rather by their activities and their endowments. Supplementary financiers include three types of actors: creditor states, private financial institutions (PFIs), and multilateral organizations. Each type has different reasons for providing financing to borrowing states, and therefore different preferences about how Fund programs should be designed. Creditor states, PFIs, and multilateral organizations thus try to influence the terms of Fund conditionality agreements in systematically different ways. Many of the over-time changes in Fund conditionality and the cross-sectional variation between Fund programs have been caused by the shifting mix of supplementary financiers. In 1952, when Fund conditionality began, nearly all of the supplementary financing came from creditor states, mainly from the United States. Now borrowers receive supplementary financing from a diverse set of creditor states, PFIs, and multilateral organizations. As the sources of supplementary financing have shifted and diversified, so have the demands on the Fund, and hence so have the Fund's activities, particularly the design of Fund conditionality programs.

In other words, there is a static aspect and a dynamic aspect to the puzzle of Fund conditionality and hence to this argument. The static argument is about why and how supplementary financiers influence Fund conditionality. Change, or the dynamic aspect of this argument, comes exogenously from the changes in the sources of supplementary financing. Each part will be addressed in turn.

Explaining the Influence: The Static Argument

THEORETICAL ANTECEDENTS

The static argument is built on the central insights from two strands of liberal theory: first, that nonstate actors may influence international outcomes, and second, that international institutions (IIs) and international organizations (IOs) help facilitate mutually beneficial exchange between international actors.[1] In other words, I am trying to harness the powerful insights of the neoliberal institutionalist turn without accepting its state-centric ontology. Although the state-centric turn in liberal theory may have had certain advantages (for example, increased parsimony; more obvious and falsifiable predictions), it encouraged scholars to narrow the range of questions they asked and the answers they considered, and it may have caused them to miss key relationships that produce important political and economic outcomes. This section focuses on neoliberal institutionalist (hereafter referred to just as neoliberal) insights and the reasons for broadening our analysis of the Fund to include nonstate actors.

The trademark neoliberal insight about IIs and IOs, including the International Monetary Fund, is that they are Pareto improving. Absent cooperation, state interaction often results in a Pareto-suboptimal outcome, often as a result of credible commitment, transaction cost, and incomplete contracting problems. IIs and IOs help states overcome barriers to cooperation and reach mutually beneficial outcomes by restructuring their incentives.[2] They can increase the benefits and reduce the costs of cooperation by lengthening actors' time horizons through iteration, fostering issue linkage and side payments, creating a focal point, and increasing information.[3] IIs and IOs, like the Fund, thereby serve the collective interests of states. They are both forums for and "agents in" interstate cooperation, enabling states to achieve greater absolute gains.[4] For example, George von Furstenberg has argued that the International Monetary Fund promotes efficient exchange—namely, financing—between debtor and creditor states, and thus helps them achieve a more efficient outcome.[5]

For neoliberals, the key actors are states, and therefore IIs and IOs help facilitate exchange between states. Although this simplifying assumption may be analytically useful and even accurate in the case of some IIs and IOs, it is misleading in the case of the IMF. The Fund's main activities—promoting exchange rate stability, helping countries resolve payments imbalances, and so on—are no longer exclusively the domain of states.[6] For instance, creditor states are no longer the main source of balance-of-payments financing, and are therefore not the only actor that might benefit from the Fund's capacity to make borrowers' commitments more credible, monitor their policies, and provide signals about borrower creditworthiness.

Consequently, previous studies of the Fund have relaxed the state-as-actor assumption, for instance focusing on the Fund's role in promoting efficient exchange—again, financing—between state and nonstate actors. Both Benjamin Cohen and Charles Lipson argued that the Fund, in reaction to the changes in balance-of-payments financing in the 1970s and 1980s, evolved from an organization focused on providing financing from its own coffers or facilitating the flow from creditor states to one focused on facilitating the flow of balance-of-payments financing from private sources.[7] Cohen and Lipson separately identified an important relationship among the IMF, borrowing states, and official and private financiers. According to both scholars, the IMF facilitated mutually beneficial exchange, including new loans and debt reschedulings, between private commercial banks and borrowing states. Theirs is a typical neoliberal perspective, except that the creditors are banks, not states.

The argument presented here draws heavily on their insights and extends their implications. It acknowledges not only the role of the Fund in facilitating supplementary financing to borrowers, but also the supplementary financiers' leverage over the Fund and their influence on its activities. The Fund is not simply a neutral arbiter, stamping programs it deems acceptable, monitoring country adherence to these programs, and thereby helping both financiers and borrowers overcome their credibility problem. The Fund itself has a vested interest in the success of its programs, and as a result, it is susceptible to influence from the financiers.

The argument advanced and tested in this book builds on the insights of neoliberalism: that international institutions and organizations facilitate mutually beneficial exchange between actors and are directed by those actors. However, the actors who direct and are served by the IMF are not only states, but also other sources of financing, including PFIs and multilateral organizations.

WHY SUPPLEMENTARY FINANCIERS ARE ABLE TO INFLUENCE THE FUND

Supplementary financiers and the IMF are locked in a mutually dependent relationship. The Fund depends on supplementary financiers to help ensure the success of its loan programs and its future bargaining leverage with borrowers. In turn, supplementary financiers depend on the Fund to help facilitate their financing transactions and make borrowers' commitments more credible. As a result, supplementary financiers are both able and willing to influence the Fund's activities.

First, consider why supplementary financiers are able to influence the IMF. The Fund is an actor with interests, and supplementary financiers help the Fund maximize those interests. The Fund is composed of an international staff of economists, most trained at a few select U.S. and Western European universities.[8] Despite their diverse national backgrounds, new staff and management join the Fund with remarkably similar shared assumptions and principles influenced by their education.[9] Both the Fund's staff and its management have been trained as economists and want to be successful economists, influencing the direction of the international economy at large and the economies of individual borrowers by applying theoretical principles.[10] The failure of an implemented Fund program damages not only the reputations of the individual staff members who designed it, but also the organization's reputation and the credibility of the principles that have been applied.[11] Therefore, individually and collectively, the staff want Fund programs to succeed in measurably improving the economies in which they intervene.[12] Supplementary financiers exercise leverage over the Fund and its activities because their financing affects the success of Fund programs in two separate ways: a direct effect on the short-run success of an individual program, and a more generalized, longer-term effect on the Fund's bargaining leverage with borrowers. I will address each in turn.

Supplementary financing is often crucial for the short-run success of individual Fund programs because the Fund provides only a fraction of the amount of money necessary for a borrowing country to balance its payments and implement the Fund-designed program successfully.[13] These financing gaps were well publicized during the 1980s debt crisis, as were the Fund's efforts to line up supplementary financing. However, gaps between borrower need and Fund loans have been commonplace throughout the history of Fund conditionality. For instance, between 1954 and 1960, in 77% of the cases of Fund stabilization programs with Latin American countries, 50% or more of the country's external financing came from supplementary financiers, not from the Fund.[14] In 64% of the cases from the 1952–1995 Conditionality Data Set, the country's current account deficit was more than the amount of the entire Fund loan agreement, indicating a likely financing gap.[15] This comparison is admittedly flawed, not least because it underestimates the frequency of the financing gap. Fund loans are generally not delivered in full when the agreement is signed, but instead in segments over several months or years. For the 36% whose Fund loan was larger than their current account deficit that year, the Fund loan was delivered in five segments over 19 months on average.[16] Because the loan was not delivered in full the first year, there is a strong chance that, even for these 36%, the country's financing needs in the first year exceeded the Fund loan disbursements. Thus in most, if not all, cases, the Fund provided only a fraction of the financing needed to balance its payments that year.

Consequently, Fund programs are designed with an assumption of a certain amount of supplementary financing. Countries come to the Fund when they face payments imbalances. The Fund programs are designed to bring them back into balance through a combination of adjustment—they often demand contraction measures that are intended to reduce the existing current account deficit—and financing of the remaining deficits with Fund loans and supplementary financing.[17] Jacques Polak, former director of research and a former executive director (ED) of the Fund, sums up the Fund's reliance on supplementary financiers in this way:

> Traditionally, a key component of any Fund arrangement was that the resources provided by the Fund together with those from the World Bank, aid donors, commercial banks, and other sources, would cover the country's projected balance-of-payments gap. In the absence of an integral financing package, the Fund could not be confident that the degree of adjustment negotiated with the country would be sufficient. To this end the Fund sought *financing assurances* from other suppliers of financial assistance. In the second half of the 1980s, however, commercial banks began to exploit this approach. No longer afraid of becoming victims of a generalized debt crisis, the banks began to realize that they could insist on favorable terms for themselves by blocking a country's access to Fund credit (and to other credit linked to a Fund arrangement).[18]

In short, the Fund relies on the supplementary financiers and this allows the supplementary financiers—in this case, Polak discusses banks in particular—to "exploit" this reliance.

Supplementary financing has been factored into these programs since the 1950s, when Fund conditionality began. For example, Venezuela's 1960 stand-by arrangement stated that their deficit would be "covered" by loans from PFIs. The stand-by "proposed to finance this deficit by credits now being negotiated with foreign commercial banks."[19] Fund agreements not only stated that supplementary financing was being sought and was necessary for the country to balance, but also sometimes required a specific amount of supplementary financing as a condition of the Fund agreement. An early—and at that time rare—example of this was Argentina's 1958 stand-by arrangement, which required Argentina "to request financial assistance from sources other than the Fund" and to borrow from the Fund and those "other credit facilities" in a "proportion of 1 to at least 2 ½."[20]

In order for a country to balance its payments and implement the Fund's program, supplementary financing was almost always needed and expected. Fund programs explicitly mentioned supplementary financing, factored it in, and even required borrowers to secure it as a condition of the Fund program. Without the additional financing, the countries would not have been able to balance their payments that year and would have been forced to abandon a Fund program designed with an assumption of incoming supplementary financing.[21]

Supplementary financing is central not only to the short-run success of Fund programs, but also to the Fund's future bargaining leverage with borrowers.[22] Borrowing countries enter into Fund programs not only for Fund financing, but also for the supplementary financing that often accompanies it. Fund staffers have consistently articulated this point. For instance, during a debate about the design of Fund programs, the head of the Western Hemisphere division, Jorge Del Canto, emphasized how stand-by agreements should help borrowing countries secure supplementary financing. He wrote, "In some cases it is the establishment of confidence rather than the use of Fund resources that is the prime objective of a stand-by arrangement . . . [and that] the confidence . . . is registered directly through a flow of supporting assistance from other sources, the availability and volume of which is tied to observance of conditions in the Fund stand-by arrangement."[23] By 1970, the staff even classified some conditionality arrangements as "symbolic" when borrowing countries had no intention of borrowing from the Fund, but instead were utilizing Fund agreements exclusively for the purpose of securing non-Fund supplementary resources.[24] Consequently, if a borrowing country signs a Fund agreement and the supplementary financing is not forthcoming, future borrowing member states may be less likely to agree to the Fund's conditions or even turn to the Fund at all. Without the inflow of supplementary financing, Fund programs may be a much less attractive prospect for many Fund borrowers.

Supplementary financing impacts both the success of Fund programs and the Fund's future bargaining leverage with borrowers. As a result, the Fund has an incentive to help secure supplementary financing, particularly because many of the other factors that influence the success of Fund programs—including inter alia natural calamities, contraction of international demand for primary product exports, and regional political instability—are outside the Fund's control. The inflow of supplementary financing, on the other hand, is neither random nor automatic.

Earlier scholarship argued that the inflow of supplementary financing was more or less automatic. According to the standard "catalytic effect" argument, a Fund loan program often serves as a "good housekeeping seal of approval," increasing the creditworthiness of debtor countries and provoking an automatic inflow of outside financing.[25] Recent empirical work has challenged that argument, demonstrating that Fund programs have not been followed by an automatic inflow of private capital.[26] The way the inflow of supplementary financing works is broader than just the spontaneous reaction to the signing of a Fund program suggested by the "catalytic effect" argument and disputed by recent empirical literature on catalysis. Instead, much of the supplementary financing, the so-called "catalytic" finance, is explicitly negotiated and controlled.[27] Supplementary financing almost always accompanies Fund programs.[28] Sometimes it comes mainly from PFIs; other times it comes from creditor states or other multilateral organizations. The Fund plays an integral role in securing these fresh funds and coordinating lenders to restructure existing debt.[29] Supplementary financing packages are often negotiated concurrently with Fund program negotiations. The Fund often acts as a mediator between financier and borrower, and helps the borrower secure necessary financing.

WHY SUPPLEMENTARY FINANCIERS WANT TO INFLUENCE THE FUND

Supplementary financiers are not only able, but also willing, to influence the individual terms of Fund conditionality agreements. They often want to influence the content of the Fund's conditionality arrangements in order to increase the likelihood that the borrowing country will use its financing in ways the financier deems appropriate. Supplementary financiers and borrowers often face a credibility problem. A supplementary financier wants to provide financing as long as it is used in certain ways (for example, invested rather than consumed), and the borrowing country often pledges to use the financing just as the financier prefers. However, the borrower's (particularly a sovereign borrower's) pledge may not be credible for two reasons.

First, as a result of informational asymmetries, the supplementary financier may not know a borrower's "type" or their true preferences regarding the use of this financing (for example, their willingness to invest rather than consume). The Fund program can serve as a signal of borrower creditworthiness and thereby help financiers and borrowers overcome this impediment to mutually beneficial financing. Scholars have argued that the Fund agreement serves as a signal—either the borrower's costly signal of its commitment to reform, or the Fund's costly signal of its assessment of borrower "type" based on its own expertise and access to private information.[30] In a world of incomplete information, where financiers may not be able to assess the reliability of the current government, the Fund can signal its approval (or disapproval) of the borrower's commitment to reform by approving (or denying) a new loan program or disbursement.[31] Alternatively, the Fund can release detailed information about the borrower via published reports, press releases, or recently, with borrower approval, by posting the loan agreement on the Internet.

Second, and more importantly for the argument advanced here, is the so-called time-consistency problem.[32] Even if the borrower is earnest in pledging to use the financing as the financier prefers, the supplementary financier knows that the borrower's incentives may change once this financing is disbursed. The Fund can help financiers overcome this problem by influencing the borrower's ex post incentives through its conditionality agreements. Attempts by supplementary financiers to impose conditionality on their own, without the Fund, have not been successful.[33] Despite notoriously uneven compliance, IMF conditionality agreements do include mechanisms that shift states' incentives and allow them to make more credible commitments.[34] First, IMF financing and supplementary financing, including loans from PFIs, are often tied to the country meeting its binding conditions. The loans are often split into separate segments, and each segment is conditioned on borrower compliance with certain conditions. Thus, borrowers' "hands are tied" in that costs will be suffered ex post if they defect from the agreed policy program.[35] Second, IMF conditionality programs allow the Fund to monitor borrowing country policies in detail and publicize transgressions, thereby "reviving the reputation mechanism."[36] The IMF, through its conditionality, facilitates cooperation between creditors and borrowers by vouching for a borrower's reputation and enabling it to more credibly commit to a particular course of action. The financiers often want to influence borrower incentives and the content of this Fund conditionality program in order to better serve their own interests.

In sum, supplementary financiers are willing and able to exercise leverage over the design of Fund conditionality agreements. The Fund is vulnerable to supplementary financier influence because their financing is necessary for the short-run success and feasibility of Fund programs and for the Fund's future bargaining leverage with borrowers, and is not automatic. Supplementary financiers want to influence Fund conditionality because they want to control how their financing is utilized, and Fund conditionality arrangements help them do that.

Explaining the Change: The Dynamic Argument

DIFFERENT INTERESTS, DIFFERENT PREFERENCES

Creditor states, private financial institutions, and multilateral organizations provide financing to developing countries for different reasons. Creditor states finance for political ends. Loans, grants, and aid are political tools used to support other states or governments. Private financial institutions finance for profit. They make loans to and investments in countries that they expect will yield a positive return. Multilateral organizations finance for policy ends. Loans or grants are made to encourage policy reform or maintenance.

The International Monetary Fund serves the interests of supplementary financiers and the recipients of that financing by making the recipients' commitments more credible. The IMF acts as a commitment mechanism, facilitating the flow of financing from financiers to developing country recipients. States, private financial institutions, and multilateral organizations each have different interests in financing and therefore have different preferences over Fund activity. Their preferences can be deduced from their interests. This section discusses these supplementary financier interests and preferences regarding the design of Fund conditionality agreements briefly. The discussion is resumed and extended in each of the empirical chapters on creditor states, private financial institutions, and multilateral organizations (Chapters 5–7).

I assume that creditor states are rational and unitary, and that they provide financing to maximize political ends. This assumption of the state as a rational, unitary, self-interested actor is one that many scholars have adopted because of its parsimony and power.[37] The assumption that states finance for political ends simply means that aid or bilateral loans are political, not financial, investments. Political (versus financial) investments are only made in governments or in government entities that the creditor states want to support. Bilateral loans and aid are only given to allies, not enemies.

This book is not specifically concerned with how states' interests are determined. Presumably domestic interest groups and national history, as well as more traditional concerns of size, proximity, and power, influence how states define their political priorities. However, when creditor states act by providing supplementary financing, they are serving these broad political interests, however aggregated and defined, not the narrow interests of particular groups. These broad political interests include which other governments or states are considered allies and the degree to which those other governments or states merit their (financial) support. This book is concerned with state interests for a narrow purpose: to understand why creditor states provide financing to other states and thereby derive state preferences over Fund activity.

Creditor states provide financing for political ends. They are less concerned with being paid back than PFIs. Aid and bilateral loans are political, not financial, investments. Aid is often—but not always—given to allies, and therefore creditor states are often interested in preserving political stability.[38] As a result, creditor states generally prefer Fund conditional loan arrangements to be relatively less stringent than the other supplementary financiers.[39] Although creditor states want borrowers to agree to certain conditions, they prefer Fund arrangements to allow borrowers to maintain some political room for maneuver. Moreover, in the Fund's earliest days, it was much less clear which countries would be creditors and which would be debtors in any given year.[40] As a result, creditor states may have had an additional reason to prefer relatively lenient loan arrangements: the looming threat that they could swing from creditor to debtor and be forced to swallow the Fund's bitter pill themselves.

Largely because creditor states want Fund programs to encourage discipline but not to destabilize an important ally, creditor states often prefer Fund conditional loan arrangements that are less constraining, offering borrowing states more political wiggle room. I operationalize this preference in two ways. First, I consider the number of "binding conditions." (Binding conditions trigger the suspension of the Fund loan if they are violated, are coded by the Conditionality Data Set, and are introduced in more depth in Chapter 3 and Appendix 1.) If creditor states prefer Fund loan agreements to be relatively less constraining, then all else equal, they should prefer Fund loan agreements with relatively fewer binding conditions. Second, I divided all binding conditions into two groups: targets or procedures. Targets specify only the ends that need to be met and allow domestic politicians to choose whichever means are politically feasible. For instance, a target may specify that the borrower limit its fiscal deficit or credit to a certain amount by whatever methods the borrower deems appropriate. Targets are less politically constraining than procedural conditions, which specify both means and ends. For instance, a procedural condition may direct the country to implement a specific social security reform plan approved by Fund staffers and with evident distributional—and hence political—consequences. If creditor states prefer relatively less constraining Fund programs, then they should prefer Fund programs with more targets relative to procedural conditions. Creditor state interests and preferences thus generate two hypotheses:

HYPOTHESIS 1   *If a country receives relatively more (less) supplementary financing from creditor states, then its Fund loan arrangement should include relatively fewer (more) binding conditions.*

HYPOTHESIS 2   *If a country receives relatively more (less) supplementary financing from creditor states, then its Fund loan arrangement should include relatively more (less) targets versus procedural conditions.*

PRIVATE FINANCIAL INSTITUTIONS

As capital mobility has increased, so has the influence of supplementary financiers from the private sector. Private financial institutions provide financing to Fund borrowers in order to make a profit.[41] They extend loans to and make investments in countries when they expect a positive return, and they want Fund programs to help ensure their profitable return. This profit assumption was induced via secondary source materials and interviews with private financiers, but it is hardly surprising. Banks and private investors loan to or invest in developing countries' public or private sectors in order to make a profit. Banks serve their profit-minded shareholders. Investors choose investments that they hope will yield better returns than known alternatives, such as interest returns on bank deposits.

Although this profit motive may seem obvious, others have argued that private financiers' international loans and investments reflect their home country's political interests rather than a profit motive. It remains an issue of debate how influential home governments are in deciding which projects, countries, or companies receive financing from PFIs and the terms of that financing. For instance, Ethan Kapstein argued that states are still the most important actor in the global economy and are able to control the activities of banks.[42] Banks themselves acknowledge a degree of political influence. For instance, in its internal booklet on credit decisions, the Bank of America states, "We do not want to make loans for purposes or to customers detrimental to the interests of the United States." However, although banks certainly do not want to lend to projects, companies, or countries antithetical to home country interests, this does not mean that home countries are able to determine who received financing and the terms of that financing. Although a small proportion of borrowers or investments may be off-limits because they are detrimental to the home county's interests, within the larger pool of possible investments and borrowers, decisions are made due to profit, not political calculations.

This study focuses explicitly on commercial banks (as opposed to, for instance, private investors) as private supplementary financiers, because they are the primary source of private supplementary financing during the period under study. Traditionally, banks make money by extending loans and charging a higher interest rate on that loan than they are paying to depositors.[43]

When considering whether or not to extend a loan to a potential borrower, banks consider potential benefits (for example, income earned from loan and interest repayment; future business resulting from establishment or solidification of banker-client relationship) and potential risks (for example, creditworthiness; recoverable assets in the case of default). Bankers are willing to make loans with a reasonable degree of risk both because of the potential for gain and because of "supply pressure." They try to maintain a balance between loan "productivity (building loan volume at a reasonable cost to the bank) and [loan] quality (ensuring that the loans we make will get paid back as agreed)."[44] In deciding whether or not to extend a loan to a potential borrower, bankers will consider the potential borrower's creditworthiness (for example, both the capacity and the willingness to repay; expected income); lower probability risks and benefits (for example, reclaimable assets in the case of default, their position in relation to other creditors with respect to collateral security or default clauses; potential for future business); and supply concerns (for example, pressure to make loans from the bank's end).[45] If they are solely concerned with the profit from this transaction, then they have a medium-term perspective: the length of the loan itself. However, in some instances—for example, if the bank does not consider this loan to be particularly profitable but hopes to initiate a longer-term, profitable relationship with this borrower—banks may have a longer-term perspective.[46]

In short, private financial institutions like commercial banks are less concerned with political stability per se; they are interested in economic returns. For most of the period under investigation, the main PFI supplementary financiers were commercial banks, and they wanted Fund loan agreements to increase the probability that their loans would be paid back. This interest may manifest itself in different preferences regarding the terms of Fund agreements. The empirical section focuses on one element of the design of Fund programs that isolates the influence of PFIs best: a certain class of binding conditions, labeled "bank-friendly" conditions, which specify that the country must pay back a commercial bank creditor as a condition of its Fund loan. In other words, this condition makes defaulting on a bank loan more costly for borrowers and thereby increases the likelihood of repayment.

When should we observe PFI influence over Fund conditional loan agreements? Whereas creditor states and multilateral organizations have legitimate, established mechanisms to coordinate their demands and influence the Fund (for instance, through the Executive Board or joint Fund-Bank missions, respectively), PFIs do not. In fact, PFIs are officially not supposed to influence the content of Fund programs at all. As a result, although creditor state and multilateral organizational influence on Fund programs should be directly proportional to their relative contribution of supplementary financing, PFI influence may not be. Instead, PFI influence hinges on their ability to generate a credible threat that substantial financing will be lost if Fund activities do not conform to their preferences. As will be discussed in greater depth in Chapter 6, the PFI threat will only be credible under certain conditions: if they are organized, and if the threat is ex post incentive compatible.

The supplementary financier argument suggests that PFIs want Fund conditionality agreements to increase the expected profitability of their loans and will be able to influence the terms of Fund conditionality arrangements when they can generate a credible threat to withhold necessary supplementary financing if their demands are not met. The PFI threat will only be credible if they are organized and if the threat is ex post incentive compatible. The supplementary financier argument thus generates the following testable hypothesis:

HYPOTHESIS 3   *If PFIs are organized and can credibly threaten to withhold/ provide financing from/for a particular country, then that country's Fund program should be systematically more likely to include "bank-friendly" conditions, holding other variables constant.*

MULTILATERAL ORGANIZATIONS

Multilateral organizations finance for policy ends. This assumption was also induced through secondary source materials and interviews. It implies that multilateral organizations are actors unto themselves, not simply empty shells implementing state preferences. Multilateral organizations are interested in certain policy ends and make loans in order to encourage the implementation or maintenance of these policies. This depiction of multilateral organizations is consistent with my depiction of the International Monetary Fund. The IMF is also motivated by certain policy interests. The Fund provides financing to borrowers in order to encourage certain policies, and it responds to the demands of external financiers by changing its programs at the margins in order to increase the likelihood of policy implementation and success. As stated earlier, external financiers exercise leverage over the Fund because they impact what the Fund values most: the success of its programs (policy outcomes) and future bargaining leverage with borrowers (future policy prescriptions).

The dominant multilateral supplementary financier is the World Bank. Of the financing from multilateral organizations that supplements Fund loans, the majority comes from the World Bank's International Bank for Reconstruction and Development (IBRD) or International Development Association (IDA). For instance, between 1970 and 1995, the World Bank provided between 58% and 81% of public or publicly guaranteed multilateral debt disbursements.[47] Because the World Bank is such a dominant actor in the multilateral external financing landscape, I take the Bank's policy interests as representing multilateral supplementary financiers' interests at large. The Bank was established, along with the Fund, in 1944 to address the broad issues of reconstruction and development. As stated in a recent World Bank history, "From the outset, the Bank's subject matter covered a broader span than that of the Fund, and over the decades, it expanded."[48] The mandate to address development concerns quickly took center stage, focusing World Bank interests on poverty alleviation and economic growth, broadly defined to include policy goals related to environmental protection, education improvement, health care, private business development, and institution building, among others.[49]

In short, multilateral organizations finance for policy ends. They deal intensively with the Fund's borrowing member states and have specific policy preferences that sometimes differ from the Fund's. The main multilateral organization providing external financing for developing countries is the World Bank. The World Bank has specific policy preferences regarding development, poverty alleviation, private sector development, and institution building (among others), which are not necessarily the same as the Fund's traditionally. In practice, this means that multilateral organizations often prefer Fund conditional loan arrangements to include procedural conditions—specific, detailed directives that specify how policies should be implemented—that relate to their specific policy preferences. They also often prefer more conditions that address developmental concerns comprehensively from multiple angles. Thus two hypotheses are generated from the interests and preferences of multilateral organizations:

HYPOTHESIS 4   *If a country receives relatively more (less) supplementary financing from multilateral organizations, then its Fund loan arrangement should include relatively more (less) binding conditions.*

HYPOTHESIS 5   *If a country receives relatively more (less) supplementary financing from multilateral organizations, then its Fund loan arrangement should include relatively more (less) procedural conditions versus targets.*

Thus, if the dominant source of state financing shifts from states to banks to multilateral organizations, the instructions that the IMF will receive on appropriate activity, and in turn, the content of its conditionality arrangements will change. Whereas a state will instruct the IMF to negotiate a conditionality arrangement with some general targets for credit expansion but few procedural reforms that may upset political stability, a private financier will prefer an arrangement with more bank-friendly conditions, and a multilateral organization will prefer a program with numerous conditions, particularly procedural conditions, to address issues of development and poverty alleviation comprehensively.

SUM OF DYNAMIC ARGUMENT

The sources of state financing have shifted and diversified since conditionality was established in 1952. Initially this outside funding came largely from the U.S. government, particularly the U.S. Treasury and the U.S. Export-Import Bank.[50] However, as the U.S. balance of payments shifted from surplus to deficit during the 1960s, U.S. bilateral loans to other countries dwindled. Starting in the 1960s, but particularly in the 1970s and 1980s, the funding stream had shifted and came not only from states, but also from banks, either through new loans or through reschedulings.[51] This marked a big change in the financing of developing countries and the balance of payments deficits. Banks, flush with petrodollars, dramatically increased their lending to developing countries. They too wanted a policy enforcer to ensure the profitability and security of their investment and benefited from the Fund's activities, encouraging economically sound policies that would help protect the long-term viability of their loans. By the late 1980s and 1990s, the providers of supplementary financing had diversified further to include other multilateral organizations and eventually private investors.

In this book, I argue that these changes in the sources of state financing, from the United States to other states, banks, and multilateral organizations, prompted the changes in Fund conditionality. The IMF now responds to the demands of creditor states, banks, investors, and other multilateral organizations.[52] One high-level Fund staff member and former ED has called the expansion of Fund conditionality "mission push" (rather than "mission creep") for just this reason.[53]

The Supplementary Financier Argument's Relationship to the Main Alternative Arguments

The supplementary financier argument is presented, and evaluated, as an alternative to the conventional arguments about international organizational activity and change—specifically, realism and the bureaucratic argument. However, before delving into the empirical chapters and assessments, it is useful to step back and consider the relationship between this argument and the alternatives in two different senses: conceptually and empirically.

CONCEPTUAL RELATIONSHIP

Conceptually, the supplementary financier argument has a unique relationship with the alternatives presented here. At times the supplementary financier argument emphasizes the influence of the same actors, although with different predictions of how that influence should manifest itself. For instance, the bureaucratic argument emphasizes the influence of IO bureaucrats. The interests of IMF bureaucrats (in the short-run success of Fund programs and the Fund's future bargaining leverage with borrowers) and the preferences of other multilateral organizations (like the World Bank's preference for more numerous and detailed conditions) are also important factors for the supplementary financier argument. However, the predictions of these two alternative arguments diverge.

Similarly, realists emphasize the influence of powerful states, and the supplementary financier argument also points to the influence of (powerful) creditor states (specifically when their financing dominates the supplementary financing pool). However, the supplementary financier argument offers predictions that directly contradict realist predictions. Realists look to states as the impetus for change in international organizational activity. International organizations serve state interests, and so a shift in IO activity would come from states' shifting demands from states, perhaps due to a shift in the distribution of power for realists. Therefore, states would be the ones demanding increasing stringent and specific Fund conditionality arrangements from the International Monetary Fund. By contrast, the supplementary financier argument suggests that states actually depress conditionality; private financial institutions and multilateral organizations have been the main forces of change, demanding new, increasingly stringent terms.

Thus, although states can and do influence the IMF's activity, according to the supplementary financier argument, the trajectory of IMF conditionality change over the last few decades has actually deviated from powerful state preferences. This is not to say that the IMF has acted wholly against state interests. State representatives on the Executive Board do approve all Fund conditionality programs. Both powerful donor states and borrowing member states clearly still find it advantageous to help preserve international financial stability and encourage growth and investments in developing countries by approving these agreements. The central point is that most Fund programs today do not reflect states' first-choice preference. If states designed Fund programs, or if the Fund followed states' directions and preferences strictly, the programs would be quite different. However, state representatives approve these loan programs because they are preferable to the alternative (which is often no program at all and great economic hardship for the potential borrower).

Some Fund programs conform more to state preferences than others. The supplementary financier argument provides a way of predicting when state influence over Fund conditionality program design should be greatest (when states are the main sources of supplementary financing) and what to expect from state influence (fewer and less stringent conditions). State influence is not determined by the dynamics within the Executive Board meeting or the percentage of weighted voting power, but by the amount of supplementary financing that that creditor state is pledging in bilateral loans or aid. And although state influence is certainly still apparent in individual cases, states have not been the force behind the general trends in Fund conditionality we have observed over the last several decades, including the increasing stringency and breadth of Fund conditionality.

EMPIRICAL RELATIONSHIP

I argue that supplementary financiers have influenced Fund conditionality, and that the shifts in the sources of supplementary financing have driven many of the over-time changes in Fund conditionality. Thus the null hypothesis is simply that there should be no relationship between supplementary financier influence and Fund conditionality (that the parameter associated with supplementary financiers would equal zero versus my own hypothesis that the parameter is not zero). The primary empirical hurdle is simply to show that supplementary financiers have influenced Fund conditionality programs in predicted ways. In the absence of this influence, Fund programs would look different: they may reflect the influence of Fund staff preferences or borrower preferences more than they do now. The changes that have been driven by PFIs and multilateral organizations in particular would be much less pronounced, if not nonexistent. In the absence of this influence, Fund conditionality would not have changed in the particular ways or as dramatically as we have observed, but that does not mean that Fund programs in 2005 would be exactly the same as Fund programs in 1965 (which in themselves were not uniform).

In other words, there have certainly been many influences on Fund conditionality programs as well as changes in those programs. To some extent, all of the alternative arguments (the primary ones discussed here, as well as others that emphasize the change in ideas, domestic variables, and so on) may explain some of the changes in Fund conditionality. Similarly, when independent variables continue to be added to a regression, the model will tend to explain more and more variation in the dependent variable. Therefore, I do not make the drastic claim that there is no value to the alternative arguments, or that these alternatives are necessarily "disproven" or "wrong." Instead, the secondary empirical hurdle is to show that changes in the terms of Fund conditionality agreements are best explained by shifts in the courses of borrower state financing—in other words, that the supplementary financier argument explains more of the change in Fund conditionality than do the alternative arguments.

In assessing the supplementary financier argument versus the alternative arguments, I employ four basic types of empirical evidence: comparing the broad observable implications of the three arguments with the actual record of Fund conditionality change, comparing the pattern of supplementary financing with the predicted changes in Fund conditionality, running statistical tests to determine whether each type of supplementary financier seems to have influenced Fund conditionality in predicted ways, and evaluating case studies of Fund conditionality agreements to uncover the causal mechanisms by which this type of supplementary financier influences the terms of Fund conditionality agreements (Chapters 5–7, respectively).

In the next two chapters, Chapters 3 and 4, I detail how Fund conditionality has changed over time and specifically consider whether the overall patterns conform to the observable implications of the main alternative arguments or the supplementary financier argument.

CHAPTER THREE

A History of International Monetary Fund Conditionality

Introduction

What is Fund conditionality? How has it changed? Because the Fund agreements themselves have been hidden from public view until quite recently, the term *Fund conditionality* has been used to mean a variety of things from a specific set of policies, to the degree of economic contraction, to a type of Fund facility or the entire ambiguous Fund agreement itself. In this study, I define Fund conditionality as the terms of an arrangement between a member country and the IMF that specify policies, performance criteria, or standards that the country must meet in order to receive resources from the Fund.[1] This definition is deliberately content-neutral and historically unspecific; conditionality is not a single set of policy requirements because the policy requirements and goals of conditionality have changed over time. The definition focuses on the terms of the contract by which the IMF attempts to influence or determine national policy, not policy enactment or the outcome of policy implementation.[2] It also does not include preconditions, which are unevenly mentioned in the arrangements themselves, or the general policy programs, which are often described in the arrangement but do not cause loan installments to be withheld. In focusing on the changes in conditionality, this chapter focuses on the change in what the IMF asks member states to do in order to receive an IMF loan, not on the change in what a country actually does.

There are at least two central reasons to focus an entire chapter describing the dependent variable—Fund conditionality—before turning directly to the analytical puzzle motivating this study. First, this chapter complements, and in some cases corrects, previous histories of Fund conditionality that are informing current policy-oriented debates about Fund conditionality. Second, it provides the reader with a broader sense of the changes in Fund conditionality before focusing on specific changes in the analytical chapters that follow.

In the last decade, scholars, politicians, and Fund staff and management have been engaged in a broad debate about the appropriate nature of Fund conditionality, motivated in part by recent expansions in Fund conditionality.[3] Much of this literature is explicitly policy oriented and includes a subtext that the current practice has gone too far. Perhaps surprisingly, though, this debate has been informed by extremely limited data on the actual changes in Fund conditionality over the last 50 years. Through most of the Fund's history, conditionality has been described vaguely by Fund staffers or country observers. Most of the existing literature on IMF conditionality is historical and includes general descriptions of how policy and practice have evolved with very little, if any, explicit empirical data.[4]

Recently there has been a push within the International Monetary Fund to develop better data on Fund conditionality. The Monitoring of IMF Arrangements (MONA) database includes a wealth of information on Fund program design (including performance criteria, structural benchmarks, and prior actions) and implementation or compliance. It has incredible depth but not as much breadth: the database only codes agreements since 1992.[5] Research utilizing the MONA database has just begun to be released and is no doubt valuable, but it clearly cannot give us a sense of over-time and cross-sectional changes in conditionality before the last decade.[6]

The data and history presented in this chapter offer a new perspective of how Fund conditionality has changed since its inception on the basis of original research. The chapter relies mainly on primary documents from the Fund's archives and the originally constructed Conditionality Data Set (Appendix 1) in order to link the history of Fund conditionality with data on how Fund conditionality agreements have actually changed. This description of the dependent variable is useful because it can serve as a corrective, and complement, to previous accounts of conditionality change that relied mainly on single case studies or staff-written histories. In addition, this chapter serves the narrow interests of this particular study. Before dissecting and analyzing particular changes in Fund conditionality over time in the chapters that follow, this chapter will provide an overview of the many different changes in Fund conditionality agreements over the past 50 years.

In short, this chapter sets out to retell the history of Fund conditionality, using new archival sources and new data on Fund conditionality. The history makes clear how dramatically Fund conditionality has diverged from the founders' original plans by reviewing the preconditionality history, development of stand-by arrangement (SBA) practices, and the introduction of the other, newer lending facilities. This history is told with deliberate, if only moderately successful, causal neutrality. In other words, I have tried to tell the history of Fund conditionality without ascribing causal influence to particular actors, like powerful states, bureaucratic actors, or supplementary financiers. Many scholars have used the story of conditionality as a backdrop to substantiate their favorite theory of international organizational influence. By contrast, I have attempted to be causally neutral in this chapter, and I assess causal explanations by considering their observable implications in the next chapter. Chapter 4 explicitly and carefully assesses how well this history and data conform to the observable implications of two common explanations of IMF conditionality change—realism and bureaucratic politics—and one not so common: the supplementary financier argument. As a brief foreshadow of the next chapter, the evidence will reveal, perhaps surprisingly, that the changes in Fund conditionality do not comport to the observable implications of the conventional wisdoms, but do lend initial support to the supplementary financier argument.

Early Debates over Fund Conditionality

Today if a member state wants to borrow Fund resources, most likely there will be conditions attached to that loan. However, this has not always been the case. In fact, when the International Monetary Fund was established at Bretton Woods, New Hampshire, in July 1944, conditionality had not yet been established. In 1952, at the insistence of the United States and through the advocacy of the managing director, conditionality in the form of a SBA was first implemented. The practices of the SBA developed through the 1950s and 1960s, establishing certain features like performance criteria and phasing, but generally keeping the individual arrangement limited to under one year and the conditions to broad macroeconomic targets. In the 1970s, the Fund's practices changed again. New loan facilities with different terms and purposes were created, including the two oil facilities, the Extended Fund Facility (EFF) and the Trust Fund. During the 1970s, the lower-conditionality oil facilities were used the most; however, these oil facilities expired by May 1976, and what remained were the high-conditionality facilities with expanded purposes. The average length of arrangements and the specificity and number of their conditions increased. In 1986 and 1987 two new facilities, the Structural Adjustment Facility (SAF) and the Enhanced Structural Adjustment Facility (ESAF), were created to deal with problems and provide solutions that would have been prohibited by the original founders. In the 1990s, still more facilities—the Systemic Transformation, Supplementary Reserve, and Poverty Reduction and Growth Facilities—were created to deal with the specific issues for transition countries; sudden, deep crises; and heavily indebted poor countries.

The history of Fund conditionality presented here begins with the pre–Bretton Woods debates. The discussion then moves to the creation of the Fund's original conditional loan arrangement, the SBA, a few important changes in the design and terms of SBAs, and finally the creation of new lending facilities. Data from the Conditionality Data Set and Fund archival material are used throughout to create a richer and more accurate portrait of this change.

The International Monetary Fund and its state principals did not invent conditional lending. Before the Fund's founding, countries had received conditional loans from (or facilitated by) the League of Nations and with the help of "money doctors."[7] However, it was not until 1952 that states formally delegated the authority to design and negotiate conditional loan agreements to the International Monetary Fund. This delegation occurred after a protracted struggle between members of the Fund's Executive Board. In the pre–Bretton Woods discussions and in the early years of the Fund itself, the battle lines were drawn between those who advocated "automaticity," or automatically approved loans from the Fund, and those who favored conditionality.[8]

Most of the founding members, except the United States, advocated "automaticity," a policy of automatically allowing countries to draw from their quota in order to allow members to truly rely on this quota as a "second source of reserves." Member countries were (and still are) required to deposit a quota—with 25% in gold and 75% in their local currency—in the Fund's General Resource Account (GRA) as a requirement of membership. Most state representatives argued that "drawing" against this quota, technically purchasing another country's currency with theirs, should be a country's automatic right; the Fund should not be able to prevent them from borrowing within a specific range.[9] For instance, the United Kingdom's John Maynard Keynes argued that countries should be able to draw (or borrow) 25% of their quota per year with no questions asked. In fact, UK negotiators had received specific instructions to oppose conditional access. The IMF should not be able to force deficit countries to introduce "a deflationary policy, enforced by dear money and similar measures, having the effect of causing unemployment; for this would amount to restoring, subject to insufficient safeguards, the evils of the old automatic gold standard," they were told.[10]

The United States, by contrast, advocated "conditional" rights to draw on IMF resources. Keynes famously described the United States' position as promoting an IMF with "wide and discretionary powers" and "grandmotherly influence and control over the central banks of member countries."[11] The United States wanted member states' borrowing rights to be conditional in order to ensure that the resources were being used in a manner "consistent with the purposes of the Fund."[12] The United States argued for conditionality to protect the Fund's resources. But despite Keynes's description, this conditionality was quite narrow by today's standards; for instance, the United States notably did not advocate an active role in member states' domestic policies. In July 1944, Harry Dexter White (then the U.S. assistant Treasury secretary) explained that the Fund should not "butt into every country's business and say, 'We don't like this or that.'" [13] The U.S. representatives argued that the Fund should be able to deny, but not suspend, loan installments because they acknowledged that countries needed the assurance that these installments would be forthcoming in order to implement tough corrective policies. [14]

The actual Bretton Woods agreement contained indecisive language on whether members had an automatic or conditional right to borrow the Fund's resources. [15] The automatic right was embodied in Article V, Section 3 (a) (i) and (iii), which stated that a member "shall be entitled" to make a drawing as long as the member "represents that it is presently needed for making in that currency payments which are consistent with the provisions of this Agreement," within certain quantitative restrictions based on the country's quota. [16] The conditional right was embodied in Article XX, Section 4 (i), and Article V, Section 5, which stated that the IMF may "postpone exchange transactions with any member if its circumstances are such that, in the opinion of the Fund, they would lead to use of the resources of the Fund in a manner contrary to the purposes of the Fund Agreement." [17] In other words, although there were no specific provisions for conditionality per se in the original Articles, they did require that borrowing state policies be consistent with the Articles of Agreement. This provision later allowed conditionality to take form. [18]

Fund conditional lending is now one of the IMF's main activities. Interestingly, Article I of the Articles of Agreement, which delineates the six purposes of the IMF, does not identify the IMF as an institution of lending or redistribution. [19] The Articles established the IMF as an institution to promote international monetary cooperation by enforcing a certain "code of conduct" based on "orderly exchange arrangements" free from restrictions and by providing temporary resources in order to facilitate the smooth running of an international system of payments, unhampered by temporary balance of payments deficits. [20] The only purpose that dealt with the use of Fund resources, and Fund lending, was Article I (v), which instructed the IMF "to give confidence to members by making the Fund's resources available to them under adequate safeguards, thus providing them with the opportunity to correct maladjustments in their balance of payments without resorting to measures destructive of national or international prosperity." Thus, Fund resources were to be used as a "second source of reserves" when countries faced temporary balance of payments deficits, thereby obviating the need to devalue one's currency or erect exchange restrictions in order to deal with that deficit.[21] Members could also make use of the Fund's resources for capital transfers under specific circumstances.[22] But Fund resources were explicitly not to be used to offset large or sustained capital flight; for relief and reconstruction; "dealing with international indebtedness arising out of war"; or economic development.[23] Instead, these four areas were the intended domains of the World Bank and other development or reconstruction venues. Today these proscriptions seem ironic, given that many of the current Fund loans are explicitly used for those purposes. But the original Articles of Agreement envisioned an organization with a more restricted mission. The IMF was established to maintain and monitor the fixed exchange rate system, and its loans were intended to narrowly serve that purpose.

The Fund's original Articles of Agreement did not mandate conditionality, but they also did not decisively resolve the automaticity versus conditionality debate. The IMF was intended to monitor and maintain the Bretton Woods par value system, and was supposed to lend money on a revolving basis to members facing short-term payments imbalances. However, members, staff, and management alike were unsure of the appropriate boundary between members' borrowing rights and the Fund's discretionary power. In the first few years after Bretton Woods, preliminary rules began to take shape.

At first, the Fund's policy stipulated that members could borrow against their quota for short periods of time and with no conditionality. A September 1946 Executive Board decision established initial guidelines for the use of Fund resources: "authority to use the resources of the Fund is limited to use in accordance with its purposes to give temporary assistance in financing balance of payments deficits on current account for monetary stabilization operations."[24] The 1946 Annual Report emphasized that the "essential test of the propriety of the use of Fund resources is . . . that its use . . . will be of relatively short duration."[25] The use of Fund resources was intended to be temporary both to protect the Fund's resources (and ensure their "revolving character") and to restrict their use to addressing only short-term payments imbalances.[26] These short-term Fund loans were supposed to help prevent short-term payments imbalances from snowballing and thus forcing a country to abandon its par value exchange rate and commitment to open monetary relations.

Although executive directors (EDs) tended to agree on the temporary use of Fund resources, they continued to disagree on the question of conditionality versus automaticity. Many EDs argued that the Fund already had too much discretionary power over when a member could draw on Fund resources. More Fund discretion would undermine the whole concept of the Fund acting as a "second source of reserves" and lead to a certain "arbitrariness" of Fund policy, they argued.[27] However, the United States' ED continued to argue that the Fund had too little discretionary power and thus its resources were at risk of being misused.[28] The Executive Board as a whole came under increasing pressure to clarify the Fund's position on the use of its resources. Members argued that in order for Fund resources to "give confidence to members," as stated in the Articles, they needed to know when their access to these resources could be assured and if they could truly rely on their Fund quota as a "second source of reserves." Fund resources would not inspire confidence, if they were unavailable during dire economic times.

Between 1948 and 1952, a more certain Fund policy developed. The United States, which was both the world's main creditor and the IMF's main source of funding, was able to bring the Fund's general position more in line with its preferences.[29] A March 1948 interpretive decision stipulated that a member's "representation" (that it needed to borrow resources in order to make "payments in that currency consistent with the provisions of the Articles of Agreement") could be challenged by the Fund "for good reasons."[30] If the member's representation was challenged, then the Fund "had the power to postpone or reject the request for a drawing or grant it subject to conditions designed to safeguard the Fund's purposes."[31] According to Sidney Dell, this decision marked a "turning point" away from automaticity; members no longer had an automatic right to borrow Fund resources.[32] In that year, the Board also sided with the United States in denying European Recovery Program countries the right to borrow dollars.[33] The shift in policy marked by these decisions resulted in a sharp drop-off in Fund transactions.[34]

U.S. ED Frank Southard, who held about 30% of the Executive Board's total voting power at that time, began demanding a more restrictive policy regarding the use of Fund resources. In May 1948, Southard announced that countries would need to satisfy four criteria in order to borrow from the Fund:

> (a) that the par value of the member was appropriate; (b) that the circumstances which gave rise to the proposed drawing were due to a temporary

rather than to a fundamental disequilibrium; (c) that the proposed drawing could not primarily be attributed, directly or indirectly, to requirements engendered by programs of rehabilitation or development; and (d) that the member was taking all the steps essential to assume, as soon as possible, its full obligations under the Articles of Agreement.[35]

Southard began applying this policy unilaterally—for example, with the proposed loan programs for Brazil and the Netherlands that year.[36] In October 1949, Southard suggested that future dollar drawings should be contingent on a country's agreeing to pay back these drawings within five years, in order to ensure that loans were temporary and short term.[37] Most other EDs initially opposed Southard's propositions.[38] They agreed that the use of Fund resources should be temporary but "thought that the proper course was for the Fund to work out ways to ensure this without imposing conditions which might force members, in order to repurchase drawings, to introduce measures which would be inimical to the Fund's basic aims."[39]

A combination of reduced demand (due to the European Recovery Program) and restricted supply (due to the position of the U.S. ED) brought IMF lending to a standstill in 1950.[40] The staff and management advanced successive compromise solutions, hoping one would finally "reinvigorate the Fund" and prevent it from being "written off . . . as moribund."[41] The SBA, the Fund's first conditional lending arrangement, was the final iteration in a series of attempts by the Fund's staff and management to break the stalemate between the United States and most of the other Fund members. However, first, in December 1949, the staff suggested that the Executive Board send out a letter notifying members that "the Fund's resources required that members should adopt corrective measures to ensure repayment." This proposal was not accepted by the Board.[42] Next, in November 1950, the Fund's managing director, Camille Gutt, tried again, suggesting "a procedure which would tie drawings to programs of action by the drawing members . . . that where a member was in difficulties the staff might assist it to work out a suitable policy for the recovery of equilibrium, and that this policy might then be supported by a drawing."[43] On May 2, 1951, the Executive Board approved a version of this proposal, which stated that "the Fund's resources could be made available to give confidence to members to undertake practical programs of action to help achieve the purposes of the Fund Agreement." Specifically, member countries would be "assured that the Fund's aid would be forthcoming" if it were needed to "achieve monetary stability, adopt realistic rates of exchange, relax and remove restrictions and discrimination, or simplify multiple currency practices."[44] However, according to the Fund's former historian, Keith Horsefield, and Gertrud Lovasy, this proposal "had little practical result" in "reviving the institution," although it did signify another important step in "the concept of eligibility from automaticity to conditionality" by establishing a link between Fund drawings and policy programs.[45]

In January 1952, the Fund's new managing director, Ivar Rooth, proposed a third plan, again to revive the use of the Fund's resources and reduce uncertainty about members' access to the Fund's resources.[46] Rooth suggested that the Fund's decision whether or not to lend to a member country "should turn on whether the policies the member will pursue will be adequate to overcome the problem within such a period. The policies, above all, should determine the Fund's attitude."[47] Rooth's plan appealed to the United States because it protected "the revolving character of the Fund's resources"; it stipulated that Fund loans needed to be repaid within three to five years and include financial incentives to discourage long-term, large loans.[48] It also appealed to automaticity advocates because it provided that a member could borrow with an "overwhelming benefit of the doubt" within the gold tranche (or first 25% of quota).[49] The Rooth Plan also suggested an avenue for "temporary automaticity," which appealed to potential borrowers. It suggested that "at other times, discussions between the member and the Fund may cover its general position, not with a view to any immediate drawings, but in order to ensure that it would be able to draw if, within a period of say 6 to 12 months, the need presented itself."[50] This mention of "discussions" was the "germ of the stand-by arrangements."[51] After debate and revision, the Executive Board passed the Rooth Plan in February 1952.[52]

On July 31, 1952, the Fund's secretary distributed a staff report to the Executive Board that finally established the SBA. A few key points in the initial staff proposal deserve highlighting. First, the staff proposal suggested the SBAs be short term, about six to twelve months. U.S. ED Frank Southard, who held over 30% of the voting power in 1952, and the elected ED from Egypt, Ahmed Zaki Saad Pasha, who represented nine countries with 4.8% of the vote, were two vocal defenders of the idea that SBAs be no more than six months in length. As Saad stated, "The Fund could not possibly foresee all developments so far in advance and it should have protections

against sudden deteriorations that would make a drawing clearly inaccept-
able."[53] Southard similarly argued:

> The period was . . . the most important issue on stand-bys. When the Fund
> agreed to the kind of arrangement the staff suggested, it gave the member a
> virtually irrevocable drawing right; as experience has shown it was highly
> unlikely that any move would be made to declare such a member ineligible
> so as to limit its exercise of the commitment. Therefore, the Fund would be
> unwise to bind itself for more than six months in advance since its ability to
> foresee a country's future much beyond that point would be questionable.

Second, the staff proposal suggested SBAs would be offered for no more
than 25% of a country's quota. Some EDs, including EDs from Mexico, Australia, and India, argued that 25% would not be enough to offset short-term
payments imbalances and restore confidence. The ED from Mexico, who represented nine other Latin American countries with 4.9% of the vote, argued
that "the member's quotas were so small in comparison to the size of their
normal imports that a 25% drawing would not give any worthwhile protection." However, other EDs and staff defended the 25% limit in order to
protect Fund resources for other countries' use. Finally, the staff proposal
stipulated that SBAs could be renewed, but not automatically. If SBAs were
automatically renewed, then any effort on the part of the Fund to terminate
a renewal "would involve, in effect, an almost public castigation of the member concerned and might cause unnecessary injury to the member."[54]

In October 1952, the Executive Board passed Decision 155–(52/57),
which established the formal procedures for the Fund's first conditionality
lending facility: the stand-by arrangement. It stipulated (as the staff proposal
suggested) that SBAs would be limited to six months in length and 25% of
quota, and would not be automatically renewable.[55] The final decision was
considered by some to be "stiffer," in the words of the UK ED, than the original staff proposal and incorporated many, but not all, of the concerns of the
U.S. ED.[56] An SBA is an agreement between a member country and the IMF
that stipulates that the country can be assured that it will be able to draw a
certain specified amount of Fund resources, within a certain window of time,
as long as the country commits to, maintains, or implements certain agreed-
upon policies. SBAs, Joseph Gold later wrote, "must be understood in the

context of the dispute about automaticity." They were "developed as a device which would give to members *ad hoc* the automaticity which the Fund had rejected as a general rule."[57] The SBA was not intended to be a loan per se, but rather an assurance of automaticity: that the Fund will loan within a certain period of time under certain conditions. SBAs thereby allowed countries to treat a portion of their Fund quota as an extension of their reserves.[58] The original logic behind stand-bys was that they would serve as a double layer of confidence protection. They would bolster the confidence of the government by allowing them to act as if they had more reserves in their central bank and would bolster investor confidence by committing the governments to certain policies.[59] The Fund effectively gave members a guarantee that it would not "review" and therefore would not "challenge a request" to borrow, unless the Fund declared the member ineligible.[60] SBAs were initially envisioned to be short-term assurances of automaticity, and to require little, if any, change in a country's policy. However, that practice changed radically in the subsequent years.

The Changing Design of the Stand-by Arrangement

> I have no hesitation in saying that there is no reason why we should really fear that stand-by arrangements will come to be universal, that they will be automatically renewed and become semi-permanent, and that they will tie up too much of the Fund's resources. Stand-by arrangements are, after all, a matter of policy and the policy can be shaped in whatever means seems reasonable and can be changed altogether if that proves necessary.[61]
> —Statement by Managing Director Ivar Rooth addressing U.S. concerns

Since 1952, the practice and policy of SBAs has developed, deviating from many of the initial elements so intensely debated by the Executive Board. In this and the next section, I discuss the history of how Fund conditionality policy evolved, focusing intermittently on seven main changes in Fund conditionality arrangements: the length; the use of protective clauses; the number of binding conditions; phasing; reviews; consultations; and the types of binding conditions (or the scope of the conditionality).

The first element to begin changing was the length of SBAs. In 1953, the staff suggested changing the policy to allow SBAs to be longer because six months was "inadequate to give assurance to members undertaking certain programs."[62] The subsequent Executive Board Decision 270–(53/95) on December 23, 1953, stated that stand-bys could extend longer than six months "if this appears warranted by the particular payments problem of the member making the request."[63]

The change in length spawned other design changes. Longer arrangements, it was argued, required more safeguards because the Fund could not be assured of a countries' economic situation beyond six months. As one ED stated,

> because of the difficulty of foretelling a member's situation for a long time in advance, a stand-by beyond six months might have to be based on the expectation that the member would maintain policies. If the member changed those policies so as to impair the character of the understanding with the Fund, the Fund should have the possibility of canceling its guarantee.[64]

Thus, the introduction of loans conditional on the implementation of, rather than the commitment to, certain policies was introduced in order to compensate for the increased risk associated with longer arrangements. In order to protect against "improper use," the staff began including certain clauses in the SBAs that allowed them to suspend a country's drawing privileges without formally declaring a country ineligible, which carried a great stigma. Before the insertion of these clauses, a country's borrowing rights were not legally conditioned on the member country adhering to the conditions specified in the SBA.[65]

A few different types of protective clauses were included in Fund SBAs initially. "Prior notice" clauses, first utilized in 1954, specified that a country had the right to borrow a specified amount from the Fund during the period of the SBA "unless the Fund has given [that country] prior notice to the contrary."[66] In other words, they provided a way for the Fund to suspend the temporary automaticity that stand-bys conferred. Prior notice clauses were almost exclusively utilized in the SBAs for Western Hemisphere (Latin American and Caribbean) countries.[67] They were discontinued in 1961 because, it was argued, they were not used uniformly and ultimately gave the staff too much discretion, undermining the notion of assurance and automaticity that undergirded the SBA.[68]

A second protective clause specified objective criteria, or binding conditions, that needed to be met in order for a country's automatic drawing rights to be maintained through the SBA period. Most SBAs, even early on, included pages of descriptions of policies that the member country planned to implement and the Fund advocated. However, only a select few of those conditions were singled out in the binding conditions protective clause and therefore whose violation could trigger a suspension of borrowing privileges. The binding condition protective clause was first used in 1957.[69] Joseph Gold described the use of this clause and its advantages to the managing director:

> The usual technique has been to get the member to undertake to observe certain fixed criteria, such as ceilings on credit, and to agree that if it departs from these criteria, it will not draw [or borrow] before consulting the Fund and agreeing on terms for subsequent drawings. Drawing rights under the stand-by arrangement are then made expressly subject to the paragraph in the member's letter in which it undertakes to consult, etc., before requesting further drawings. The normal Fund procedure under such a clause, when a request is received, is to ascertain that the criteria are being observed. If they are not, the request is not a proper one within the terms of the stand-by arrangement, and we can either call for consultation before meeting the request or inform the Board that the criteria are not being observed and propose to meet the request notwithstanding the failure (e.g., because it represents a small and temporary excess over a ceiling). . . . Thus, one advantage of this clause is that the problem raised by the member's failure to carry our certain aspects of its promised program can be handled without publicity of any kind.[70]

This clause remained in SBAs in various forms and was widely and uniformly incorporated in upper-credit tranche SBAs by the late 1960s.

Phasing was another innovation in the structure of SBAs. It involved dividing the SBAs into segments or tranches that would be disbursed in installments, each often conditioned on meeting binding conditions specified in the arrangements.[71] Phasing was first introduced in March 1956, and by the late 1950s, the majority of SBAs were phased.[72] SBAs were officially phased for two reasons. First, staff argued, it was in the interest of both the Fund and the borrowing country to have Fund resources borrowed over an extended period rather than in one lump sum. Second, "it was felt that phasing was

TABLE 3.1
Phasing in Stand-by Arrangements, 1952–1963

Year	Total No. of SBAs	Percentage SBAs with Phasing	No. of Western Hemisphere SBAs	Percentage Western Hemisphere SBAs with Phasing
1952	2	0%	0	NA
1953	0	n/a	0	NA
1954	3	0%	3	0%
1955	1	0%	1	0%
1956	8	25%	5	40%
1957	10	30%	7	43%
1958	13	54%	9	78%
1959	13	77%	11	91%
1960	17	82%	11	91%
1961	21	90%	14	100%
1962	17	82%	9	100%
1963 partial	7	86%	5	100%

SOURCE: Data from Memo from Joseph Gold, April 12, 1963, IMF Archives; and International Monetary Fund Annual Reports, various years.

NOTE: SBA = stand-by arrangement.

necessary in order to ensure observance of the member's commitments [or binding conditions]."[73] Phasing helps give the binding conditions and the binding condition clauses teeth; it requires countries to borrow Fund resources in tranches and over extended periods of time. The more phasing, the more opportunities the Fund has to enforce adherence to the binding conditions. Table 3.1 provides data from internal Fund memos on the prevalence of phasing from 1952 to 1963. In 1956, the first year of phasing, 25% of SBAs were phased. By 1962, 82% of SBAs initiated were phased, and 100% of Western Hemisphere SBAs.

Table 3.2 provides data from the Conditionality Data Set on phasing over a longer period. It provides the number of arrangements that had no phasing (represented as one phase, or loan installment), two phases, three phases, four phases, or between five and 18 phases for three different time periods: 1952–1973, 1974–1982, and 1983–1995. Two phases means that the loan can be disbursed in two installments, the first portion at the start of the arrangements and the second portion after a specified date if certain conditions have been met. Table 3.2 reveals not only the increase in the prevalence of phasing over time, but also the increase in the average number of phases per arrangement. In the 1952–1973 period, 12% of the Fund conditional

TABLE 3.2
Changes in the Use of Phasing, 1952–1995

| | PHASES, N(%) | | | | | |
Year	0	2	3	4	5–18	Total
1952–1973	31 (27%)	12 (10%)	25 (22%)	34 (29%)	14 (12%)	116 (100%)
1974–1982	12 (25%)	1 (2%)	5 (10%)	11 (23%)	20 (41%)	49 (100%)
1983–1995	1 (1%)	1 (1%)	7 (10%)	8 (11%)	55 (76%)	72 (100%)
Total	44 (19%)	14 (6%)	37 (16%)	53 (22%)	89 (38%)	237 (100%)

SOURCE: Data from the Conditionality Data Set.

NOTE: Percentages are rounded and therefore may not add to 100.

loan arrangements in my sample had between 5 and 18 phases; between 1974–1982, 41% and by 1983–1995, 76% of the Fund conditional loan arrangements had between 5 and 18 phases. Arguably the Fund has improved its mechanisms of enforcement over time by making the inclusion of a binding condition clause universal by the 1990s and by increasing the average number of phases per arrangement.

In the early 1960s, a debate ensued over what the general policy on phasing should be. As noted, a disproportionately high percentage of SBAs for Western Hemisphere countries included phasing.[74] Practices regarding the inclusion of binding conditions also varied between Area Departments, which are the geographically based departments that are primarily responsible for designing the conditionality agreements. The staff and the Executive Board tried to develop guidelines about when phasing or binding conditions should be required in a Fund conditionality program in order to encourage uniform practices. At first, in 1962 and 1963, staff debated the guidelines between themselves and decided that binding conditions and phasing should not be required for relatively small "gold tranche" drawings (generally the first 25% of quota drawn), "except perhaps where the member insists on conditions"; binding conditions would be included for first-credit tranche drawings (the second 25% of quota drawn); drawings and stand-bys beyond the gold tranche should also generally include phasing unless there are special circumstances.[75] By 1966, transactions in the gold tranche were granted "on a virtually automatic basis," and in the first-credit tranche "on a liberal basis." Drawings beyond the first-credit tranche were normally drawn with "substantial justification" under a one-year SBA that was both phased and required the borrowing country to meet certain binding conditions.[76]

TABLE 3.3
Average Number of Performance Criteria by Tranche and Time Period

Stand-by Arrangements Reaching Into:	1957–1960	1961–1964	1965–1967	Average 1957–1967 (tranche)
Gold tranche	—	—	—	—
First tranche	—	1.5	2.1	1.2
Second tranche	2.5	3.1	5.1	3.7
Third tranche	2.5	4.8	5.8	4.4
Fourth tranche	1.5	5.2	5.4	4.9
Average (time period)	2.0	4.1	5.1	3.9

SOURCE: SM/68/128, Supplement 3, September 4, 1968, IMF Archives.

These general practices were codified in the First Amendment to the Articles of Agreement, adopted by the Board of Governors in 1968 and effective in 1969. The decision stipulated that gold tranche drawings would be approved virtually automatically.[77] Drawings above the gold tranche—including first-credit tranche drawings—would be subject to conditionality, thus presumably denying the Fund the opportunity to grant "de facto automaticity" to these other requests.[78]

In 1968, after this decision was passed, the Executive Board weighed in on these matters again. Despite staff efforts, the Executive Board continued to argue that Fund conditionality had generally become too stringent and programs were insufficiently uniform.[79] According to the Fund's own estimates, displayed in Table 3.3, the number of performance criteria (or binding conditions) included in Fund programs more than doubled—from 2 to 5.1 in less than a decade. By 1967, relatively small first-credit tranche SBAs required countries to meet 2.1 binding conditions on average, according to this data. New rules for guiding staff activity on Fund conditionality were passed on September 20, 1968, at Executive Board Meeting 68–132. In contradiction with the policy developed by the staff and codified by the First Amendment, first-credit tranche SBAs would now neither be phased, nor include binding conditions. However, all arrangements beyond the first-credit tranche (that is, all upper-credit tranche SBAs) would now be phased and would have binding conditions and consultation clauses; exceptions to the phasing, but not the binding condition or consultation, requirements would be allowed for "exceptional cases." In addition to establishing uniform design criteria for SBAs of different sizes, the Executive Board also instructed the staff to limit the number of binding conditions to those "necessary to evaluate the implementation and achievement of the objectives of the program" and "keep the number of criteria [or conditions] to the minimum necessary, for the success of the program."[80]

In the late 1970s, the Executive Board returned to the question of conditionality program design. The Second Review of Conditionality was passed by the Executive Board in March 1979 and again provided new guidelines for IMF conditionality.[81] The 1979 Conditionality Guidelines are known for being partly in response to developing countries' concerns, specifically a September 1978 Group of 24 resolution that asked for medium-term balance-of-payments assistance for developing countries with limited conditionality, among other things.[82] However, the similarities to the 1968 Conditionality Guidelines are striking.

A number of the instructions from these guidelines are noteworthy. First, reiterating the 1968 review, the Second Review also stipulated that phasing and performance clauses would be omitted from SBAs or drawings below the first-credit tranche, and included in all others. Second, the 1979 Conditionality Guidelines introduced the notion of preconditions, which require countries to enact certain policies or reach certain performance criteria before they are allowed to draw funds. These preconditions arguably had the effect of increasing conditionality for first-credit tranche SBAs. After 1979, the Fund started asking for preconditions or prior actions before many drawings were made.[83] First-credit tranche arrangements were not supposed to have performance criteria; preconditions enabled the IMF nevertheless to secure policy control over first-credit tranche borrowers by requiring policy changes before the first drawing.[84]

Third, the maximum length of arrangements was extended from 6 months to 12 months and "up to but not beyond three years."[85] This length change was somewhat controversial. For instance, Joseph Gold expressed "caution" that the original goals of the agreements could be blurred by extending the time periods. However, this change in the formal policy had simply followed a change in practice. As Figure 3.1 indicates, by 1979 the average conditionality program was designed to be about 18 months. Figure 3.1 represents the average length, in months, of all stand-by, EFF, SAF, and ESAF arrangements from 1952 until 1995, as specified in the original agreement between the member country and the IMF.[86] This is the entire population of stand-by,

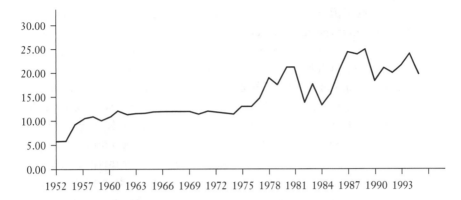

Figure 3.1. Average length of arrangements in months, by year (1952–1995)
SOURCE: From IMF Annual Reports, 1952–1996.

NOTE: The average length represents the average length of all stand-by, Extended Fund Facility (EFF), Structural Adjustment Facility (SAF), and Enhanced Structural Adjustment Facility (ESAF) arrangements initiated in that year according to the original agreement. The average length is in months.

EFF, SAF, and ESAF arrangements, not the sample of arrangements included in the Conditionality Data Set. As the graph indicates, the average length remained relatively stable in the 1950s and 1960s. From 1956 to 1959, the average length increased from 9.43 to 10.46 months. From 1960 until 1969, the average length remained stable at around 11 months (between 11.14 and 11.93 average months). In the early 1970s, the average length continued to stay within the narrow range of 11.7 and 12 months. However, starting in 1975, that stability ended. From 1974 until 1980, the average length almost doubled, from 11.7 months to 21.4 months. Excluding two dips from 1982 to 1984 (an average of 14.1 and 13.4 months, respectively) and a dip in 1990 (to 18.3 months), the average length of IMF conditionality arrangements increased rapidly from 1974 until 1991. In the 1990s, the average length varied between 20 and 24.2 months. Although the average length of programs has remained under three years—the upper limit set by the Second Guidelines—individual loan programs have exceeded it.

Fourth, the 1979 guidelines stated that all SBAs would include clauses that provide for "consultation from time to time during the whole period in which the member has outstanding purchases in the upper credit tranches." For stand-bys longer than one year and in other "exceptional" circumstances, the arrangement would specify at least one review in which the member country and the IMF could review the program and possibly reach new understandings about the reforms the country should undertake.

Consultations and review clauses both provide Fund staff with opportunities to sit down with borrowing country representatives, assess their program implementation, and possibly come up with new program criteria. Reviews are scheduled events, which are explicitly included in the conditionality arrangement and are requirements of the Fund program. Reviews must be conducted at certain points in the program (usually at certain prespecified dates) in order to receive subsequent loan installments. Sometimes borrowing countries and the Fund review the country's economic performance, policies, and appropriateness of the Fund program in their entirety. At other times, the reviews are more circumscribed and concern only certain policy areas, sectors, or prescriptions. Consultations are also included in the Fund conditionality agreement, but are generally required under special circumstances. Consultations were generally required under five circumstances that were separately specified in the arrangement: as a matter of course through correspondences, letters, and visits; in order to resume drawings when binding conditions had been violated; in order to resume drawings if the borrower's drawing rights were suspended as a result of ineligibility or another decision by the ED or managing director; if the managing director requested it; and after the program had ended, but while the loan was still outstanding.

The inclusion of both consultations and reviews had become prevalent before the 1979 Conditionality Review. For instance, only 19% of all arrangements sampled between 1952 and 1973 required reviews, compared to 62% between 1974 and 1982, 98% between 1983 and 1990, and 93% of those samples between 1991 and 2000 (incomplete sample). Consultations were an even more common requirement by the time the Executive Board passed the 1979 guidelines. Table 3.4 provides the percentage of sampled loan arrangements in each of four time periods that specified that consultations would be required in each of these five circumstances. Consultations via letters, visits, and other correspondences were almost universally required from the start. Consultations to resume drawings suspended either because binding conditions had been violated (second column) or because of a decision by the managing director or Executive Board that the country is ineligible (third column) were also common through the entire 1952 to 2000 time period. However, consultations that were required at the discretion of

TABLE 3.4
Changes in Consultation Procedures, 1952–2000

Time Period	1. Regular Correspond	2. Binding Conditions	3. MD/EB Ineligible	4. MD Requests	5. Funds Outstanding
1952–1973	92%	71%	81%	36%	15%
1974–1982	100%	85%	100%	96%	34%
1983–1990	100%	85%	77%	98%	81%
1991–2000	100%	100%	87%	100%	87%

SOURCE: Data from the Conditionality Data Set.
NOTE: The 1991–2000 period is incomplete. MD = managing director; EB = Executive Board.

Fund management and staff were relatively rare from 1952 to 1973 (fourth column). By 1974–1983, nearly all Fund conditional loan arrangements required countries to agree to consult with the Fund if the managing director requested such a consultation. The last type of consultation clause, which required countries to continue to consult with the Fund after their SBA ended but while a certain portion of their loan was still outstanding, began being used in 1970 (fifth column).[87] This clause has been included in over 80% of the Fund conditional loan agreements since 1983. As a result, borrowers often have to consult with the Fund for years after their official loan agreement ends.

Finally, the 1979 guidelines returned to the question of how many and what type of binding conditions (or performance criteria) should be included in Fund programs. The First Review had instructed staff to limit the number of binding conditions. Those instructions had not been heeded. Even during the 1970s, when, according to many scholars, competition from low- and no-conditionality lending vehicles (like the oil facilities) forced the Fund to offer easier terms, conditionality actually continued to increase. According to the Fund's own research (Table 3.5), the average number of binding conditions required by an upper-credit tranche between 1969 and 1977 was 5.8. Recall that the Fund staff estimated the average number of binding conditions between 1965 and 1967 was 5.1, indicating a modest increase during the decade between the first and second Conditionality Reviews. Table 3.5 also reveals that some Fund stand-by arrangements, particularly those for the European and Western Hemisphere borrowers, required countries to meet fiscal binding conditions, and that the average number of binding conditions and type of binding conditions varied substantially by region.

TABLE 3.5

Stand-by Arrangements in Upper-Credit Tranches (1969–April 1977): Distribution of
Performance Criteria by Tranche and Region

Arrangement	TRANCHE				REGION				
	Second	Third	Fourth	All	Africa	Asia	Europe	Middle East	Western Hemisphere
No. of stand-bys	36	36	18	90	18	18	13	10	31
Total binding conditions	201	225	97	523	74	138	81	62	168
Monetary BC									
Ceiling on credit expansion	33	34	16	83	11	18	13	10	31
Ceiling on credit to government	26	23	13	62	15	10	8	6	23
No reduction in reserve requirements	4	9	1	14	2	8	2	—	2
Other*	8	13	3	24	3	8	7	2	4
Foreign borrowing BC	20	32	8	60	7	27	2	5	19
Exchange and trade BC									
Balance of payments test	8	11	5	24	—	11	—	2	11
On exchange restrictions	72	82	34	188	30	48	28	31	51
On trade or import restrictions	24	16	9	49	5	8	12	5	19
Other†	1	2	—	3	—	—	2	—	1
Fiscal BC	5	3	6	14	1	—	5	1	7
Other BC‡	—	—	2	2	—	—	2	—	—
Average per stand-by	5.58	6.25	5.39	5.81	4.11	7.67	5.85	6.20	5.45

SOURCE: Data from SM/77/128, 6 June 1977, Tables 1–6, IMF Archives.

NOTE: BC = binding condition.

* Ceiling on credit to specialized financial institutions or public entities; ceiling on export financing; no reduction in interest rates or rediscount rates.

† Reduction in exchange guarantees; limit on deficit in trade account; limit on international convertible reserves.

‡ Quarterly consultation; ceiling on price index.

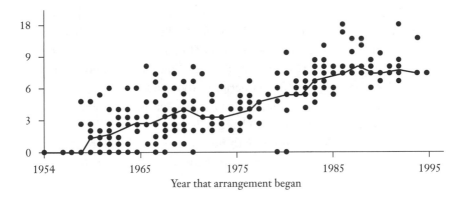

Figure 3.2. Total number of binding conditions, 1952–1995
SOURCE: From the Conditionality Data Set.

In the Second (1979) Conditionality Guidelines, the Executive Board instructed the staff to "pay due regard to the domestic social and political objectives, the economic priorities, and the circumstances of members" and also to apply "nondiscriminatory treatment" in its dealings with member states.[88] And once again the Executive Board instructed the staff to limit the inclusion of binding conditions "normally" to "macroeconomic variables" and "those necessary to implement specific provisions of the Articles of policies adopted under them."[89] The message was that binding conditions should be limited in both number—to only "those that are necessary to evaluate the implementation of the program"—and type—to macroeconomic, not structural, conditions. In short, these guidelines attempted to limit the increase in conditionality by reducing the "number of performance criteria, insisting on their macroeconomic character, circumscribing the reasons for reviews, and keeping preconditions to a minimum."

In practice, these guidelines were ineffective in containing the increase in conditionality. The number of binding conditions, for example, continued to increase.[90] Figure 3.2 is a scatterplot of Fund conditionality arrangements by the year that the program commenced and the number of binding conditions. The line is a smoothed median line and indicates that the average number of binding conditions has been climbing since around 1958 with a slight dip in 1974 and a stabilization in the 1990s (although there are fewer coded cases in the 1990s, due to archive access issues, so this may not be entirely representative). Note that this line represents the average for stand-by, EFF, SAF, and ESAF programs sampled; therefore, after the creation of the EFF in 1974, the average is not strictly comparable with the Fund estimates from Table 3.5. The mean value of the average number of binding conditions for arrangements initiated between 1952 and 1973 was 4.2; between 1974 and 1982, 7.1; between 1983 and 1990, 12.1; and between 1991 and 1995, 12.4.

The types of binding conditions also continued to change and became more structural in nature. Those changes have been linked, in part, to the creation of new lending facilities with new purposes. Therefore, it is useful to introduce those facilities before discussing the changes in the types of binding conditions.

The End of Bretton Woods and the Proliferation of Lending Facilities

In addition to the SBA, the International Monetary Fund created several other lending facilities. While stand-bys were explicitly intended to address short-term payments imbalances and serve as a second source of reserves, these new facilities were often designed to address new goals and had varying design features to match. This section reviews the new lending facilities developed by the Fund. Appendix 3 provides a brief summary of all the lending facilities and their features and terms. Because many of the different lending facilities were explicitly created to be "high," "low," or "medium" conditionality lending vehicles, some have considered this history of the creation (and use) of the new lending facilities as a proxy for the change in conditionality itself. By contrast, in most of the figures and tables presented here and in the statistical analyses that follow, I combine data for stand-bys, EFF, SAF, and ESAF arrangements. At the end of this section, I compare data from the four different lending facilities in order to debunk the myth that the increase in conditionality has been driven by the creation of these new facilities while leaving the design of stand-bys relatively untouched.

The first new lending facility, the Compensatory Financing Facility (CFF), was established by the Executive Board in 1963 as a low-conditionality facility to help primary product producers facing shortfalls in export earnings. The facility was "designed to extend the Fund's balance of payments support to member countries suffering from fluctuations in receipts from exports or primary products caused by circumstances largely beyond their control."[91] Member countries facing these circumstances could almost automatically draw up to 100% of their quota and, unlike under SBAs, the IMF would not explore the problems of, or solutions to, the country's economy.[92] In 1966, the facility was modified to make it even easier for members to use, and this increased its use.[93] For instance, in 1966 the "floating feature" was first introduced for the CFF; the floating feature allowed countries to make drawings under this facility that would not count as their (no conditionality) gold tranche or (low conditionality) first-credit tranche drawings.[94] In this way, the new facility was supposed to give countries more flexibility to receive immediate financing.[95]

Most of the new lending facilities were created after the collapse of the Bretton Woods system. On August 15, 1971, U.S. President Richard Nixon announced that the United States would no longer convert foreign holdings of dollars into gold. By March 1973, most industrial countries, including the United States, had adopted floating exchange rates, and the par value system established at Bretton Woods came to an end. Sharp increases in the price of oil caused widespread and deep balance-of-payments deficits, and it was in this tumultuous environment that four new lending facilities emerged from the IMF.

First, the 1974 Oil Facility was opened for six months, from June to December 1974, to assist countries facing payments imbalances due to the worldwide increases in oil prices. It provided low-conditionality loans; drawings were not linked to performance criteria and were not phased, but they did "float" alongside regular tranche drawings.[96] The amount that could be drawn was also not determined by the policies that a country followed, but rather by a formula based mainly on the increase in oil- and oil-related costs based on 1974 purchases.[97] The 1975 Oil Facility, which was open from January 1975 until May 1976, addressed the same problem, but required countries to agree with the Fund on a policy program and was therefore considered a higher conditionality facility.[98] As the 1975 Annual Report stated:

> Stricter conditionality applies to the use of the oil facility for 1975 compared with that for 1974. Under the 1974 facility a member was *expected to consult* with the Fund on its balance of payments prospects and policies . . . whereas use of the 1975 facility *requires* the purchasing member to *describe* its policies to achieve medium-term solutions to its balance of payments problems and an *assessment by the Fund of the adequacy of these policies.*[99]

In addition to requiring an agreed-upon policy program, the 1975 oil facility gave "greater weight to a member's quota in calculating a member's access to the facility and somewhat less weight to the increase in oil costs," making it more closely resemble a SBA.

Three months after the Executive Board created the first oil facility, it established the Extended Fund Facility (EFF), a higher-conditionality, medium-term loan program to address deeper, more structural balance of payments problems and chronic low growth.[100] These loans tended to be larger (up to 140% of quota) and longer, both in terms of the time of the arrangement and the period for repayment, than previous loan programs. EFF loans also required more detailed policy programs than previous loan programs in order to address the country's structural imbalances.[101] In certain ways, this facility appears to be an early deviation from the original intentions of the Articles, which specify that the Fund should provide funds for temporary payments imbalances, and specifically not for developmental assistance (or structural reform). It provides funds for longer periods and in larger amounts (relative to the quota).[102] The EFF initially required a comprehensive policy program for the first 12 months and then progress reports and subsequent plans every 12 months for up to three years.[103]

In May 1976, the Trust Fund, the fourth lending facility created during the 1970s, was established to provide "eligible developing members" with "additional balance of payments assistance on concessionary terms."[104] The Trust Fund loans required a 12–month program; they required a program of action and lent money on a "highly concessional" basis.[105] Thus, over the early to mid-1970s, the Fund innovated in many directions, creating four facilities of varying stringency to meet different purposes.

As mentioned previously, at the end of the 1970s, the Executive Board passed the second amendment to the Articles and the Second Review of Conditionality, which was discussed at length in the previous section. The second amendment, which entered into force on April 1, 1978, codified the new post–Bretton Woods policies of the International Monetary Fund.[106] It helped create a new system by formally abandoning the par value, gold-backed system and establishing a new surveillance mechanism for monitoring exchange rates and ensuring their stability.[107] It codified some of the existing practices by referring to "stand-by arrangements" for the first time in the Articles and also extended the domain of IMF conditionality arrangements by stipulating that "special" policies were needed for special balance-of-payments problems.[108]

Immediately after the Second Review of Conditionality, drawings increased.[109] In 1981, the Executive Board decided to provide certain members with "enlarged access" or to allow larger amounts (relative to quota) to be drawn from the GRA. By 1981, the new maximum drawings were 150% of quota per year, 450% over three years, and 600% as a total access limit.[110] By 1981 (and as opposed to 1971), the majority of drawings were in the "upper-credit tranche," or high-conditionality category. As larger percentages of the quotas were able to be drawn under larger and longer SBAs, stricter conditionality requirements were imposed.[111] In 1981, Managing Director Jacques de Larosière wrote, "In the period following the first oil shock, approximately three quarters of the resources provided by the Fund to its members were made available on terms involving a low degree of conditionality. At present, by contrast, some three quarters of our new lending commitments involve 'upper credit tranche' programs, that is to say, they require rigorous adjustment policies."[112] Part of the reason that countries entered into higher tranche arrangements was because IMF quotas were not increased as quickly as the world economy grew. Inflation led the real value of quotas to fall, even as IMF quotas were increased at the in 1970 to $28.8 billion, in 1974–1978 to $78.1 billion, in 1983 to $95 billion, in 1990–1992 to $204 billion and in 1998 to SDR 212 billion (about $283 billion).[113]

Not only were the absolute and relative (to quota) amounts of lending in the 1980s larger than before, but also the content of the programs was changing. This is reflected partially in the Fund's closer working relationship with the World Bank, as the two organizations started addressing similar structural (rather than simply in the short term, as originally intended for the Fund) problems.[114] These sister institutions, established at Bretton Woods, worked jointly on three new lending facilities, including the Structural Adjustment Facility (SAF), the Enhanced Structural Adjustment Facility (ESAF), and the Poverty Reduction and Growth Facility (PRGF), which allowed the Fund to get involved in longer-term growth-oriented structural reforms. In March 1986, the Executive Board established the SAF "to provide concessional balance of payments assistance—in conjunction with the World Bank and other lenders—to low-income countries eligible for loans from the International Development Association that were facing protracted balance of payments problems and were undertaking comprehensive efforts to strengthen their balance of payments position."[115] This facility included "a number of major innovative features" such as the requirement to adopt a comprehensive three year program that "incorporates explicitly the structural policy elements of a member's reform program" and the institutionalized cooperation between the World Bank and the Fund.[116] The structural adjustment facility allowed countries to draw up to 70% of their quotas "to support a one-year program," delineated in a detailed policy framework paper that has been drafted by country representatives.[117] In December 1987, the Executive Board replaced the SAF with the ESAF, which was quite similar to the SAF except that it allowed larger amounts to be drawn (normally 250% of quota over three years, but could be up to 350% of quota), and the amount of financing was based on "the strength of the country's adjustment effort and the size of its balance of payments need."[118] (Appendix 3 provides details about these and other facilities.)

Innovations in the late 1980s and early 1990s further expanded the purposes for which Fund resources were utilized. In 1988 the CFF was reformed and renamed the Compensatory and Contingency Financing Facility. This newly named facility differs from its predecessor in that it not only compensates for export shortfalls, but now also assists members who have already entered into arrangements (that is, extendeds or stand-bys) and are faced with exogenous shocks.[119] In April 1993, the Executive Board established a temporary facility to deal primarily with the economic transitions of former Soviet and Eastern European countries. This Systemic Transformation Facility expired at the end of December 1995. In 1995 the Emergency Financing Mechanism was established to "allow for quick Executive Board approval of IMF financial support to a member facing a crisis in its external account that required an immediate Fund response." The Debt Initiative for Heavily Indebted Poor Countries (HIPCs) was established in September 1996 as a joint World Bank–Fund initiative to "provide exceptional assistance to eligible countries following sound economic policies to help them reduce their external debt burden to sustainable levels." The program was then modified in September 1999 to provide more debt relief and "strengthen the links between debt relief, poverty reduction, and social policies."[120] In response to the Asian financial crisis, the Supplementary Reserve Facility was established in 1997 to "provide financial assistance for exceptional balance of payments difficulties owing to a large short-term financing need resulting

TABLE 3.6
Comparisons of Different Fund Lending Vehicles, 1986–1995

Vehicle	Length (months)	No. of Phases	Total No. of Binding Conditions	Total No. of Procedural Conditions
Stand-by	14.8/24	5.4/9	11.9/17	2.1/8
EFF	36/36	12.25/18	11.3/12	2.0/3
SAF (1986–1988)	36/36	3/3	15.2/18	4.8/7
ESAF (1988–1995)	36/36	6/6	15.2/18	4.0/5

SOURCE: Data from the Conditionality Data Set.

NOTE: Data are presented as mean/maximum. EFF = Extended Fund Facility; ESAF = Enhanced Structural Adjustment Facility; SAF = Structural Adjustment Facility.

from a sudden and disruptive loss of market confidence."[121] In November 1999, the ESAF was renamed the Poverty Reduction and Growth Facility in order to give it a "more explicitly antipoverty focus." Programs are "based on country-designed poverty reduction strategies, and formulated in a participatory manner involving civil society and developmental partners."[122]

These new loan programs addressed new problems, such as chronic low growth and poverty.[123] Whereas IMF funds were initially intended to be used to offset temporary balance of payments crises and then to support stabilization programs, now they also support structural adjustment programs with deeper, longer-term, supply-side reforms. As the goals of Fund programs change, invariably new stipulations and requirements are added to the conditionality arrangement between the Fund and borrower. As a result, many point to the creation of these new facilities as an explanation for the changing terms of Fund conditionality arrangements.

However, the differences between, for instance, SBAs and ESAF programs should not be exaggerated. Certainly these programs, and others, differ in some systematic ways, including the interest rate charged on the loan and the repayment period. But the number and type of binding conditions required, and the length and phasing, differ less than previous characterizations suggest. Table 3.6 provides data on the mean and maximum length in months, number of phases, number of binding conditions, and number of procedural conditions for each of the four types of Fund conditional loan arrangements included in the Conditionality Data Set between 1986 and 1995.[124] The averages are restricted to the post-1985 period because SAFs were first used in 1986 and it is useful to compare the programs during the same time period. As Table 3.6 notes, EFF and SBAs do tend to have three or four fewer binding conditions, including about two fewer procedural conditions, than do SAF or ESAF programs on average. However, these differences are not consistent across cases. Individual SBAs required as many as 17 binding conditions and 8 procedural conditions during this period. SBAs tend to be shorter than EFFs, SAFs, and ESAFs; however, they are no longer only one year, as stipulated by the Second Conditionality Guidelines. SBAs during this period extended as long as two years. Finally, SBAs vary widely in the number of phases in which their loan is disbursed, but the mean number of phases (5.4) is similar to the ESAFs' mean of 6. The EFF arrangements, by contrast, apparently tend to include more phasing than stand-bys, SAFs, or ESAFs.

Changing Types of Conditions

How have the types of binding conditions changed across the population of Fund conditional loan arrangements? Fund publications have described shifts in the content of Fund programs.[125] Initially Fund programs were stabilization programs that attempted to solve temporary balance of payments problems with short-term, demand-side policies, like fiscal or monetary austerity. Now Fund programs are mainly structural adjustment programs that address chronic balance of payments shortfalls and low growth, and often entail long-term, supply-side policies, such as deregulating domestic goods, eliminating price controls, deregulating financial markets, eliminating interest rate ceilings, liberalizing trade, and "strengthening [the] social and economic infrastructure and promoting administrative and other microeconomic reforms."[126] Today Fund programs do not only address the original goals of correcting short-term payments imbalances, but also address much broader goals like economic growth and poverty alleviation.[127] The typical Fund program has shifted, according to official publications, from consisting of four main elements—credit controls, fiscal controls, exchange rate adjustment, and price and wage controls—to a three-pronged approach of securing external financing, "reining in domestic demand," and increasing economic growth.[128] Other Fund staff members or scholars have written that up until the early 1970s, performance criteria for Fund stabilization programs consisted of broad economic targets "significant enough to serve as a basis for an appraisal of the economy as a whole," whereas current performance criteria tend to be more detailed and numerous, reflecting a shift toward "microconditionality."[129] Most recently, work within and outside the Fund has focused on the purportedly recent increase in "structural conditionality." These descriptions offer an official and general picture of changes in binding conditions. Data reveal that this simple portrait is somewhat misleading.

Tables 3.5 (discussed earlier) and 3.7 present data on the use of specific types of binding conditions between 1969–1977 and 1957–1967 respectively, according to internal Fund documents. Between 1957 and 1967, 52% of all binding conditions included in upper-credit tranche Fund SBAs were monetary conditions, and 34% were exchange and trade conditions. Nine percent of all included binding conditions were fiscal in nature, whereas 5% concerned foreign borrowing, according to these data. The changes between 1957–1967 and 1969–1977 seem to be mainly related to the number of binding conditions, and the shift in priorities from monetary conditions to exchange and trade conditions. In the 1969–1977 time period, 50% of all binding conditions in upper-credit tranche stand-bys were related to exchange and trade, 35% were monetary, 11% were related to foreign borrowing, and 4% were related to fiscal and other conditions. These data give us a good sense of which conditions Fund staff were more or less likely to use during this period, but not how widespread the inclusion of these conditions was, or how their usage changed after 1977.

By contrast, Table 3.8 shows some central aspects of how the types of binding conditions in Fund conditionality programs have changed, according to the Conditionality Data Set. In this data set, I coded the binding conditions as belonging to one of 13 different substantive groups. Table 3.8 provides data on the change in the relative frequencies of 9 of these 13 binding conditions groups (or in nine different types of conditionality).[130] Each column in Table 3.8 represents a substantive grouping of binding conditions, and the cell values represent the percentage of arrangements initiated in each time period that contained these types of conditions. Column 1 represents the percentage of arrangements that included all four basic requirements as binding conditions; the basic requirements include a prohibition on any new restrictions on payments and transfers for current international transfers, quantitative restrictions on imports, multiple exchange practices, or bilateral payments agreements. (These would be considered exchange and

TABLE 3.7
Distribution of Binding Conditions for Selected Countries*

Area	Country	Number of Stand-bys	Monetary BC	Fiscal BC	Foreign Borrowing BC	Exchange and Trade BC	Total BC	Average BC per Stand-by
Africa	Liberia	5	4	11	5	5	26	5.2
	Morocco	4	4	—	—	4	8	2.0
	Tunisia	4	12	—	2	7	21	5.2
Asia	India	4	4	—	—	—	4	1.0
	Philippines	4	6	—	—	4	10	2.5
Europe	Turkey	7	34	—	—	—	34	4.9
	UK	4	—	—	—	—	—	—
Western Hemisphere	Argentina	6	11	2	1	4	18	2.3
	Bolivia	9	26	—	2	12	40	4.4
	Brazil	4	8	6	2	19	35	8.7
	Chile	8	14	11	—	25	50	6.2
	Columbia	9	14	1	—	27	42	4.7
	Costa Rica	5	17	1	3	8	29	5.8
	Ecuador	6	18	1	—	24	43	7.1
	El Salvador	7	11	—	—	9	20	2.8
	Guatemala	4	12	—	2	9	23	5.7
	Haiti	9	36	25	6	16	83	9.2
	Honduras	7	21	1	4	—	26	3.7
	Nicaragua	5	8	—	—	9	17	3.4
	Paraguay	5	10	4	—	2	16	3.2
	Peru	9	22	—	2	12	36	4.0

SOURCE: SM/68/128, Supplement 3, September 4, 1968, IMF Archives.
*All countries with four or more stand-by arrangements in the upper credit tranche over the period 1957–1967.

TABLE 3.8
Changing Frequencies of Certain Categories of Binding Conditions

Time Period	Basic Requirements	Credit Targets	Foreign Debt Targets	Fiscal Targets	Bank Reform	BoP Targets	Economic Policy Reform	Rel. with Fund	Bank Friendly
1952–1973	3%	77%	23%	44%	44%	12%	14%	0%	3%
1974–1982	57%	35%	63%	63%	26%	30%	2%	0%	20%
1983–1990	98%	39%	94%	91%	30%	43%	26%	64%	79%
1991–2000	100%	93%	100%	100%	40%	67%	40%	67%	73%

SOURCE: Data from the Conditionality Data Set.

NOTE: BoP = balance of payments; Rel. = relations. The 1991–2000 period is incomplete.

trade conditions according to the Fund staff's classification.) Column 2 represents the percentage of arrangements that have at least one limit on credit expansion, another long-standing and common type of condition. Columns 3 and 4 represent the percentage of arrangements that have at least one limit on the contraction of foreign debt and targets related to reducing the government deficit (including fiscal targets), respectively. Columns 5 and 6 represent the percentage of arrangements that have at least one binding condition related to domestic bank reform and balance of payments targets, respectively. Column 7 represents the percentage of arrangements that have at least one binding condition related to economic policy reform. This group of conditions best captures the trend toward "microconditionality" noted by Fund observers. For instance, economic policy reform conditions may specify how a borrower should reform its tax system, liquidate, or reform a particular state enterprise, implement a public investment program, or reform the social security system. Column 8 represents the percentage of arrangements that have at least one binding condition related to maintaining good financial relations with the Fund (for example, no overdue financial obligations to the Fund). Finally, column 9 represents the percentage of arrangements that have at least one binding condition that is "bank-friendly" (for example, a country must stay current in payments on its commercial bank loans).

Table 3.8 provides only a partial picture of the changes in the content of conditionality arrangements. Some reforms that were required elements of Fund programs, like exchange rate adjustments that are often required as prior actions, do not appear in the arrangements as ongoing binding conditions. Not all coded binding conditions are even listed in the table. However, the groups of binding conditions included in the table do reveal some interesting trends. Arrangements in the first period, between 1952 and 1973, generally had at least one credit target (77%), and nearly half of them had some sort of government deficit or spending target and a condition regarding domestic bank reform. Between 1974 and 1982, the Fund increased its use of credit, government deficit, and balance of payments targets, and especially basic requirements and foreign debt targets. Use of bank reform and economic policy reform decreased from the previous time period. In the last period, programs have become more uniform and consistent in their stringency.

During the 1983–2000 period, basic requirements, credit, foreign debt, and government deficit targets were used in nearly all arrangements included in the sample. Conditions ensuring good financial relations with the Fund were introduced during this period and utilized in nearly two-thirds of the arrangements. Three-fourths of all arrangements included bank-friendly conditions; half included balance of payments targets; 60% stipulated conditions pertaining to good financial relations with the Fund; 40% required bank reform; and about one-fifth included economic policy reform conditions.

The Executive Board's third comprehensive review of conditionality in April 1988 demonstrates just how much conditionality had changed since 1952, and even since 1979. For instance, the examination considered such issues, previously outside the purview of the Fund, as "the means of ensuring that adjustment programs foster growth, how programs affect poverty, the monitoring of structural adjustment, and technical issues in program monitoring."[131] The focus on the implications of Fund programs on poverty represents a real shift, given the Fund's previously quite vocal neutrality on the effects of their programs on poverty. As opposed to the emphasis on temporary balance of payments crises prevalent in the 1950s, 1960s, and early 1970s, this examination stated that it is "accepted that Fund-supported adjustment programs should foster sustainable economic growth in a *medium-term* perspective."[132] Moreover, the policy tools for structural adjustment are different and more specific than those used in the 1950s through 1970s. Policy tools emphasized by the 1988 Review include "policies aimed at strengthening domestic savings and improving resource allocation, . . . price reforms, . . . actions to strengthen the efficiency of the capital structure, in part by raising the quality of public sector investment; and steps to lessen the distortions caused by monopolies, skewed incidence of taxation, and trade restrictions."[133] The review also acknowledged that the goals and policies of Fund programs had changed:

> While certain structural measures are clearly within the Fund's traditional areas of responsibility, others, such as the rationalization of public sector investment programs, strengthening social and economic infrastructure, and promoting administrative and other microeconomic reforms, are less directly related. Deeper Fund involvement in these areas must involve very close collaboration with the World Bank.[134]

In fact, the Fund has increasingly become involved in "microconditionality." Whereas in the 1950s, 1960s, and early 1970s the Fund would have simply established macroeconomic targets and remained agnostic as to how a government reduced its deficit (for instance, its burden on the poor), by 1988 the Fund required much more specific policy enactments.[135] By 1988 the Fund also provided technical assistance to determine how countries should achieve the expanded Fund goals of a balanced budget, economic growth, and equity—for instance, which taxes should be cut and how. The Fund also remained involved with the borrowing country for much longer periods of time as these extensive reforms were being implemented.[136]

Conclusion

This chapter provides a new account of the changes in Fund conditionality, relying heavily on Fund archival materials and the original Conditionality Data Set. The history starts by tracing the beginning of Fund conditionality, from the pre–Bretton Woods "automaticity versus conditionality" debates to the eventual establishment of the SBA in 1952. Next it follows the development of Fund conditionality policy and practice, and the changes in program length, the use of protective clauses, the number of binding conditions, and the use of phasing, reviews, and consultations. The history then focuses on the creation of new lending facilities with new purposes from the 1970s through today and debunks the myth that changes in conditionality have been driven mainly by the establishment of these new facilities by the Executive Board. Finally, the history provides a portrait of how the types of Fund conditions have changed over time, relying on documents from the Fund archives and the Conditionality Data Set. The next chapter evaluates whether this history and data appear to support the two dominant conventional wisdoms.

CHAPTER FOUR

Observable Implications and Explanations of Longitudinal Change

Introduction

The previous chapter provided a detailed portrait of the changes in Fund conditionality since its inception in 1952. In retelling this history, scholars could emphasize different factors as important in influencing changes in Fund conditionality. For instance, in explaining the creation of the stand-by arrangement (SBA), scholars could emphasize how the powerful United States imposed its preferences on other members and the Fund itself, or they could emphasize how the staff and management scrambled to prevent the IMF from becoming "moribund." In fact, this history has generally been told either approvingly by Fund staff historians recounting how the Fund bent to the winds of change, or disapprovingly by economists dismayed by the unforeseen expansion. Sometimes the history has been used as a backdrop against a story of U.S. dominance or a tale of bureaucratic expansion.

In this chapter, I explicitly consider how well the pattern of changes in Fund conditionality conforms with the observable implications of two of the most prominent explanations for these changes—the realist argument and the bureaucratic politics argument—or with the observable implications of the supplementary financier argument.[1] This section focuses on particular elements of the change in conditionality discussed in the previous chapter to see whether the observable implications of conventional wisdoms hold true. I present new evidence of the details of how conditionality has changed, relying on data directly extracted from Fund archival documents and from the Conditionality Data Set (also constructed using documents from the Fund archives). For instance, I compare the instructions from the Executive Board, the Fund's formal collective principal dominated by certain powerful states including the United States, with the actual changes in Fund conditionality revealed by this data. By comparing the instructions provided to the staff in three Fund Conditionality Guidelines from 1968, 1979, and 2002 with actual changes in Fund conditionality, this chapter roughly assesses whether the growth in Fund conditionality seems to have originated from the instructions of the Fund's formal principals, the member states represented on the Executive Board and Board of Governors.

In short, the history casts doubt on the two conventional explanations. State control of the Fund is elusive. Consistently, executive directors (EDs), including those from powerful states like the United States, have argued for less stringent conditionality during policy debates, and consistently these policy decisions have been followed by increases in the stringency of Fund conditionality arrangements. Similarly, staff members, the other obvious culprit for increases in Fund conditionality, have consistently opposed many of the changes in the Fund's conditional loan arrangements. The history does, however, provide initial support for the supplementary financier argument. Changes in Fund conditionality broadly conform to global changes in the provision of supplementary financing.

Realist Argument and Observable Implications

Realist scholars argue that changes in the activities of international organizations—in this case the International Monetary Fund—have been driven by the interests of powerful states.[2] If realists are correct, then certainly the changes that we observe in Fund activity should reflect U.S. preferences over Fund activity. In other words, one key observable implication of this argument is that the changes we observe ex post reflect ex ante U.S. preferences. But how does one discern U.S. preferences over Fund conditionality? This section focuses on U.S. expressed preferences. In other words, despite the potential drawbacks, I have accepted statements by U.S. officials, often the U.S. ED, at face value as accurate representations of U.S. preferences over Fund activity. Second, this section focuses mainly on U.S. expressed preferences over *Fund conditionality policy*, rather than individual conditional loan arrangements.

Why not focus on individual conditionality agreements instead? After all, pundits and scholars alike have often used *individual* conditional loan arrangements as their central piece of evidence to substantiate claims that the United States controls Fund conditionality (a claim about causality) and that the United States has pushed for more conditionality (a claim about preferences). Russia in 1998 and Mexico in 1995 are two favorite examples. However, this anecdotal case evidence is at best inconclusive with regard to both preferences (the focus of the discussion here) and causality. One could just as easily cite examples of conditionality agreements that support the realist claims as one could cite examples of conditionality agreements that cast doubt on them. For example, one could cite examples of arrangements where the United States explicitly opposed a loan program that was nonetheless passed (disputing the causal claim), such as the 1957 Indian SBA or the 1981 Indian Extended Fund Facility (EFF). In the case of the 1957 agreement, the U.S. Treasury secretary explicitly stated that he was willing to support an Indian SBA for $127.5 million, but not for $200 million, because he believed the larger amount would endanger Fund resources. The managing director did not agree and decided, even during this heady period of U.S. power, to ignore U.S. preferences in order to preserve close relations with India.[3] In the case of the 1981 agreement (for SDR 5 billion, which was at that time the largest Fund program to date), the United States again strongly and loudly opposed this arrangement, but it was still approved, with the U.S. ED abstaining from the final vote.[4] Alternatively, one could offer examples where the United States pushed for weaker conditionality on an individual agreement and was not successful (disputing both the claims about preferences and causality). Consider the case of the 1969 UK SBA. The United States (and UK) opposed inclusion of monetary conditions in this arrangement but was "overruled," according to one of the Fund staff members who negotiated that arrangement.[5] In the end there was one binding condition required for this loan arrangement—the first condition in any UK arrangement to date. (There had been eight previous UK SBAs.) Finally, one could discuss cases where the United States pushed for weaker conditionality and did appear to be successful (disputing only the claim about preferences). The case of Brazil's 1965 SBA, discussed at length in Chapter 5, fits this description. U.S. policy with regard to individual conditionality agreement cases has certainly fluctuated—the United States has appeared to have decisive influence in some cases and little influence in others, and has appeared to support stronger and weaker conditionality in different cases.

Individual case evidence is not useful for evaluating U.S. preferences over Fund conditionality for two basic reasons. First, there is the case selection problem. The cases just mentioned are likely to be outliers. The American press rarely covers Fund conditional loan arrangements. It is likely that the programs that are covered deviate in some way from the mean. In order to be able to generalize from such case evidence (to glean broad U.S. preferences over conditionality from individual cases), one should select representative conditionality agreement cases at several points in time from 1952 to 1995 and observe whether the United States tended to advocate higher, status quo, or lower conditionality at each of these points. Even this ideal (but time-consuming!) research design is fraught with problems. How do you determine representativeness so that you can generalize from the United States' expressed preferences regarding a few select cases to the United States' general position on conditionality? Policy discussions and decisions are clearer expressions of preference over conditionality than are discussions and decisions regarding individual country cases.

Second, the Executive Board (and the United States) does not appear to be controlling Fund conditionality through changes of, or debates over, *individual* conditionality arrangements. Typically draft agreements are written by Fund staff in anticipation of a loan request. The details of each stand-by, EFF, Structural Adjustment Facility (SAF), or Enhanced Structural Adjustment Facility (ESAF) arrangement are negotiated by the staff and borrowing country representatives, often during a staff mission trip to the prospective borrowing country. Although powerful states may be involved in these negotiations (as, for instance, the Brazil case study in Chapter 5 indicates), this is not the standard practice. Once an agreement is reached, the staff place this arrangement on the Board's agenda for discussion. Sometimes the Board discussions get heated and there are disagreements about specific measures; however, these proposed agreements are almost always approved by Board consensus without being amended in any way. In practice, the Executive Board rarely, if ever, exercises its veto power, particularly with respect to Fund loan arrangements.[6] There are only a few instances in the entire Fund history of the Executive Board, much less the United States, turning down or even modifying a request for a conditional loan arrangement.[7] Some may hypothesize that the Executive Board does not exercise its veto power because the staff accurately anticipate the Board's preferences. Interviews with numerous EDs and their staff actually suggest otherwise.[8] Interviewed Executive Board members made clear that proposals do not always reflect their preferences.[9] The Board's veto threat regarding individual loan arrangements is too costly, both in terms of harm to the borrowing country and to the Fund's future bargaining leverage with borrowers.

Because on a case-by-case basis the Executive Board is often not able to influence the terms of Fund conditional loan arrangements, the Board issues policy directives that are intended to guide and constrain future Fund activity. The debates over these policy directives are better reflections of U.S. and Board preferences over Fund conditionality (and they are also more consistent) than debates over individual Fund conditional loan arrangements that generally do not impact the contours of those individual arrangements.

The evidence from debates over Fund conditionality policy suggests that ex ante U.S. preferences did align with subsequent changes in Fund conditionality from the 1940s through the early 1960s. As discussed earlier, the United States pushed for lending to be conditional on the maintenance of certain policies and supported the new terms introduced in the 1950s—for instance, that SBAs be short term and that they be repaid within three to five years.[10] In the words of the U.S. ED during that period (and later the deputy managing director of the Fund), Frank Southard, "In the 1950s the U.S. voice in the Fund was decisive. . . . The practical question in those years, in any prospective large use of Fund resources, was whether the United States would agree—and the answer was obtained by direct inquiry."[11]

However, observing U.S. preferences during this early period alone— from the 1940s through the early 1960s—is not a good test of the realist argument for two reasons. First, many of the dramatic changes in conditionality—concerning the length, number of conditions, types of conditions, and review and consultation procedures—occurred after the early 1960s. Therefore, if we are interested in what drove these changes, we should be more concerned with the conformity between ex ante U.S. preferences and subsequent changes in Fund conditionality after the early 1960s. Second, the supplementary financier argument also predicts that changes in Fund conditionality will reflect ex ante U.S. preferences from the 1940s through the early 1960s when the United States was the dominant source of supplementary financing. As a result, the period since the late 1960s offers a better test of the realist argument via-à-vis the supplementary financier argument.

Since the late 1960s, a different pattern has emerged regarding ex ante U.S. preferences and subsequent changes in Fund activity. During policy reviews and debates over general Fund conditionality policy, the United States and many other powerful states have consistently pushed for policies to constrain staff activity and limit Fund conditionality. Despite Executive Board efforts to constrain Fund activities during the 1968 and 1979 reviews, as well as during more recent policy discussions, Fund activity has continued to deviate from those constraints.

As mentioned in the previous chapter, between 1966 and 1968, the Executive Board debated Fund conditionality policy. In the debates preceding the 1968 decision, nearly all EDs, *including* the United States ED, advocated less stringent conditionality and fewer binding conditions.[12] According to the Fund's own estimates, the number of performance criteria (or binding conditions) included in Fund programs had more than doubled—from 2 to 5—in less than a decade.[13] By 1967, even the relatively small first-credit tranche SBAs required countries to meet 2.1 binding conditions on average. The U.S. ED, William Dale, did urge the use of some binding conditions; those binding conditions were meant to encourage supplementary financing from the United States. At one Executive Board meeting in 1966, he argued, "By establishing performance criteria related to public finance, credit policy, and the balance of payments, stand-by arrangements have in many cases provided an essential part of the basis on which sizable amounts of U.S. assistance have been committed."[14] Dale and other EDs agreed that the use of fiscal performance conditions, however, should be minimized. Fiscal conditions tended to impact social policy, and as the UK ED stated, "the Fund should bow before the economic and social priorities set by any country."[15]

These debates eventually culminated in the 1968 Conditionality Guidelines passed by the Executive Board in September 1968 as EBM 68–132.[16] The Guidelines included two main instructions for staff. First, in contradiction with the guidelines that staff had developed for themselves in 1963 and in response to demands from members for greater flexibility, the Executive Board decided that first-credit tranche SBAs would not be phased and would not include binding conditions. However, all arrangements beyond the first-credit tranche would be phased and would have binding conditions and consultation clauses. "Exceptional cases" would not be required to be phased. In other words, the Executive Board tried to establish some uniform design criteria for loan programs that were in and above the first-credit tranche. Second, whereas the Executive Board instructed the staff to include binding conditions and consultation clauses for all upper-credit tranche SBAs, the Executive Board agreed that binding conditions had "proliferated" in previous SBAs and hereafter should be limited to the "minimum necessary for the success of the program."[17] The decision also stated that Fund staff should limit binding conditions to those

> necessary to evaluate the implementation and achievement of the objectives of the program in support of which the stand-by arrangement is granted. While no general rule as to the number and content of performance criteria can be adopted because of the diversity of the problems and institutional arrangements of members, every effort will be made to keep the number of criteria to the minimum necessary, for the success of the program.[18]

Some EDs had wanted the Fund to establish uniform criteria for all SBAs (for example, Alexandre Kafka, an elected ED from Brazil) in order to ensure fairness and uniformity. The Executive Board decision did not end up establishing uniform criteria, but it did instruct Fund staff to limit the number of binding conditions. This 1968 decision allowed the EDs to express their general concerns about the "proliferation" of binding conditions, the use of phasing and binding conditions for first-credit tranche drawings, and the lack of uniformity between programs.[19]

The 1968 decision was an effort on the part of the Executive Board to define and constrain Fund conditionality and the terms of Fund SBAs. The Executive Board revised an earlier staff policy on Fund conditionality, urging the staff to apply fewer binding conditions and to not include phasing and binding conditions for first-credit tranche drawings. In other words, the Executive Board decision attempted to reduce the stringency of Fund programs and constrain Fund activity.

However, the practice of Fund conditionality continued to deviate from the policies set ex ante by the Executive Board and advocated by the U.S. ED, William Dale. Despite clear instructions for uniformity and fewer binding conditions, Fund programs continued to vary, and the average number of binding conditions continued to increase (if slightly during the immediate postdecision period). Fund programs did not become more uniform during this period, as the Executive Board had instructed and hoped. Table 3.5 indicates that, according to the Fund's own estimates, the average number of binding conditions and types of binding conditions varied substantially by region.[20] Despite explicit instructions to include fewer binding conditions, the number continued to increase. Again according to the Fund's own research, the average number of binding conditions required by an upper-credit tranche between 1969 and 1977 was 5.7. Recall that the Fund staff estimated the average number of binding conditions between 1965 and 1967 was 5.1, indicating a modest increase. According to the Conditionality Data Set, the average number of binding conditions in SBAs also increased during this period. In 1968 the average number of binding conditions required by a Fund SBA was 5.6; in 1970 it was 6.3; in 1976 it was 6.5; and in 1978 it was 8.[21] Despite Executive Board pressure, including from the United States' own ED, to refrain from using fiscal performance conditions, their use also increased widely between 1969 and 1978. In fact, between 1973 and 1978 only six upper-credit tranche programs did not include a fiscal binding condition.[22]

In 1978 and 1979, the Executive Board resurrected the discussion of conditionality guidelines. In the debates on Fund conditionality policy that preceded this review, Sam Cross, the U.S.-appointed ED with 21% of the vote in 1978, argued that the Fund staff should stick to broad macroeconomic targets as binding conditions, rather than specific policies. The Fund may offer advice regarding specific policies, like fiscal policies, but these specific policies should not be included as binding conditions (or performance criteria) whose violation prompts the withholding of Fund resources. The following is an excerpt from Cross's statement, as recorded in the Executive Board meeting minutes:

> As to whether the Fund concerned itself in too much detail with matters of social equity and the allocation of resources in member countries, Mr. Cross observed, he had no objection to the Fund advising members on such matters as part of the consultation process. Ideally, performance criteria ought to be directed toward macroeconomic problems, such as overall budget deficits and levels of external borrowing. But *great care should be taken not to inject the Fund into the choice of measures by a country for achieving the objective sought*, especially where matters of social equity were involved. To require any action in that sphere as a condition of Fund financing called for very delicate judgments about how far the institution should go. . . . The Fund should not try to determine what structural changes should be made, but should accommodate itself to those that the member wished to introduce, especially where social and political decisions were being made.[23]

Most other EDs concurred that the Fund should not include fiscal criteria or detailed policy criteria as binding conditions, but instead require binding conditions that related to broad economic indicators and that would help ensure that Fund resources are not improperly used. For instance, R. J. Whitelaw, an ED from Australia who also represented four other countries with 3% of the vote in 1978, agreed that the Fund had gotten too "involved in the details of economic policy."[24] As he stated:

> Requirements had been made of countries to reduce subsidies, or to raise the prices of government services, change the structure of taxes, and so on. While no doubt appropriate from an economic point of view, it might have been better if those requirements had not been raised to the status of performance criteria [binding conditions], but left on the level of well intentioned advice.[25]

The limitation of performance criteria to only macroeconomic variables was intended to restrain the IMF from micromanaging. Developed and developing country EDs alike agreed that the Fund should not include more structural policies as binding conditions. Cross argued that the "Fund should not try to determine what structural changes should be made, but should accommodate itself to those that the member wished to introduce, especially where social and political decisions were being made."[26] Alexandre Kafka, the elected ED from Brazil, also recommended limiting binding conditions and Fund recommendations to nonstructural, demand-side policies. He argued that "performance criteria should be strictly limited to the macroeconomic variables which would guarantee appropriate progress toward a viable balance of payments. . . . I have no doubt at all that microeconomic matters are not a proper subject for performance clauses. A distinction must be made between good ideas and performance clauses."[27]

Related to this preference for broad binding conditions, rather than detailed procedural ones, Cross warned against a drift into longer-term developmental lending, reiterating a concern U.S. representatives have articulated since the Bretton Woods days of 1944. He argued that the Fund should generally stick to short-term balance of payments financing, as originally mandated. For instance, in response to a suggestion for longer arrangements, Cross stated, "It was necessary to maintain institutional integrity, so to speak, between the Fund's balance of payments financing for purposes of adjustment, and other forms of financing, for development, for instance. Therefore, the Fund should confine itself to the shorter range . . . in order not to blur the distinction between it and other institutions."[28] In short, Cross and others expressed a preference for shorter programs that addressed payments imbalances with broad macroeconomic conditions, rather than longer programs addressing developmental concerns with detailed structural conditions.

The Second Review of Conditionality was passed by the Executive Board in March 1979 and again provided new guidelines for IMF conditionality.[29] Three of these instructions are noteworthy in their attempt to define and constrain future Fund activity. First, reiterating the 1968 Review, the Second Review also emphasized uniformity across loan programs, this time stipulating that phasing and performance clauses would be omitted from SBAs below the first-credit tranche, and included in all others. Second, the decision again provided the staff with instructions about the length of these supposedly short-term loan programs. The permitted length of Fund programs was extended to reflect the then-current practice, but an explicit limit was set. Most new arrangements were now supposed to last around 12 months and at most three years. The maximum length of arrangements was extended from 6 months to 12 months and "up to but not beyond three years."[30] This change was a controversial one, but basically it just followed practice. By 1979, the average conditionality program was about 11 months.[31] Third and finally, the guidelines returned to the question of how many and what type of binding conditions (or performance criteria) should be included in Fund programs. The First Review had instructed staff to limit the number of binding conditions, but those instructions had not been heeded. Through the Second Review, the Executive Board instructed the staff to "pay due regard to the domestic social and political objectives, the economic priorities, and the circumstances of members" and also to apply "nondiscriminatory treatment" in its dealings with member states.[32] And once again the Executive Board instructed the staff to limit the inclusion of binding conditions in both number and type. Binding conditions should "normally be confined to (i) macroeconomic variables, and (ii) those necessary to implement specific provisions of the Articles of policies adopted under them."[33] Binding conditions should also be limited to only "those that are necessary to evaluate the implementation of the program"—and type—to macroeconomic, not structural conditions. In short, these guidelines attempted to limit the increase in conditionality by reducing the "number of performance criteria, insisting on their macroeconomic character, circumscribing the reasons for reviews and keeping preconditions to a minimum."

As with the debates preceding the 1968 Review, the United States expressed preferences in the debates preceding the 1979 conditionality Review to constrain conditionality and the subsequent decision reflected many of these expressed preferences. And as with the 1968 Review, the constraints on Fund activity decided by the Board and advocated by powerful states like the United States were subsequently abrogated. As Jacques J. Polak wrote, "These restraining provisions [from the 1979 decision] have not prevented the intensification of conditionality in every direction that the guidelines attempted to block."[34] First, the Executive Board had instructed the Fund to design uniform SBAs, and in some ways, uniformity did increase after the 1979 decision. For instance, of the 75 SBAs in the Conditionality Data Set from 1979 to 1995, only four did not include phasing, and only three did not include any performance clause with binding conditions. However, the number of binding conditions and the amount of phasing continued to vary widely across SBAs even after the 1979 decision. Between 1979 and 1995, the average number of binding conditions for an SBA was 10.1, with a standard deviation of 3.0 (and ranging from 0 to 17); the average number of phases was 5.4, with a standard deviation of 2.3 (and ranging from 1 to 15). Second, Fund arrangements continued to get longer on average. According to the Conditionality Data Set, the average SBA between 1968 and 1978 was 11.7 months by design, whereas the average SBA between 1979 and 1995 was 15.3 months by design. Moreover, 40 of the 78 SBAs in the sample (between 1979 and 1995) were longer than 12 months. Third, the number of binding conditions also continued to increase.[35] According to the Conditionality Data Set, in 1979, the average number of binding conditions for an SBA was 7.2; in 1981 it was 8.25; in 1983, it was 9.3; in 1985, it was 10.6; in 1989, it was 12; and by 1994, it was nearly double the 1979 average at 13.5.

Fourth and finally, the types of binding conditions also continued to change and become more structural in nature, despite Executive Board instructions. Particularly after 1982, the use of procedural conditions became more prevalent.[36] The Conditionality Data Set codes all binding conditions as either targets and procedures. A target, for instance a fiscal deficit limit, can be met by whatever means the borrowing member state's government chooses and thus is less of an infringement on the country's (Westphalian) sovereignty than a procedural condition.[37] Procedures require countries to implement a one-time action, like devaluing the exchange rate, or a longer-term policy reform, like tax reform; they specify both ends and means. Procedures directly dictate borrowing country policies, constrain domestic politicians options, and violate Westphalian sovereignty.[38] They may require borrowers to reduce import restrictions by changing specific licensing requirements, reform the social security or tax system in specific ways stipulated by the Fund agreement, implement a public investment program, or reform a state enterprise in ways spelled out in the Fund program.[39] Figure 4.1 depicts the increase in the use of procedural conditions over time. Procedures were included occasionally in Fund programs in the 1950s and 1960s. The steady increase in the absolute number of procedural conditions began around 1982.[40] In addition, the use of fiscal policy and other economic policy binding conditions became much more common. In other words, it appears that subsequent changes do not reflect ex ante U.S. or Executive Board preferences. In fact, they may reflect the exact opposite!

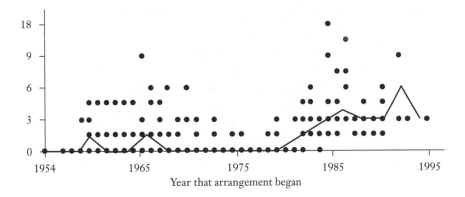

Figure 4.1.   Absolute use of procedural conditions
SOURCE: From the Conditionality Data Set.

Since that 1979 Review, the United States has continued to criticize the IMF's expansion of conditionality and shift into longer-term adjustment loans as straying from its mandate.[41] The Reagan administration opposed the IMF's "drift" into "longer-term adjustment programs" from its mandated short-term balance of payments loans.[42] The Clinton administration expressed similar preferences over Fund activity. In December 1999, Treasury Secretary Larry Summers presented a reform program that included the phasing out of the Fund's low-interest financing, increasing Fund transparency and returning to the Fund's core mandate of emergency financing (with fewer conditions), rather than the current load of developmental lending (with more conditions and a broader policy focus).[43]

In September 2002 the Executive Board concluded another review of conditionality and approved new Conditionality Guidelines and a related decision on SBAs to replace the Second Review of Conditionality Guidelines, which had been officially instructing staff activity since 1979. As with the Executive Board's previous guidelines on conditionality for the staff, these emphasize uniformity and attempt to reign in the increases in conditionality. These guidelines also include some new features, like an emphasis on country "ownership" of programs and Fund-recommended reforms. However, it is noteworthy how many of the instructions appear to reiterate points from the First and Second Guidelines. Through these new guidelines, the

Executive Board has once again instructed the Fund staff and management to reign in conditionality and apply it uniformly. In short, the changes in Fund conditionality that have been observed, including longer arrangements with more conditions and greater specificity, do not appear to reflect U.S. preferences or the preferences of the Executive Board at large. If anything, the United States—from Dale in the 1960s, to Cross in the 1970s, to the Reagan and Clinton administrations in the 1980s and 1990s—appears to be trying to reverse those trends in Fund conditionality.

In sum, one of the key observable implications of the realist argument is that subsequent changes in Fund activities reflect ex ante U.S. preferences. In this section, I have assessed evidence regarding U.S. preferences from the 1968 and 1979 reviews of conditionality, as well as later statements from both Republican and Democratic administrations. This evidence suggests that since at least the mid-1960s the United States had relatively consistent preferences regarding Fund conditionality, namely a return to the Fund's original mandate, to short-term balance of payments lending with fewer and macroeconomic conditions, rather than longer-term development lending with more conditions, particularly structural ones. If this assessment of U.S. preferences is correct, it casts doubt on the realist argument that powerful states, particularly the United States, have primarily driven changes in the activities of the International Monetary Fund.

Bureaucratic Argument and Observable Implications

Another conventional explanation is that the Fund's bureaucracy has driven the observed changes in Fund conditionality. This bureaucratic politics argument comes in a two different guises. Scholars employ either a more rationalist or sociological logic to argue that the IMF should be understood as an actor unto itself, not just a conduit for state preferences, with autonomy to pursue its own interests or goals. The two variants of this argument differ both in how they conceive of the source of organizational autonomy and in the purposes to which this autonomy is put.[44] Rationalists tend to argue that international organizations (IOs) achieve a degree of autonomy due to principal-agent issues of informational asymmetry and incomplete monitoring.[45] IOs use their autonomy to pursue the narrow, self-interested goal of survival, often operationalized as budget or task expansion. For instance, in a series of articles, Roland Vaubel focuses on the Fund bureaucracy's efforts to "maximize their budget, their staff, and their independence." Vaubel views Fund conditionality as a mechanism to pursue those interests.[46] By contrast, sociological or cultural approaches emphasize that the international organization is a product of its institutional environment, not actor interests per se, and achieves a degree of independence from states as a result of its expertise and externally derived legitimacy.[47] For scholars from the sociological school, IOs use that autonomy to pursue activities determined by their specific bureaucratic culture, such as by their professional disposition or other particularistic factors. For instance, Michael Barnett and Martha Finnemore argue that Fund activities reflect the intellectual, causal models developed and used by Fund staff members.[48]

Although these two variants share an emphasis on the Fund bureaucracy in driving changes in Fund activity, they imply somewhat different observable implications. As a result, I will evaluate them separately.

OBSERVABLE IMPLICATIONS OF THE RATIONALIST VARIANT

Vaubel argues that Fund activity, including the changes in Fund conditionality, is driven by self-interested bureaucrats. Bureaucrats want to increase the power and independence of their organization, and Vaubel has argued that Fund bureaucrats have expanded Fund conditionality in order to pursue those interests. I interpret Vaubel's argument as mainly applying to Fund staff, who are largely careerists, versus Fund management, many of whom are political appointees. Hence, if Fund staff have truly driven the changes in Fund conditionality, then presumably the staff would have advocated the inclusion of the new conditions that marked conditionality change. Certain conditions—for instance, those that appear to increase the latitude of staff advice and hence staff influence and power—might be more likely to be advocated by the staff, according to this argument.

Thus one observable implication of this argument is simply that we should observe staff advocating the introduction of new conditions (and perhaps particularly certain types of conditions). However, this is surprisingly difficult to assess. The problem is that if we do *not* observe staff advocating the introduction of new conditions, it does not necessarily mean that it is not occurring. We may simply not have looked hard enough or in the right places. Moreover, if we do observe staff advocating the introduction of one or the other binding conditions, we cannot be sure that this is representative. We may have observed the single outlier condition that staff advocated among many that they opposed. Because of these difficulties, I have searched for the converse observation: instances when staff oppose the introduction of new binding conditions. These may also be outliers: single instances of opposition among many more instances of advocacy. Therefore I am considering "most likely cases": conditions that increased the latitude of Fund advice and were subsequently widely incorporated in Fund conditional loan arrangements and hence would be most likely to be initiated by the staff according to the bureaucratic argument.[49] If staff opposed conditions that subsequently became widely used, then this observation casts doubt on the claim that changes in Fund conditionality have been driven by the staff.

Are there instances of widespread staff opposition to the introduction of new binding conditions that were subsequently widely incorporated? In fact, staff have frequently expressed a preference to stick with activities (and binding conditions) that relate to their traditional concerns and strengths, rather than searching for or advocating new activities (and conditions). One particularly notable example of staff opposing the introduction of a type of binding condition that subsequently became a central feature of Fund programs concerns fiscal criteria in the 1960s and 1970s. (Recall that in the previous section regarding the realist argument, powerful states were also noted to have opposed the inclusion of fiscal criteria.)

In the 1960s and 1970s, staff debated among themselves which binding conditions were appropriate and how they should be applied. These debates make clear that staff as a whole did not advocate the introduction of detailed fiscal binding conditions. For instance, a 1968 staff paper advised the Board:

> In many stand-by arrangements in the past, in addition to a ceiling for government or public sector borrowing, the member has set criteria in the performance clause on other fiscal actions. These criteria have related to the surplus in the current account of the budget, budgetary revenues, investment expenditures, aggregate budgetary expenditures, and also the operations of the public agencies. . . . But normally it would be desirable not to include the fulfillment of any of the fiscal targets in the performance clause.

Budgetary operations as well as the operations of public agencies reflect the social and economic priorities of the member; they represent compromises often arrived at after difficult negotiations among interested economic and social groups or geographic subdivisions. If they are made performance criteria and included in a performance clause, the impression may be created that the Fund is making a judgment on the priorities of the member.[50]

Fiscal binding conditions (referred to in the quote above as "performance criteria") were to be avoided not only because they involve judgments on policy priorities, but also because "there are important technical difficulties in the use of fiscal criteria."[51] Fiscal imbalances were acknowledged as a leading problem for borrowing member states. However, in 1968, the staff still advocated using an overall or public sector credit ceiling to impose fiscal restraint, rather than a fiscal target or procedural condition, because monetary data were easier to measure, more available, and of better quality than fiscal data. Fiscal measures were still to be included in Fund-recommended stabilization programs, but generally only the monetary conditions were to be made binding both "for technical reasons and because credit ceilings are less likely to convey the impression that the Fund is making an unnecessary judgment on the social and economic priorities of the member country."[52] As stated in the staff report, "A credit ceiling on the public sector can enforce adequate restraint on the expansive influence of the sector as a whole, while allowing the Fund to maintain neutrality between the alternatives provided by increased taxation vs. reduced expenditure and among types of taxation and types of expenditure."[53] This staff opposition to the inclusion of detailed fiscal criteria continued into the 1970s. When the EDs again debated conditionality policy in the late 1970s, the staff report guiding their discussion stated, "the purpose of conditionality is not to modify or influence basic features of economic organization maintained or desired by the member. Social objectives or priorities of members are taken as given, provided the policies proposed in the program are consistent with the objective of obtaining a sustainable balance of payments position." Staff, like Executive Board, advocated a narrower set of binding conditions and opposed detailed fiscal binding conditions.

In short, staff generally opposed the inclusion of fiscal criteria as binding conditions because such conditions could interfere with the political priorities of the borrowing country and because fiscal data were often less dependable than monetary data. Despite their opposition—and opposition from the Executive Board, discussed previously—the inclusion of fiscal criteria as binding conditions increased steadily. By the late 1970s, their inclusion in Fund loan arrangements was virtually ubiquitous. As mentioned previously, between 1973 and 1978 only six upper-credit tranche programs did not include a fiscal binding conditions.[54] Of the arrangements included in my sample, 91% included a fiscal target between 1983 and 1990, and 100% of the arrangements sampled between 1991 and 2000 included fiscal targets. According to Vaubel's argument, one would have expected the staff to have advocated the inclusion of fiscal binding conditions. Instead, the staff actually opposed the inclusion of fiscal criteria, which were nonetheless subsequently widely incorporated in Fund programs.

The general sentiment of Fund staff—gleaned from staff writings, Fund archives, and interviews I conducted—toward new conditions and forays into new policy areas for conditionality has been opposition. They prefer to include tried-and-true conditions, which are both quantifiable and tested. The staff's aversion to new, nonquantifiable conditions is evident in the following quote from a long-time Fund staff member. This staff member stated that since the 1970s, and particularly when Michel Camdessus was managing director, conditions increased and are now no longer easily quantifiable. As he stated, "the fact that these things are unobserved makes them very difficult to measure . . . and also, in a sense, takes the rigor away from the process. . . . [Earlier], it was very clear that the Fund was rigorous and the [World] Bank was fluffy. This extension of conditionality of the Fund over a very large range [of issues], it is inevitable that it must get fluffier too."[55] A recent staff survey provides further substantiation of this point. Only 30% of Area Department staff (who often negotiate and draft conditionality agreements) consider structural measures to be "'critical' for the program's macroeconomic objectives," despite their widespread inclusion.[56] Staff members have often interpreted the Fund's role narrowly. They prefer to design Fund programs that are precise, limited, quantifiable, and measurable. New policy areas and new goals are not generally supported by Fund staff. Staff opposition to fiscal binding conditions, which were later widely required in Fund programs, and the general staff opposition to forays into new areas of conditionality weakens support for the bureaucratic argument.

Michael Barnett and Martha Finnemore argue that international organizations often derive a certain power and independence from their expertise and "the legitimacy of the rational-legal authority they embody."[57] Specific aspects of international organizations' bureaucratic culture contribute to "pathological behavior," which they define as behavior that deviates from the IO's stated objectives. They specifically address the puzzle of expanding Fund conditionality, arguing that the Fund staff's expertise gave them a great deal of latitude to develop and adjust certain intellectual models, which in turn justified the expansion in Fund conditionality. In their account, this expertise leads to an expansion of Fund conditionality, seemingly against the wishes of not only the state principals but also the "reluctant" Fund staff members themselves.

The argument itself is not framed in terms of testable hypotheses, but certain observable implications are nonetheless implied. In particular, Barnett and Finnemore suggest that we should observe program convergence or increased program uniformity during periods of "normal science," when the coherent, shared knowledge model is being employed by Fund staff. They identify the post-1970, when the Bretton Woods system collapsed, and post-1990 periods as ones of program failure that prompted "pathological" organizational activity and the adoption of new, noncore conditions. Have we observed program convergence and divergence, as the Barnett and Finnemore suggest we should? I evaluate Fund program convergence/divergence in three separate ways. First, I consider the uniformity of inclusion of staple conditions, like credit and fiscal targets. In other words, did most programs include the conditions considered central by the Fund's dominant intellectual models in the pre-1990 or pre-1970 periods, as this argument suggests? Second, other nonstaple binding conditions have also become frequently used. I evaluate the timing of the introduction of nonstaple conditions. Were they introduced during periods of paradigm crisis? Have they been included uniformly in Fund programs? Finally, I consider the variation in the number of binding conditions over time. Has the spread around the mean value of binding conditions increased in the post-1990 or post-1970 periods, as Barnett and Finnemore suggest?

Uniformity of Inclusion of Staple Conditions

Barnett and Finnemore are not alone in characterizing fiscal and (particularly) credit targets as staple conditions that are included in all Fund programs. It is widely perceived that Fund program design was guided by the absorption and monetary (or Polak, named after Jacques J. Polak) models, which considered credit and fiscal targets key. Many also contend that Fund programs, at least through the 1970s, tended to be strictly informed by these models, so that most Fund programs included credit controls, fiscal controls, and exchange and trade liberalization measures as the sole binding conditions.[58] Binding conditions used in the pre-1970 period were supposed to include broad targets "significant enough to serve as a basis for an appraisal of the economy as a whole."[59] Is it true that Fund programs were (and are) uniform in their inclusion of staple conditions, like credit and fiscal controls?

Data from internal Fund memos and the Conditionality Data Set suggest that early Fund programs were far less uniform in terms of their inclusion of staple binding conditions than previous scholarship, including Barnett and Finnemore, suggest. Initially, most binding conditions were broad and limited to certain monetary policies, like reducing the growth of the money supply or maintaining open monetary relations. However, practices varied between different Area Departments regarding how many and which binding conditions would typically be included in SBAs. Practices initially developed within Area Departments, rather than by a central, coordinating division.[60] In fact, during the 1960s, both the Fund management and the Executive Board expressed concern about the lack of uniformity across Fund programs.

The Fund staff and management debated program uniformity between themselves during the early 1960s. They were mainly concerned about the lack of uniformity regarding the inclusion of binding conditions and phasing for different levels of tranche drawings.[61] In 1963, Joseph Gold, the general counsel and director of the Legal Department at the Fund, wrote the managing director that "the Fund practice is less than uniform but also . . . the Area Departments hold different views on what the practice should be."[62] Gold suggested a uniform policy whereby gold tranche and first-credit tranche drawings would not have any binding conditions, unless specifically desired by the borrowing country.[63] However, certain staff members strongly opposed the omission of binding conditions from first-credit tranche SBAs. For instance, the head of the Western Hemisphere department, Jorge Del

Canto, argued that binding conditions in the first-credit tranche are necessary to restore confidence and "facilitate obtaining parallel assistance," or supplementary financing.[64] The head of the African Department also wanted to be free to include binding conditions in the first-credit tranche because "for the majority of African countries Fund guidance would be most desirable."[65] The staff and management resolved that binding conditions should not apply to borrowing from the gold tranche, "except perhaps where the member insists on conditions." Conditions would still be allowed for first-credit tranche drawings, as the Area Heads had preferred. The staff tried to develop and establish this policy of uniformity independently, without Executive Board involvement. In a memo to the managing director, Gold wrote, "I do not think that this is a matter which needs to go to the Board. Policies in relation to, and the drafting of, stand-by arrangements have been worked out by the management and staff within the framework of the general policies adopted by the Board, and the Board comments, if it sees fit, on particular stand-by arrangements as they are recommended to the Board."[66] The staff initially tried to establish a uniform policy regarding the inclusion of binding conditions on its own.

However, the staff's independent attempts apparently did not satisfy the Executive Board. By 1967, the Executive Board began focusing on the continued lack of uniformity across Fund programs and asked the staff to compile a database of upper-credit tranche (that is, above first-credit tranche) SBAs to compare how much conditionality varied across programs. Tables 3.7 and 4.1 show the distribution of certain types of binding conditions (or performance criteria) for all upper-credit tranche SBAs from 1957 to 1967, according to the internal Fund staff documents produced in response to this Board request. The staff grouped binding conditions in four substantive categories: monetary, fiscal, foreign borrowing, and exchange and trade conditions. Table 4.2 lists typical binding conditions in each category.[67] Table 3.7 indicates that between 1957 and 1967, most arrangements did include monetary binding conditions. However, the inclusion of fiscal binding conditions varied widely. No European or Asian upper-credit tranche SBA included fiscal binding conditions during this period. Certain African and Western Hemisphere countries, including Morocco, Tunisia, Bolivia, El Salvador, Guatemala, Nicaragua, and Peru, also were never required to include a fiscal binding condition in their upper-credit tranche SBA from 1957 to

TABLE 4.1
Stand-by Arrangements in Upper Credit Tranche,
1957–1967 Distribution of Binding Conditions by Area

Area	No. of SBAs	Monetary BC	Fiscal BC	Foreign Borrowing BC	Exchange and Trade BC	Total BC	Average BC per SBA
Africa	27	53	11	10	36	110	4.1
Asia	12	20	—	2	10	32	2.7
Europe	24	45	—	—	2	47	2.0
Middle East	9	25	4	1	17	47	5.2
Western Hemisphere	103	256	55	23	191	525	5.1
Total	175	399	70	36	256	761	4.3

SOURCE: SM/68/128, Supplement 3, 4 September 1968, IMF Archives.
NOTE: BC = binding condition; SBA = stand-by arrangement.

TABLE 4.2
Typical Examples of Binding Conditions

Binding Condition Group	Examples
Monetary	• Ceiling on domestic assets of central bank • Ceiling on central bank financing of government budget • Ceiling on central bank credit to private sector • Ceiling on central bank credit to commercial banks • Ceiling on central bank credit to government • Reserve requirements • Interest rate changes
Fiscal	• Ceiling on current and/or capital expenditures • Ceiling on government fiscal and/or nonfiscal expenditures • Increasing revenues by improving tax collection or adjusting prices of state-produced goods
Foreign borrowing	• Ceiling on new government foreign debt • No new short- or medium-term debt incurred by government
Exchange and trade	• Floor on foreign reserves • No new exchange restrictions • No new trade restrictions • Limit on central bank sale of foreign exchange • No quantitative restrictions on imports

SOURCE: SM/68/128 and Suppl. 2, August 12, 1968.

1967. However, according to Table 3.7, other countries like Liberia, Brazil, Chile, and Haiti were required to include more than one fiscal binding condition per loan agreement on average during this period.

According to the Conditionality Data Set (as opposed to the above-mentioned Fund staff-generated data), between 1952 and 1973, 77% of Fund conditional loan arrangements included credit targets as binding conditions, and 44% included some sort of fiscal or deficit target. In other words, at the height of the Polak model, programs did not uniformly include credit and fiscal targets. In fact, program uniformity by this metric (consistency with regard to including credit or fiscal targets) increased in later years. In the 1990s, 93% of conditional loan programs included credit targets as binding conditions, and 100% included fiscal or deficit targets as binding conditions, according to the Conditionality Data Set.

In short, staff debates and Executive Board concern about lack of program uniformity, Fund staff-generated data, and the Conditionality Data Set all concur that Fund programs varied widely in terms of their inclusion of staple conditions, including credit and fiscal targets, during the 1950s and 1960s. Data reveal that programs were not as uniform as previously thought.

Introduction of Nonstaple Conditions

The second metric of program coherence concerns the timing of the introduction of nonstaple conditions. In the pre-1970 and pre-1990 years, few new conditions should be observed. Those that are observed should represent extensions of existing intellectual models and should thereafter be somewhat uniformly included. In the post-1970 and post-1990 paradigm crisis years, many new conditions should be included in a more haphazard fashion, as staff try new methods in the face of program failure. Received wisdom on changes in conditionality similarly suggests that the Fund initially limited its binding conditions to broad targets and that the introduction of new conditions has increased in recent years. Is it true that early programs only included staple conditions and that nonstaple conditions were introduced after 1970 or after 1990? In fact, evidence suggests that many noncore binding conditions were introduced in the 1950s and 1960s. Of the conditional loan programs sampled in the Conditionality Data Set that were initiated between 1952 and 1973, 14% included binding conditions that required countries to implement a specific, detailed economic policy reform, rather than simply meeting an economic target.

During the 1950s and 1960s, the Fund required certain borrowing countries to implement specific reforms, often relating to import liberalization or fiscal policy. For instance, in addition to credit and fiscal expenditure ceilings, reserve requirements, and prohibitions on new exchange and import restrictions, the 1959 Haiti SBA also included more specific binding conditions relating to fiscal policy. First, the government had to establish a separate "nonfiscal" account with the National Bank. If revenues exceeded budgeted expenditures, then these excess revenues would be deposited in this "nonfiscal" account. Nonbudgeted or "nonfiscal" expenditures could only be paid from this account. Second, revenues from a coffee export tax were "earmarked for retirement of public debt obligations," according to the arrangement's binding conditions. Those revenues would be directly deposited in the National Bank, which "will see to it that the tax proceeds are so applied without exception." Third and finally, the arrangement did not simply set general limits on the credit that could be extended to the government, as was common. Instead, the arrangement set more specific credit limitations, stipulating that the National Bank could only "extend to the Government of Haiti overdraft facilities only to finance fiscal expenditures within the ceiling [specified] under paragraphs (a) and (d) above, and for periods not exceeding sixty days."[68]

Later SBAs with Haiti were even more constraining in terms of budgetary management. The 1966 Haiti SBA included detailed binding conditions concerning the amount of fiscal revenues that needed to be collected and expenditures that were allowed to be spent on a *quarterly* basis, rather than setting a simple fiscal deficit target. Expenditures were limited to "G 10 million per month . . . except for December 1966 when expenditures may exceed this limit by not more than G 5 million to permit advances of salary payments to public employees during the Christmas holiday." Moreover, it required that 5% of fiscal revenues be deposited in a separate account, which could be used "solely to provide matching funds to complement foreign or international loans or grants." Another 10% of fiscal revenues had to be set aside for servicing public debt as a condition of the Fund loan.[69]

There are many other examples of arrangements in the 1950s and 1960s that specified noncore binding conditions, including very detailed procedural conditions, that needed to be implemented. The 1959 Bolivia SBA specified certain adjustments in certain prices and wages. The 1961 Brazil SBA included a condition with instructions on how to run the state-run Brazilian Coffee Institute, including how much coffee it should buy from the general market. The 1966 Yugoslavia SBA required a specified list of imports to be liberalized.

TABLE 4.3

All Stand-by Arrangements, 1957–1967, Performance Criteria by Area and Tranche

Area	Average (area)	Gold Tranche	First Tranche	Second Tranche	Third Tranche	Fourth Tranche
Africa	3.9		—	3.7	4.2	2.6
Asia	2.0	—	1.0	1.2	3.4	—
Europe	1.6		—	2.4	2.2	0.6
Middle East	4.7		—		5.6	4.7
Western Hemisphere	4.8	—	2.6	4.9	4.8	6.1
Average (tranche)	3.9	—	1.3	3.7	4.1	4.9

SOURCE: SM/68/128, Supplement 3, September 4, 1968.

NOTE: According to staff documents, "In determining tranche positions drawings under compensatory financing scheme were excluded." Similarly, staff documents noted, "There were five stand-by arrangements (Chile 1964, 1965, and 1966; Costa Rica 1966 and 1967) under which Fund holdings of the member's currency could have reached into the fifth credit tranche. However, phasing of drawings under the stand-by arrangements was linked to repurchase commitments falling due during the period of the stand-by arrangement so that the Fund's holdings of the member's currency would not exceed the fourth credit tranche."

In short, the Fund has been requiring different types of binding conditions outside of the standard credit and fiscal targets informed by the Fund's guiding intellectual models since the early days of Fund conditionality. Although the prevalence of nonstandard binding conditions has certainly increased over time, particularly after 1983 and in the 1990s, so has the prevalence of standard binding conditions like fiscal or monetary targets. In other words, contrary to what Barnett and Finnemore's argument implies, binding conditions outside of the intellectual models that guided Fund staff appear to have been included in the early years of Fund conditionality when the monetary model was still in its heyday.

Uniformity in Number

A third measure of program uniformity is the variation in the number of binding conditions. As discussed earlier, in the 1960s, the staff, management, and Executive Board were concerned about the lack of uniformity in the number of binding conditions required for first- and upper-credit tranche SBAs. For instance, Table 4.3 provides the number of binding conditions (or performance criteria) required by tranche level and region. It demonstrates how widely practice differed between Area Departments. On average, upper-credit tranche SBAs for Middle Eastern and Western Hemisphere countries had twice as many binding conditions as those for Asian and European

TABLE 4.4
Variation in the Number of Binding Conditions

Year	N	Mean	Standard Deviation	Minimum	Maximum
Total	222	7.05	4.34	0	18
Pre-1971	96	4.03	3.28	0	12
Post-1970	126	9.34	3.57	0	18
Pre-1990	206	6.65	4.21	0	18
Post-1989	16	12.19	2.20	10	18

SOURCE: Data from the Conditionality Data Set.

countries.[70] For instance, Table 3.7 indicates that although the UK had four SBAs from 1957 to 1967 with no binding conditions and India averaged one binding condition per arrangement for its four SBAs, Brazil's four arrangements averaged 8.7 binding conditions each. Only Western Hemisphere and Asian arrangements appeared to follow the Fund's stated rule that higher credit tranche drawings require more "justification" (or conditions).

Is it true that programs were more uniform in terms of their number of binding conditions in the pre-1990 or pre-1970 periods than in the post-1990 or post-1970 periods, respectively, as Barnett and Finnemore's argument suggests? In both cases, the earlier period (which according to their argument is supposed to be more uniform) is actually less uniform with respect to the number of binding conditions. Table 4.4 indicates that the average number of binding conditions for conditional loan arrangements initiated in the 1990s is 12.2 with a standard deviation of only 2.2. For the pre-1990 period, by contrast, the mean is 6.7 and the standard deviation is 4.2. In other words, absolutely and relatively, conditional loan arrangements appear to vary much more before 1990 than during the 1990s in terms of the number of binding conditions stipulated in the arrangement. The comparison of pre-1971 and post-1970 generates somewhat different results. The standard deviation actually increases slightly from the pre-1971 to the post-1970 period. In other words, there is slightly more absolute variation or spread about the mean after 1970 than before it. However, relative to the value of the mean, there is much less variation in the number of binding conditions after 1970 than before 1971. Before 1971 the average number of binding conditions was 4.0 with a standard deviation of 3.3, whereas after 1970 the average number is 9.3 with a standard deviation of 3.6. Relative to the value of the mean, the number of binding conditions varies much less after 1970 than before it.

In sum, evidence suggests that programs do not appear to have been more uniform in the pre-1990 days, when the Fund's intellectual models were supposed to have still tightly guided Fund activity. Inclusion of fiscal and monetary conditions varied widely across countries in the 1950s and 1960s. Other types of binding conditions, including procedural conditions and those that required specific economic policy reform, were included as binding conditions in Fund conditional loan arrangements in the 1950s and 1960s. Pre-1971 and pre-1990 programs varied much more widely in terms of the number of binding conditions than programs after 1970 or during the 1990s. If anything, it appears that post-1990 programs may be more uniform than previous programs. All or nearly all post-1990 arrangements sampled required the four basic requirements and credit, fiscal, and foreign debt targets.[71]

Observable Implications of the Supplementary Financier Argument

Does the general history of Fund conditionality change conform to the observable implications of the supplementary financier argument? The next three chapters address specific predictions of this argument, considering the influence of each of the three groups of supplementary financiers—creditor states, private financial institutions, and multilateral organizations—on different features of Fund conditionality change. The most significant observable implications of this argument—that we observe the influence of supplementary financiers under certain conditions specified by the argument—will be addressed in the subsequent chapters.

Here I will deal briefly with another observable implication of the supplementary financier argument. If supplementary financiers exercise influence over the Fund's activities and Fund conditionality, then we should expect the Fund staff, and perhaps even the EDs, to discuss the importance and interests of supplementary financiers explicitly in debates over the design of Fund conditionality arrangements. Do they? In studying the Fund's archival files in depth, I found that Fund staff and EDs frequently reference "parallel credits," which is the Fund's term for supplementary financing. There are explicit references to the interests and preferences of supplementary financiers during debates over the design of Fund conditional loan arrangements. In fact, Fund staff tracked, planned, linked, and often required additional supplementary financing as a condition of the Fund program. In addition, supplementary financier interests and preferences were frequently invoked (and appeared to influence) the broader policy debates concerning Fund conditionality policy. In this section, I will present some of this evidence in greater detail.

I have argued that supplementary financing is crucial for the success of Fund programs. Fund staff and the Executive Board seem to be well aware of its importance. Fund staff and EDs have tracked the supplementary financing accompanying Fund programs, planned for a certain amount of supplementary financing in the design of their programs, linked supplementary financing and Fund loan disbursements, and required certain levels of supplementary financing as a condition (or precondition) of Fund programs.

Fund staff have tracked supplementary financing since the early days of Fund conditional loan arrangements. For instance, internal memos from 1960 presented data on "parallel credits" and discussed the importance of these parallel credits for the success of Fund programs. Table 4.5 presents data from one of these memos on "parallel arrangements" between supplementary financiers and Latin American borrowers between 1954 and 1960. The table indicates that most Fund stabilization programs (purpose A) were accompanied by parallel arrangements, whereas loan programs that were identified as offering a seasonal second line of reserves (purpose B) universally were not accompanied by parallel arrangements. For all 20 arrangements that were recorded as being supplemented by external financing, 50% or more of the financing committed in the year of their Fund arrangement came from supplementary financiers, the majority from the United States. The most dramatic case is Bolivia in 1957, when 90% of its new commitments came from the United States and only 10% from the Fund loan arrangement. On average for all 20 loan agreements, 27% of the new commitments that year came from the Fund loan agreement, 53% from the United States (often the U.S. Treasury or Export-Import Bank), and 20% from other supplementary financiers, often private U.S. commercial banks.

Not only was supplementary financing tracked since the early days of Fund conditional loan arrangements, but disbursements of Fund and supplementary financing were linked since the 1950s as well. During the 1950s, much of this linked external supplementary financing came from the

United States. For instance, a 1959 Fund SBA with Haiti for $5 million was linked to a $6 million grant from the United States. A Fund staff memo explained how this link worked: "Disbursement of the [U.S.] grant fund was made subject to Haiti complying with the stabilization program agreed with the Fund and had to be matched by drawings under the stand-by arrangement in amounts equal to one sixth of the [U.S.] grant fund disbursements."[72] Peru had "continuous stand-by arrangements" with the Fund between 1954 and 1960 that were linked to U.S. government financing. An internal Fund memo described how Peru's Fund agreements from 1954 to 1958 were linked to U.S. financing: "In the first four years Peru's stand-by arrangements with the Fund were for $12.5 million and were paralleled by a stabilization credit from the U.S. Treasury for $12.5 million and a $5 million credit from one private U.S. bank." In 1958, Peru entered into a $25 million SBA with the Fund. Concurrently, Peru received a $17.5 million stabilization credit from the U.S. Treasury, a $17.5 million credit from three private U.S. banks, and a $40 million balance of payments support loan from the Export-Import Bank. The bilateral and private supplementary financing was explicitly tied to the Fund program. As an internal Fund memo stated:

> Peru, after it had drawn $10 million under its stand-by arrangement with the Fund, could draw on the Export-Import Bank up to $20 million in installments not exceeding $5 million a month, and the remaining $20 million if such further drawings were matched by equal drawings on the Fund and/or private U.S. banks, provided that at least 50 per cent of the matching funds were withdrawn from the U.S. banks.[73]

In other words, the United States' supplementary financing was explicitly linked to the disbursement of the Fund loan.

Supplementary financing from private financial institutions and multilateral organizations has also been explicitly linked to Fund programs. Commercial banks have linked their loans to Fund loans, so that disbursements of commercial bank loans are contingent on the disbursement of the Fund loan. The disbursement of the Fund's loan is a signal of the country's compliance with the Fund program. Similarly, World Bank loans have been linked to Fund financing via the joint World Bank–Fund programs: the SAF, the ESAF, and now the Poverty Reduction and Growth Facility (PRGF).

TABLE 4.5

Fund Stand-by Arrangements with Latin American Countries, 1954–1960

(in millions of dollars)

Member Country	Purpose	Date of Agreement	Amount Granted	"PARALLEL ARRANGEMENTS" U.S. Supplementary Financing	Other Supplementary Financing
Argentina	A	12/19/58	$75	$124.75 Eximbank; $50.0 UST; $24.75 D.L.F.; $17 rollover loan from Fed Reserve Bank of NY	$54 Private U.S. banks
Argentina	A	12/2/59	$100	$50 U.S.T (of which $25 million usable)	$75 Private U.S. banks; $75 Private European banks
Bolivia	A	11/29/56	$7.5	$7.5 UST; $26 (approximate overall U.S. aid)	
Bolivia	A	11/28/57	$7.5		
Bolivia	A	12/29/57	$3.5	$7.5 UST; $25 (approximate overall U.S. aid)	
Bolivia	A	12/29/58	$8.5	$19.0 (approximate overall U.S. aid)	
Brazil	C	6/30/58	$37.5	$100 Eximbank	$58 Private U.S. banks
Chile	A	4/1/56	$35.0	$10 UST	$30 Private U.S. banks
Chile	A	4/1/57	$10	$10 UST	$30 Private U.S. banks
Chile	A	4/1/58	$10	$10 UST; $15 Eximbank; $10 I.C.A.	$15 Private U.S. banks
Chile	A	4/1/59	$8.1	$15 UST; $50 Eximbank; $1.5 I.C.A.	$55 Private U.S. banks; $21.5 Germany; $11.2 U.K.; suppliers' credits
Colombia	A	6/19/57	$25	$78 Eximbank	$25 Private U.S. banks
Colombia	A	6/19/58	$15	$25 Eximbank	$25.75 Private U.S. banks
Colombia	A	10/22/59	$41.25		
Cuba	B	12/7/56	$12.5		
Dominican Republic	B	12/22/59	$11.25		

Country	Type	Date	Amount	Other credits	Private banks
El Salvador	B	10/1/58	$7.5		
El Salvador	B	10/1/59	$7.5		
Haiti	B	7/14/58	$5		
Haiti	A	7/14/59	$5	$8 I.C.A.	
Haiti	A	10/1/59	$4		
Honduras	B	11/12/57	$3.75		
Honduras	B	1/29/59	$4.5		
Honduras	A	3/7/60	$7.5		
Mexico	C	4/16/54	$50	$75 U.S. Treasury	
Mexico	A	3/5/59	$90	$75 UST; $100 Eximbank	
Nicaragua	B	11/21/56	$3.75		
Nicaragua	B	10/7/57	$7.5		
Nicaragua	B	9/15/58	$7.5		
Paraguay	A	7/30/57	$5.5	$5.5 U.S. Treasury	
Paraguay	A	7/30/58	$1.5		
Paraguay	A	8/13/59	$2.75		
Peru	A	2/18/54	$12.50	$12.5 U.S. Treasury	$5 Private U.S. banks
Peru	A	2/10/58	$25	$17.5 U.S. Treasury; $40 Eximbank	$17.5 Private U.S. banks
Peru	A	2/10/59	$13	$17.5 U.S. Treasury; $40 Eximbank	$17.5 Private U.S. banks
Peru	A	2/1/59	$13	$17.5 U.S. Treasury; $35 Eximbank	$17.5 Private U.S. banks
Peru	A	2/1/60	$27.5		

SOURCE: Memo from Jorge Del Canto, Head of the Western Hemisphere Area Department, to Mr. Per Jacobsson (Managing Director) and H. Merle Cochran (Deputy Managing Director), March 11, 1960, IMF Archives.

NOTE: This tabulation was made in March 1960 and includes only stand-by arrangements, not ordinary credits. UST = U.S. Treasury; A = stabilization program; B = second line of reserves to be used seasonally; C = other.

In addition to being tracked and linked, as early as the 1950s and 1960s, supplementary external financing was also often explicitly mentioned in the text of Fund agreements as being necessary for the implementation of the program. For instance, SBAs with Peru in 1955, 1956, 1957, 1958, and 1959 explicitly noted that Peru was also negotiating $12.5 million stabilization credits with the U.S. government and $5 million credits with "private New York" banks. Venezuela's 1960 SBA stated that supplementary financing was needed to ensure the implementation of its program. It read, "It is proposed to finance this [cash] deficit by credits now being negotiated with foreign commercial banks. If the Government succeeds in obtaining from these commercial banks the full US$200 million sought, it would be able to cover the cash deficit of Bs 352 million and Bs 314 million to its cash balances." A 1959 SBA with Spain relied on credits from the U.S. government, other governments, multilateral organizations, and commercial banks to ensure the implementation of its trade liberalization reforms and strengthen its reserves. That arrangement read:

> The Spanish Government has indicated that to carry out its stabilization program it must have sufficient resources at its disposal to meet all eventualities, including a margin for strengthening reserves, and that for this purpose it wishes to obtain the assistance of international organizations and of certain foreign governments. The staff understand that, in addition to the request of $75 million from the Fund, Spain is arranging to get further financial assistance from the OEEC and from U.S. commercial banks. At the same time aid from the United States is expected to continue, and further loans will probably be available from the Export-Import Bank for specific projects.[74]

Later arrangements have continued this practice of stating that supplementary financing is necessary for program implementation, but have gone a step further.

In later years, Fund agreements actually required a specified amount of external financing to be raised as a condition of the Fund agreement. An early, and at that time rare, example of this was the 1958 Argentina SBA. In addition to requiring that Argentina maintain credit expansion limits and reserve requirements as a condition of the loan, it also required that Argentina secure supplementary financing. The following clause was singled out as binding. In other words, the agreement stipulated that if this clause was violated, Argentina would not be able to automatically draw its next loan tranche under the SBA: "The Argentina Government intends to request financial assistance from sources other than the Fund. Drawings under the stand-by arrangement with the Fund and under the other credit facilities will be in the proportion of 1 to at least 2¼."[75] In later years, the Fund continued to require certain countries to secure supplementary financing as a condition of the Fund loan.

In addition, during staff debates over Fund conditionality policy, staff frequently and explicitly refer to supplementary financier interests as a rationale for including certain terms and features in Fund conditionality arrangements. During the time when my archival research was completed, the Fund archives only allowed the public to access memos between staff members up until 1970. As a result, I was restricted to debates on conditionality policy until 1970. Nevertheless, these memos and archival files reveal that Fund staff invoked the supplementary financier preferences over at least four key aspects of Fund conditionality design that were being debated at the time: phasing, the use of binding conditions, the inclusion of phasing and binding conditions in first-credit tranche SBAs, and the length of Fund programs.

For instance, one argument used in favor of phasing was that it provided "assurance" to supplementary financiers. In an internal memo on phasing written to the acting managing director, Joseph Gold noted that phasing had been used for four general reasons. It was often in the "best interest of the member and the Fund" to have the money delivered in multiple installments, rather than all at once; it helped "ensure observance of member's commitments"; it supported the requirements of the particular program; and it assured supplementary financiers. As he wrote, "One consideration that has not been absent from our minds in some cases has been the fact that there was a quasi-consortium and that the other lenders looked to the Fund for assurance that the member's commitments were being observed. This assurance was obtained by periodic drawings, sometimes quite small, under phasing provisions."[76] Another internal memo from 1963 discussed phasing specifically in the context of encouraging supplementary financing from the United States, the dominant supplementary financier at the time: "If the United States wants to make its aid conditional upon performance and if it regards the elements isolated by the Fund as binding commitments as significant for its purposes, the existence of phasing provides a ready check that some performance is occurring."[77] In other words, staff clearly considered phasing as being in the interests of the supplementary financier because it provided supplementary financiers with information about country compliance with the Fund program.

In another series of memos, staff discussed the importance of attracting supplementary financing and the role of Fund programs in attracting this outside capital. Binding conditions, it was argued, provided supplementary financiers with "added confidence" in providing loans to borrowing member states. As one memo clearly stated:

> In many instances support by the Fund has been supplemented by financial assistance from other sources, for example, governments and commercial banks. The knowledge of the existence of a program which formed the basis for the stand-by arrangement has afforded added confidence in the furnishing of these outside credits. Crucial to such added confidence has been an awareness of the legally binding commitments undertaken by the member to ensure the success of the program. The observance of the ceilings assured the member of the continuing right of access and at the same time offered substantial evidence that the stabilization program was being carried out effectively.[78]

The memo went on to discuss potential ways to communicate to supplementary financiers whether or not the member was observing the binding conditions—in other words, to clarify the Fund's signal to supplementary financiers. The memo suggested a certification process: "However, hitherto no procedure has been established whereby outside creditors have been able to learn whether or not the prescribed ceilings have been observed. As a measure for facilitating such parallel assistance the Fund might consider adopting a procedure whereby it could certify on request the member's conformity with its binding commitments."[79] This certification idea (discussed briefly in Chapter 2) was never approved. Instead, the Fund developed other mechanisms to clarify its signal to supplementary financiers including increased phasing, increased reviews, and more detailed press releases on Fund programs.

In the 1960s, debate over whether or not to include binding conditions and phasing in first-credit tranche SBAs, the interests and preferences of supplementary financiers were clearly raised in the staff debate. Jorge Del Canto, the head of the Western Hemisphere Department, was one of the strongest advocates for including both binding conditions and phasing in first-credit tranche stand-bys. In a memo to the managing director stating his case, Del Canto emphasized the important role of SBAs in helping borrowing members obtain supplementary financing and argued for the inclusion of phasing and binding conditions in first-credit tranche SBAs largely because of their impact on supplementary financiers. In his words:

> The intent of the understandings we have with members requesting stand-by arrangements is to give certainty and precision to the execution of financial policies because of their own merits, but also so that confidence will be quickly established. In some cases it is this establishment of confidence rather than the use of Fund resources that is the prime objective of the stand-by arrangement. Thus, the present stand-by arrangement with Jamaica was primarily to achieve such confidence through the endorsement by the Fund of precisely defined financial policies. This particular arrangement, as it involved little more than the first credit tranche, is one which would have had little virtue if the proposed new policies on conditions [of not including binding conditions for the first credit tranche arrangements] had been adopted. In other cases the confidence required on the basis of new financial policies is registered directly through a flow of supporting assistance from other sources, the availability and volume of which is tied to observance of conditions in the Fund stand-by arrangement. Here, too, there are examples of operations which would be drastically affected by the proposed changes. In 1961, the Fund had with Mexico a stand-by arrangement through the first credit tranche only, but with conditions which were used as performance standards by other agencies [or supplementary financiers].[80]

Del Canto argued aggressively for the inclusion of binding conditions and phasing because they helped attract supplementary financing. As was discussed in Chapter 3, the staff decision ended up concurring with Del Canto, but a later ED decision reversed it.

Supplementary financier preferences regarding the length of Fund programs were also discussed in Fund staff memos. In an internal memo to the Executive Board, the staff argued that supplementary financiers prefer longer programs and that this was a reason to approve longer programs. It stated that longer-term "continuous and uninterrupted Fund support" are preferred by supplementary financiers: "Creditors and lending agencies have also shown an interest in the maintenance of stabilization efforts by the borrowing country; a longer-term program supported by the Fund may provide greater assurance in this respect. It may be useful to explore means of giving Fund support beyond one year in selected cases."[81] The staff decision that followed this memo did not restrict the length of Fund programs in any way. After 1974, the average length of Fund conditional loan arrangements did increase beyond a year, possibly in response to supplementary financier preferences.

In short, the interests and preferences of supplementary financiers have clearly been considered by the staff as they debated and devised Fund practice and policy with regard to Fund conditionality. Staff memos suggested that these considerations may have been decisive in certain cases. For instance, in one internal staff memo, John Woodley wrote, "There have been a number of examples where the stand-by arrangements with the Fund are designed mainly to increase the general credit worthiness of the country, and to show to other creditors that the government's policies have the Fund's stamp of approval."[82] One observable implication of the supplementary financier argument is that we should observe the staff actively discussing and considering supplementary financier interests in the design of Fund conditionality arrangements and the debates over Fund conditionality policy. The evidence presented here suggests that supplementary financing is clearly a consideration in the construction of Fund conditional loan arrangements. Fund staff track the supplementary financing that borrowing countries receive and link the disbursement of supplementary financing to Fund loan tranches. Fund arrangements often contain wording that either mentions the importance of supplementary financing for the success of the program and the intention of the borrower to raise such financing, or requires the borrower to secure such financing. Finally, Fund staff members frequently invoke supplementary financier interests and preferences when debating conditionality policy.

The evidence presented in this chapter suggests the initial plausibility of the supplementary financier argument and casts some doubt on the realist and bureaucratic conventional wisdoms. Staff certainly consider the interests of supplementary financiers. The next three chapters will more carefully and systematically assess whether or not this consideration amounts to influence over individual Fund programs and ultimately the changes in Fund conditionality.

Conclusion

Changes in Fund conditionality have diverged not only from what the original founders intended, but also from what the Executive Board has instructed over time. This suggests that the impetus for the change may have come from someplace else. Perhaps the most common alternative argument is that bureaucrats have pushed for this change. However, staff have opposed the inclusion of the conditions that were later widely incorporated in Fund programs. And the patterns of program uniformity and diversity do not mimic the cultural bureaucratic argument, as articulated by Barnett and Finnemore. Initial evidence does suggest that supplementary financiers may have influenced the changes in Fund conditionality. For example, Fund staff, management, and even EDs frequently refer to supplementary financiers and explicitly discuss supplementary financier interests in debates over conditionality policy. The next three chapters evaluate whether the three types of supplementary financiers have been successful at influencing the design of Fund conditional loan agreements, using both large-N statistical analyses and small-N case studies.

CHAPTER FIVE

Creditor States as Supplementary Financiers

Introduction

The supplementary financier argument challenges state-centric explanations of international organizational activity and Fund conditionality. But states clearly do have some influence over international organizations, over the Fund, and over Fund conditionality. The relevant questions are: When? And how?

In this chapter, I discuss creditor state influence over Fund conditionality in detail. The chapter begins with a discussion of why creditor states are interested in providing supplementary financing and consequently what their preferences over Fund conditionality are. I argue that creditor states provide financing for political reasons, and thus prefer relatively less stringent Fund conditionality agreements than do private financial institutions (PFIs), multilateral organizations, and often the Fund's staff and management. These assumptions about creditor state interests and preferences run somewhat against conventional (and realist) wisdom. As a result, I provide various types of empirical evidence to substantiate these assumptions. The third section describes the patterns of creditor state financing to Fund borrowers in the last 50 years, or the variation in the independent variable. The last two sections provide the empirical testing (and empirical support) of the supplementary financier argument. The fourth section tests whether countries are more likely to have relatively weaker Fund conditionality when they receive more supplementary financing from creditor states using the Conditionality Data Set (Appendix 1). The fifth section discusses a specific Fund conditionality agreement in detail in order to unpack how states influence Fund conditionality agreements.

Assumptions Regarding Creditor States

According to the supplementary financier argument, creditor states provide financing for political ends. They are less concerned with being paid back than PFIs and multilateral organizations. Aid and bilateral loans are political, not financial, investments.[1] Aid is often given to allies, and therefore creditor states are often interested in preserving political stability.[2] In practice, that means that they generally prefer Fund conditional loan arrangements to be relatively less stringent than the other supplementary financiers—PFIs and multilateral organizations.[3] When states get involved in influencing the terms of Fund conditionality arrangements, they also usually push for weaker conditionality than the staff and management do.

Although creditor states want borrowers to agree to certain conditions, they prefer Fund arrangements to allow borrowers to maintain some political room for maneuver. In practice, this means that creditor states often prefer Fund conditional loan arrangements that stipulate relatively fewer conditions and include conditions that are less constraining. In this study, I divide all binding conditions into two groups: targets or procedures. Targets are the less politically constraining group of conditions. They specify only the ends that need to be met (for example, fiscal deficit or credit target) and allow domestic politicians to choose whichever means are politically feasible. Procedural conditions, by contrast, specify both means and ends (for example, implementation of a specific social security reform plan) and therefore are more constraining for domestic politicians in borrowing countries. Creditor state interests and preferences generate two specific predictions:

HYPOTHESIS 1   *If a country receives relatively more (less) external financing from creditor states, then its Fund loan arrangement should include relatively fewer (more) binding conditions.*

HYPOTHESIS 2   *If a country receives relatively more (less) external financing from creditor states, then its Fund loan arrangement should include relatively more (less) targets versus procedural conditions.*

Although the supplementary financier argument assumes that creditor states push for relatively weaker conditionality, conventional wisdom suggests the opposite. For instance, the realist model, discussed in Chapters 1 and 4, predicts that powerful (creditor) states prefer *more* stringent agreements (versus the supplementary financier argument, which suggests states prefer *less* stringent agreements). Similarly, much of the literature on the United States and its relations with the IMF suggests that the United States generally wants increases in conditionality and has pushed for the increases that we have observed. This literature overwhelmingly focuses on two periods: the early years when the United States pushed (successfully) for the development of Fund conditionality, and the Reagan administration period.[4] Although the United States preference for conditionality in the early years is undisputed, it also bears little relevance to the question at hand: whether the United States has subsequently pushed for increases in conditionality and is the driver of the increases that we have observed.

By contrast, the argument that the Reagan administration preferred higher conditionality and succeeded in increasing Fund conditionality—articulated for instance by Miles Kahler—is quite relevant to this discussion. However, Kahler's claim is unsubstantiated: little or no evidence is presented (first) that the United States actually preferred higher conditionality, or (second) that changes in conditionality were caused by U.S. influence.

First, Kahler provides little evidence that the United States actually preferred higher conditionality. He argues that the Reagan administration's preference for limited long-term Fund financing and a return to short-term lending (which has actually been a relatively consistent U.S. preference) translates into a preference for higher conditionality. As he writes, "Less finance meant sharper adjustment. . . . Conditionality should be tightened rather than loosened; the balance between financing and adjustment had to be shifted in favor of the latter." [5] However, this logic is questionable. As James Boughton has pointed out, and as I also argue, shorter programs may just as easily be considered to be of weaker, rather than more stringent, conditionality.[6]

Although no doubt the Reagan administration did take a strong stand on a few programs at the beginning of the first term (for example, Grenada, India, and Pakistan in 1981), this was more of an aberration than anything else.[7] In the 1970s, particularly the late 1970s, there had been an active and vocal push for weakening conditionality from debtor and creditor countries alike.[8] This led to not only a possible decrease in conditionality, but a definite increase in overall lending and drawings.[9] Thus the Reagan administration's early and public rebuke of lax conditionality came at a time when Fund lending was skyrocketing, and concern about the Fund's liquidity was shared among several member countries. But this push for stricter conditionality did not last long. Soon enough, the Reagan administration earned more of a reputation as pushing for weaker, rather than tighter, Fund conditionality. As one *New York Times* article on the 1987 World Bank–IMF annual meetings noted, "Delegates from the third world welcomed the willingness of Treasury Secretary James A. Baker 3rd to . . . soften often-crushing I.M.F. loan conditions." [10] The Reagan administration's adversarial relationship with the World Bank, and its willingness to vote against World Bank loan proposals, was not mimicked at the International Monetary Fund.[11] Instead, according to Anne Krueger, the United States did "use the multilateral lending institutions for its own short-term political purposes." [12] Although that might have meant voting against loan proposals at the Bank, it generally meant pushing for weaker conditionality at the Fund. As she continues, "the United States has supported lending to countries whose policy reforms were clearly insufficient, suggesting even to casual observers the loans could not be used productively." [13]

Second, Kahler discusses the "pronounced changes in IMF conditionality after 1980" as "evidence of continuing American dominance of the organization's policies." [14] However, the evidence of "pronounced change" upon which Kahler bases his claim—a 1982 study by John Williamson—has since been discredited.[15] As Boughton states, "Williamson was working with one hand tied behind his back, in that he did not have access to data on performance criteria in the Fund's lending agreements. His often-cited study therefore relied on two indirect indicators, neither of which provides unambiguous information."[16] By contrast, the discussion of changes in Fund conditionality from Chapter 3—which is based on the actual Fund agreements and their performance criteria or binding conditions—demonstrates Fund conditionality did not abruptly change after 1980. But even if the empirical observation of abrupt conditionality change after 1980 were true, Kahler's causal claim is stated, not tested. Williamson himself provides several plausible explanations for what he perceives as a change in conditionality, and he does not conclude that U.S. influence was necessarily decisive.[17]

Instead, several independent pieces of evidence confirm that, consistent with the assumptions of the supplementary financier argument, when the United States has intervened in Fund conditionality negotiations, it generally prefers and pushes for weaker conditionality. Later in this chapter, I specifically test the predictions of this argument and these assumptions by using the Conditionality Data Set and by discussing a case of a Fund conditionality agreement in detail. However, because of the dominant perception that the United States and other creditor states usually prefer increasing the stringency of Fund conditionality, it may be useful to review additional evidence to justify the supplementary financier assumptions about creditor state preferences.

Four types of evidence support the assumption used here: that creditor states like the United States have generally preferred and, when interested, pushed for relative decreases in the stringency of Fund conditionality. First, as was discussed in detail in Chapter 4, the United States and other creditor states have vocally advocated decreases in Fund conditionality during Executive Board debates on conditionality policy. These preferences are reflected in the Conditionality Guidelines, which were (and are) supposed to guide staff activity. Some may suggest that these Executive Board debates and decisions are simply "cheap talk."[18] However, evidence of U.S. preferences from its own aid policies, from Fund staff accounts of creditor state pressure, and from detailed case studies researched by other scholars supports the assumptions I use here.

Consider how the United States has administered its own aid program.

Analyzing U.S. aid policies and practices may be a more reliable way of revealing its true preferences over Fund conditionality than considering statements made by U.S. representatives. And the United States has generally not required reforms such as those required by Fund conditionality programs. Instead, U.S. aid is often granted to allies in order to support military expenditures or specific development projects. The economy-wide aid, which would be most likely to resemble Fund loans and support economic reform, is actually considered to be the most politicized and least likely to require policy change.

Certainly the United States has encouraged reforms with its aid program at certain times, but most U.S. economic aid has supported projects, not policy reforms; moreover, efforts at advising aid recipients on broad economic, rather than particular sectoral, policies have largely dwindled. In the early years, when U.S. aid accounted for a large proportion of some recipients' capital inflows, the United States maintained large staffs in recipient countries and provided extensive technical assistance. The United States focused on "economy-wide" policy dialogues—about projected revenues, expenditures, and the like—with aid recipients in the 1950s and 1960s. President Kennedy's Latin American Alliance for Progress initiative specifically encouraged policy reform.[19] However, by the 1970s, that had changed, and the United States switched to more project-oriented lending.[20] The Peterson Commission, appointed by President Nixon, recommended that the United States Agency for International Development (USAID) focus on project-oriented aid, and defer to the World Bank and IMF on policy advice. According to Krueger, the Peterson Commission

recommended that the economic assistance component of the U.S. aid program focus on project lending. Consistent with this thrust, it also recommended that the United States support the lead of the IMF and World Bank in evaluating the overall policy framework of each developing country. USAID thus reduced its staff capacity for analysis of overall economic frameworks, relying instead on the IMF and World Bank and shifting its emphasis back to project aid and technical assistance. Increasingly, USAID personnel were specialists in health, education, population, nutrition, agriculture and other sectoral or subsectoral fields. Focus on overall economic policies was left largely to the multilateral institutions.[21]

In other words, USAID advised countries on sectoral policies and largely shed their experts and accompanying expertise on macroeconomic, economy-wide policy. That policy advice would be handled by the multilateral organizations, mainly by the International Monetary Fund.

In reaction to this project focus and also to the debt crisis, the Reagan administration did initially try to reform U.S. aid policy and use it to encourage economy-wide macroeconomic policy reform through aid, in the style of Fund conditionality.[22] The Reagan administration stated it would refocus U.S. aid policy around "four pillars," one of which was a macroeconomic "policy dialogue," and started new aid initiatives like the African Economic Policy Reform Program, which also encouraged economy-wide policy reform.[23]

However, in practice, U.S. aid policy under Reagan, as under previous and subsequent administrations, supported political objectives, not economic reform. By the 1980s, USAID had lost its expertise is economic policy reform, making advising on macroeconomic policy impractical. As Sewell and Contee write, "Nor is A.I.D. well equipped to participate in discussions of macroeconomic—either in Washington or in its field missions. . . . The agency is insufficiently staffed with economists to provide the data and analysis for sophisticated macro-economic policy discussions."[24] Moreover, those aid vehicles that were supposed to provide economy-wide balance-of-payments relief (rather than project support) and presumably encourage economic reform, such as the Economic Support Fund (ESF), were actually considered to be the most politicized. In the 1985 fiscal year, 59% of ESF's funding went to just five strategically important countries. As Sewell and Contee state, "the political objectives of ESF funding prevent A.I.D. from pressing too hard for development objectives for fear that this might cause political friction." They discuss the case of an aid program for Jamaica where "the United States had not pressed for policy reforms . . . 'because Jamaican resistance was strong and for political reasons the State Department did not want to require the reforms even though they would enhance development.'"[25] In the Cold War era, the majority of U.S. aid was directed at "countries where U.S. political and strategic interests [were] perceived to be threatened by the Soviet Union and its proxies."[26] In the 1990s, USAID was reorganized in order to reflect this foreign policy focus and "was formally brought under the authority of the State Department."[27] In short, the focus of U.S. aid has been on supporting political allies and strategic interests, not encouraging specific economic reforms.[28] As Sewell and Contee write, "the existence of American political goals often makes economic and development aims a secondary priority for the United States."[29]

In recent years, politicians have again argued that aid should be used to encourage reform—both economic and political. For instance, during the 1990s and early 2000s, the major bilateral donors have emphasized the role of "good governance" in aid giving.[30] In 1990, USAID launched its "democracy initiative," which stipulated that "within each region of the world, allocations of USAID funds to individual countries will take into account their progress toward democratization."[31] Even more recently, President George W. Bush proposed sweeping changes in U.S. aid policy through the Millennium Challenge Account, which proposes to refocus a portion of aid on economic development and depoliticize the aid granting process by using "publicly available, development-oriented criteria to choose the [recipient] countries."[32] Perhaps unfortunately, this rhetoric of encouraging reform through aid has earned a faddish, cyclical quality. The historical record suggests that aid has served U.S. political interests and supported U.S. allies, but has neither successfully encouraged reform nor reflected changes in Fund conditionality.[33]

In short, U.S. aid policy is political. Aid is used to support allies and ensure strategic interests. At times, economic reforms have been encouraged, but the bulk of aid supports allied governments, not specific reforms. U.S. aid policy does not reflect the observed changes in Fund conditionality, but it does reflect creditor state preferences over Fund conditionality: that Fund conditionality should be adjusted for political purposes and thus decreased for its allies. As Anne Krueger has observed, "In countries with economic policies clearly inimical to development, political considerations may prevent aid officials from insisting on policy changes as a precondition for aid. . . . In some instances, the U.S. government has been so eager to support new regimes that aid officials have had almost no room to question development plans."[34]

Creditor states have generally advocated decreases in the stringency of Fund conditionality and have instructed Fund staff to design programs with fewer, less-intrusive conditions. The United States, as the most powerful creditor state, has not encouraged economic reforms (like those included in

Fund conditionality agreements) through its own bilateral aid programs. Testimony from Fund insiders provides the third piece of evidence suggesting that, despite conventional wisdom to the contrary, creditor states like the United States have generally preferred and pushed for decreases in Fund conditionality.

Fund staffers are famously tight-lipped, and they rarely discuss pressure from states or others to change the contents of the Fund programs. However, one famous incident occurred in March 1987, when C. David Finch, a Fund staffer since 1950 who was the Fund's counsellor at that time, "abruptly resigned in . . . protest over what he judged to be political interference with the evaluation of proposed stand-by arrangements."[35] Finch, who was "widely respected as a balanced arbiter on the design of Fund programs," resigned as a result of pressure from creditor states to weaken Fund conditionality. As Boughton writes, "Finch objected to efforts by major creditor countries to push the Fund into approving financial arrangements for Egypt, Zaire, and Argentina when the staff believed that the proposed economic programs were too weak to justify support."[36] According to the *Financial Times*, Finch charged

> that the US has pressured the IMF to reduce conditions it places on some of its loans. Over the past year, as the international debt crisis has worsened, the IMF has been under pressure to relax the strict conditions of its loans. Diplomats in Washington said yesterday the US had argued for a relaxation in the IMF's lending policy towards Mexico and Egypt. Mr. Finch, in his resignation, was said to have cited in particular for softening conditionality for Zaire and Egypt.[37]

Finch's subsequent publications provide even further insight into the nature of creditor state preferences and pressure. In 1988, he described how "in many cases, creditors' interests lay in short-term order, not in long-term reform. As a result, they became less comfortable with the IMF. And they reacted by pressuring the IMF to accept weaker economic reforms."[38] For Finch, who had held several positions of authority over 37 years at the Fund, "political pressures" from creditor states meant pressure to loan without "adequate" reform or to weaken Fund conditionality.

For instance, Finch cited the case of Egypt, historically the second largest beneficiary of U.S. aid from 1962 to 1990. Egypt had had problems with debt repayments, particularly of military debt owed to the United States, and the Paris Club required a Fund loan before rescheduling.[39] Finch wrote, "To maintain even a semblance of its traditional concern for timely repayment, the IMF had to insist on major changes in Egypt's economic policies. But the Egyptian government, fearing a domestic political backlash, refused to take the required action. Instead, it sought protection from other governments. The Fund was told to reach an 'agreement' with Egypt without insisting on the necessary policy changes."[40] The *New York Times* stated, "Washington, which regards Egyptian economic and political stability as vital to the Middle East peace process," had put special pressure on the Fund for Egypt's agreement.[41] The same *New York Times* article quotes a U.S. State Department official as stating, consistent with the assumptions of the supplementary financier argument, "our interest is to make sure that Egypt stays stable."

According to Anne Krueger, now deputy managing director of the Fund, "the Egyptian case was far from unique."[42] Argentina in the late 1980s was another case where "the IMF has been forced to continue lending to maintain the façade of the debt strategy."[43] Zaire's 1987 loan is also cited as an example, where the United States pushed for a loan with weaker conditionality.[44] Krueger herself mentions the case of Argentina in the early 1990s, when "the IMF was initially unwilling to lend to Argentina. But the United States was adamant that the Argentine government . . . should be supported."[45] According to the *Financial Times*, "Pressure by US officials is reported to have overcome opposition by IMF technical staff to the loan. Argentina has signed five standby loans since 1983, but has yet to comply with any of the loan conditions."[46]

In short, Finch's resignation provides a unique glimpse at the pressure Fund staff sometimes receive from creditor states. Finch and others describe creditor states as pressuring Fund staff "to act on inadequate programs."[47] They have different interests and preferences than do the Fund staff. Creditor states, according to Finch, "frequently provided aid in order to give political support to an incumbent government." And when they successfully influenced "the independence of [the Fund's] judgments," according to Finch, the success of Fund programs suffered.[48]

Fourth and finally, one may rely on systematic case studies by other researchers to confirm or refute the assumptions about creditor state preferences used by the supplementary financier argument. Although many scholars have assumed U.S. (or other creditor state) influence in one direction or the other, Randall Stone is unique in his use of both diverse methods and diverse sources of evidence to substantiate his claims. Stone focuses his study on the enforcement, not the design, of Fund conditionality agreement, but his findings are consistent with my assumptions. He argues that when the United States weighs in, it pushes for easier terms and easier enforcement for its allies. As he writes, summarizing his model and empirical results, powerful states "urge the Fund to be lenient toward their favored clients."[49] When powerful states do not intervene, the Fund tends to enforce its programs more strictly; anticipating this, countries comply more and have better economic results. Not surprisingly given the logic of this study, powerful states tend to intervene in those country programs where they have greater strategic interests and provide more bilateral financing.[50]

Stone substantiates this claim through large-N empirical analyses and fascinating case studies of postcommunist countries in the 1990s. For instance, in the case of Russia's 1992 loan agreement, Stone writes that IMF negotiators initially demanded a strict program with "a monthly inflation target no higher than 3 percent, with strict limits on the money supply and federal spending." However, the United States "urged the IMF to soften its usual requirements." The Fund's managing director stepped in and "watered down" the terms of the proposed stand-by: "Russia consented to cut its budget deficit and control inflation, but its goal for monthly inflation remained a generous 10 percent."[51] Similarly, Stone writes that in 1993, "President Clinton publicly called on the IMF to forgo its tough conditionality and lend Russia $13.5 billion per year."[52] The United States and other bilateral creditors committed large amounts of external financing—including $1.6 billion in new aid from the United States, a broader $28 billion package committed from the G-7 countries, and the rescheduling of $15 billion debt by the Paris Club—and the Fund subsequently fell into line with the states' preferences. Stone writes, "Under severe pressure from the United States and other governments, the Fund announced on April 10 [1993] that it would change its approach to Russia and offer up to $4.5 billion without the usual conditions concerning inflation and the budget deficit."[53]

In short, an overwhelming array of evidence—including policies passed by the Executive Board, U.S. aid policy, statements by Fund insiders, and case studies researched by other scholars—suggests that creditor states like the United States have frequently preferred and pushed for weaker Fund conditionality. On the other side, some (realist) scholars have contended, but with very little evidence, that the United States has pushed for increases in Fund conditionality. Consequently, the assumption that creditor states prefer relative reductions in conditionality seems warranted. Now we turn to a direct discussion of the independent variable—changes in creditor state supplementary financing—and testing of the argument itself.

The Independent Variable: Creditor State Financing in the Post–World War II Period

Economics teaches us that in an open economy, countries with capital surpluses are able to loan money to or invest in countries with capital deficits. Countries whose exports exceed their imports, or whose savings exceed their investments, often invest in or lend to countries whose imports exceed their exports or who want to invest more than they have saved. Political and financial institutions, like the IMF, often facilitate this flow of financing from capital-rich to capital-poor individuals, entities, and countries. These flows can include official loans and grants, direct investment, portfolio investment, bank lending, and private export credits.

In the past 50 years, there have been some important changes in the flow of external financing to developing countries regarding who is providing the financing, how, and to whom. This book concerns the impact of the changes in the sources of supplementary financing—financing that supplements a Fund loan—on certain political outcomes: the policies and activities of the International Monetary Fund. And this chapter focuses specifically on the impact of changing patterns of creditor state supplementary financing on the terms of Fund conditionality agreements. These changes in creditor state supplementary financing reflect, and therefore should be understood in the broader context of, changes in the external financing of developing countries.

In the 19th century and until World War I, external financing of developing countries was dominated by private actors, mainly individual bondholders and the banks, which served as underwriters of these bonds issued from Great Britain, as well as Germany and France. After World War I,

official flows generally became more important and the United States became a more important player, both in terms of private and official external
financing flows. Major sources of official lending included U.S. Allied war
loans and the British and French loans to other European governments.[54]

The International Monetary Fund and its sister institution, the World
Bank, were created in the rubble of World War II. And from the end of
World War II through the 1960s, bilateral lending, particularly from the
United States, was the main form of external and supplementary financing.
The United States, Canada, and Britain provided bilateral loans and credits
in the immediate postwar period to a number of European countries facing
reconstruction. Between May 1945 and late 1946, the United States provided European countries, including Britain, with $8.7 billion dollars in
loans and credits, mainly through U.S. Treasury credits and U.S. Export-
Import Bank loans. U.S. aid dominated the external financing landscape in
1946 and 1947. The United States gave $3.4 billion in aid to Europe in 1946
and $4.7 billion in 1947, when the lion's share of U.S external financing was
directed toward rebuilding Europe (Table 5.1). For instance, Latin America,
which was historically a major recipient of U.S external financing, received
only 14% of Export-Import Bank loans during 1946–1950 and little other
official bilateral financing or loans.[55]

Through the Marshall Plan program, which ran from April 1948 until
1952, the United States gave $12.3 billion in aid to European recipients of
Marshall Plan aid. This aid was provided mainly in the form of goods, including $10.8 billion in goods such as food, coal, oil, and machinery.[56] As
with the United Nations Relief and Rehabilitation Administration (UNRRA)
aid before it, governments sold Marshall Plan aid (goods) and received "counterpart funds" in return. These counterpart funds would then be allocated
with the permission of the European Cooperation Administration. On average, 29% of these Marshall Plan counterpart funds were used to service public debt (with a full 97% of Britain's used for this purpose), whereas the rest
was largely invested in long-term productive capacity.[57] The United States
also gave grants through the Marshall Plan program for specific purposes—
for instance, to encourage intra-European trade and restore multilateral
payments clearing with a European Payments Union grant.[58]

During the post–World War II period, there have been two major
changes with respect to bilateral external financing of developing countries: a

TABLE 5 . 1

United States Overseas Loans and Grants 1946–1998, by Region and Activity

Program	Postwar Relief (1946–1948)	Marshall Plan (1949–1952)	Mutual Security Act (1953–1961)	FAA (1962–1994)	Total FAA Period (1962–1998)	Total (1946–1998)
Total economic assistance ($US million)	$2,482	$18,634	$24,051	$244,513	$284,884	$332,926
Total military assistance ($US million)	$481	$10,064	$19,302	$125,797	$141,033	$173,423
Total economic and military assistance ($US million)	$12,963	$28,698	$43,353	$370,310	$425,917	$506,349
Near East (% of total)	0.34%	0.64%	7.27%	29.75%	30.94%	27.41%
Sub-Saharan Africa (% of total)	0.07%	0.02%	1.48%	6.31%	6.65%	5.52%
Latin America (% of total)	0.76%	0.50%	4.80%	9.22%	8.74%	7.51%
Asia (% of total)	17.38%	14.32%	43.71%	21.60%	19.33%	20.48%
Europe (% of total)	72.63%	82.15%	33.92%	8.59%	8.44%	16.32%
NIS (% of total)	0.00%	0.00%	0.00%	0.93%	1.50%	1.24%
Oceania and other (% of total)	0.13%	0.03%	0.18%	0.31%	0.28%	0.26%
Interregional (% of total)	8.69%	2.31%	8.59%	23.29%	24.12%	21.25%

source: U.S. Agency for International Development (1998).

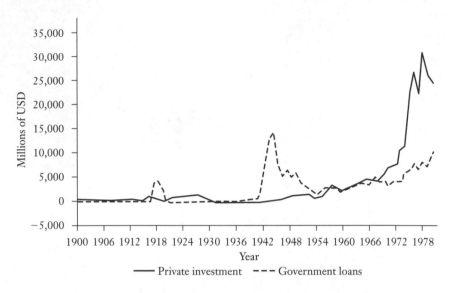

Figure 5.1.   U.S. capital export to all regions, 1900–1980 (in US$ millions)
SOURCE: From Stallings (1987, appx1).

precipitous decline in bilateral financing in relative terms, and a shift from bilateral external financing being provided mainly by the United States to it being provided by numerous advanced industrial countries.

Bilateral external (and supplementary) financing has declined in relative terms during the post–World War II period. From the 1940s to the 1960s, official lending, particularly bilateral lending, was the main form of external financing. For instance, Figure 5.1 shows the dominance of U.S. government loans compared to U.S. private foreign investment in the 1940s and 1950s. Much of this bilateral lending in the 1940s and 1950s was devoted to European reconstruction. In the case of the United States alone, flows of U.S. private investment skyrocketed past U.S. government loans around 1970. This is also evident as a global trend. Figure 5.2 depicts the absolute change in disbursements of long-term debt to developing countries since 1970 according to World Bank data (which are not available before 1970). The World Bank defines long-term external debt as "debt that has an original or extended maturity of more than one year and that is owed to nonresidents and repayable in foreign currency, goods or services." Disbursements are "drawings or loan commitments in the year specified." As Figure 5.2 indicates,

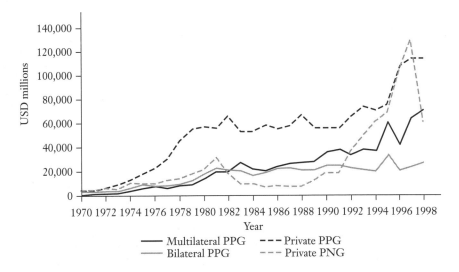

Figure 5.2.   Total disbursements for all developing countries, 1970–1998
SOURCE: From World Bank (2000).

bilateral disbursements sank below private disbursements in the 1970s and early 1980s. Later in the 1980s, multilateral disbursements also exceeded bilateral disbursements.[59]

In addition to the overall decline in bilateral external financing, the sources of that bilateral financing have also diversified. In the initial postwar period in the 1940s and 1950s, bilateral external financing was dominated by the United States. Since then, numerous countries have become active in providing external financing, particularly Japan. In the 1960s, bilateral flows from other industrial countries increased as U.S. bilateral loans and grants fell relatively (and private flows to the developing world also began to increase). Figure 5.3 shows the amount of net total bilateral financing from the United States, United Kingdom, Japan, Arab countries, and EC and EU countries according to Organisation for Economic Co-operation and Development (OECD) Development Assistance Committee (DAC) data.[60] As Figure 5.3 indicates, U.S. bilateral external financing exceeded bilateral external financing from other countries in the 1960s. In 1972, external financing from all of the EC/EU countries combined exceeded U.S. bilateral financing, and it has climbed rapidly ever since.[61] By 1980, EC/EU external financing was more than double official U.S. financing. While Germany's

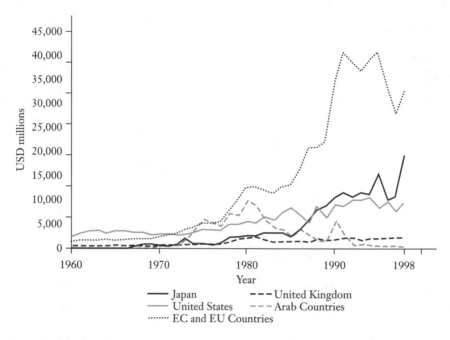

Figure 5.3. Changes in the sourcing of bilateral external financing, 1960–1998 (in US$ millions)

SOURCE: From OECD (2000).

NOTE: This figure depicts the OECD's "Total Official Net" to "Total by Income."

individual official financing did not exceed that of the United States until 1993, external financing from Arab countries (again, this is a label used by the OECD DAC) exceeded external financing from the U.S in the late 1970s and early 1980s. Japan's external financing of developing countries bypassed U.S. external financing in 1988 and continued to exceed U.S. external financing through 1998. In 1998, Japan's official net flows stood at $19.2 billion, whereas the United States' stood at only $9.3 billion.

In short, there have been two main changes with respect to bilateral external and supplementary financing of developing countries. First, there has been an overall decline in bilateral external financing in relation to financing from other sources, namely private financial institutions and multilateral organizations. Second, bilateral external financing now comes from a diverse set of creditor states and is no longer dominated by the United States. Broadly, these trends in bilateral financing suggest that state influence over

Fund conditionality should be strongest during the pre-1970 period. Before 1970, bilateral supplementary financing still outweighed private and multi-lateral supplementary financing. In addition, most bilateral supplementary financing was still being provided by the United States. As a result, U.S. preferences could be communicated more clearly, and the threat to withhold financing could be made more credibly, than when several states offered bi-lateral supplementary financing. In those early, pre-1970 years, Fund condi-tionality agreements generally conformed to creditor state preferences. As the data presented in Chapters 3 and 4 indicate, during the period when bi-lateral supplementary financing still dominated, Fund conditionality agree-ments remained relatively less stringent, requiring fewer conditions and of-ten no procedural conditions. In other words, the longitudinal changes in Fund conditionality roughly conform to the predictions of the supplemen-tary financier argument.

Large-N Econometric Analyses

The pattern of longitudinal change in Fund conditionality may roughly con-form to the predictions of the supplementary financier argument, given the corresponding changes in bilateral and multilateral external financing, but this evidence is hardly conclusive support for the supplementary financier argument. Within any given year, there is wide variation in the number of binding conditions or use of procedural conditions. For instance, in 1965, the average number of binding conditions in the Conditionality Data Set sample was 5.125. Bolivia's agreement was near the mean, with 5 binding conditions in that year, but Brazil's Fund loan agreement included 12 bind-ing conditions, and Yugoslavia's included only one. In 1971, the average number of binding conditions was 5.43. Brazil, Yugoslavia, and Morocco all initiated Fund loan agreements with five binding conditions in that year. In that same year, the Philippines' agreement included 12 binding conditions, and Haiti and Mali's agreements included only 3 binding conditions. In 1980, the average number of binding conditions was 7, but the Central Af-rican Republic and El Salvador had no binding conditions in their agree-ments. The Philippines, on the other hand, had 14 binding conditions in its Fund loan agreement in 1980. Even in the 1990s, there was wide variation in the number of binding conditions included in Fund loan agreements. The average number in 1992 was 12.8 binding conditions; Argentina had 12 binding conditions; Mali had 18, while Romania had only 10. In this section, I use the Conditionality Data Set to assess whether creditor states seem to have influenced Fund conditionality arrangements in the predicted ways, controlling for several other significant variables.

INDEPENDENT VARIABLES

Recall that the supplementary financier argument suggests that powerful creditor states want relatively fewer binding conditions in Fund conditionality agreements. By contrast, realists would presumably argue that powerful creditor states have pushed for the increasing number of binding conditions we have observed. To test these competing arguments about the influence of powerful states on conditionality, two proxies of creditor state influence are used. The first proxy is the (previously mentioned) *U.S. influence* variable, which is the total amount of U.S. loans and grants to a given Fund borrower in the year of its Fund agreement, divided by (and normalized by) the amount of the Fund loan agreement. It varies between 0 and 33.49.[62] In other words, it is the amount of the United States' contribution to this country's financing in relation to the Fund's contribution. The logic behind this proxy is that the United States contributes more resources to those countries in which it is interested, and in turn should have more influence over their Fund conditional loan arrangements.[63] The second proxy of creditor state influence (*creditor state*) is the total amount of public or publicly guaranteed debt outstanding and disbursed (PPG DOD) owed to bilateral creditors divided by the total amount of PPG DOD owed to all creditors.[64] The logic behind this proxy is that creditor states should have more interest in and influence over the programs of countries to which they have lent relatively large sums of money. These two proxies are used to test both the supplementary financier argument and the realist argument. One focuses more narrowly on the influence of the United States, whereas the other focuses more broadly on the influence of all creditor states.[65] Although the supplementary financier argument would expect the coefficients on these proxies to be negative (because creditor states push for fewer conditions and less constraining conditions), the realist argument would expect the coefficients on these proxies to be positive (because powerful creditor states should have pushed for increases in the number and stringency of Fund conditions).

Another plausible alternative hypothesis is that Fund conditionality and the changes in Fund conditionality have been driven by the Fund's bureaucracy. For instance, in a series of articles, Roland Vaubel focuses on the Fund bureaucracy's efforts to "maximize their budget, their staff and their independence." Vaubel views Fund conditionality as a mechanism to pursue those interests.[66] The *salary increase* variable is the proportional increase in the average staff salary since the previous year; it varies between −0.016 and 0.192.[67] This variable mimics a proxy for bureaucratic power and autonomy used in Roland Vaubel's work on the Fund.[68] The logic is that as Fund bureaucratic power and autonomy increase (indicated in an increase in average salaries that year), it is apt to insert more conditions and more constraining and "discretionary" conditions that further serve to "increase its power."[69] Thus, according to the bureaucratic argument as articulated by Vaubel, the coefficient on this variable should be positive and significant.

I use this proxy because it mimics Vaubel's own empirical work; however, I believe this is a flawed proxy of bureaucratic influence. Many of the increases in staff salaries are proposed according to a formula meant to mimic market and inflation increases.[70] As a result, this variable may not actually be a great metric of staff power. Alternative proxies for bureaucratic influence have been considered, but are equally, if not more, problematic. For instance, the number of regular full-time Fund staff members (another metric of bureaucratic power used by Vaubel and others) is almost perfectly correlated with a simple year-tracking variable (at 0.9863).

The Fund may also interact with borrowers differently on the basis of borrower attributes. Scholars have considered the influence of borrower attributes on borrower demand for Fund loans.[71] Less work has been done on the supply side (how borrower attributes may influence Fund activity, including the design of Fund programs) despite the fact that the Fund often claims that programs are tailored to the specific needs and demands of borrowers, or to borrower attributes. It certainly seems plausible that Fund conditionality agreements would vary systematically on the basis of borrower attributes.

Three variables are included to test the general premise that Fund conditionality is responsive to the changing needs or demands of borrowers. Fund lending was originally intended to help countries offset temporary payments imbalances. Over time the Fund has increasingly lent to countries facing "protracted balance of payments problems" and impediments to growth.[72] The Fund has argued that Fund program design has changed to meet the objective needs of borrowers facing increasingly severe payments imbalances and economic crises.[73] To control for the severity of the borrower's balance-of-payments problem, I include the *reserves* variable, which is the ratio of foreign reserves to imports in the year that the country began its Fund conditional loan agreement.[74] This measure should be negatively related to the dependent variable.

Second, the Fund has also argued that less developed countries require different Fund conditionality—including more or different binding conditions—than more developed countries.[75] As a result, the Fund has created new lending facilities for less-developed countries, like the Structural Adjustment Facility (SAF), Enhanced Structural Adjustment Facility (ESAF), and now the Poverty Reduction and Growth Facility, that require more detailed conditionality. A constant *GNP per capita* variable is included in the analysis to control for this effect.[76] The predicted coefficient should also be negative for this variable.

Third, democracies may interact differently with the Fund. Democracies may tend to have systematically higher conditionality programs because they demand increased conditionality in order to tie their own hands.[77] Alternatively, democracies may have systematically lower conditionality programs because they resist tougher conditions out of fear of voter retribution. A *regime*-type variable, that ranges from −10 (full autocracy) to +10 (full democracy), is included to capture this effect.[78]

The seventh independent variable tests the general Fund's policy on loans: that larger loans (in relation to the country's quota) require more "justification" or stricter conditionality.[79] The *tranche* variable tests whether the Fund actually follows this policy. It is the amount of the Fund loan, divided by the amount of the country's Fund quota. The predicted relationship between this variable and the dependent variable is positive.

The eighth independent variable tests whether the borrower's size influences the terms of its Fund conditional loan agreement. Some have argued that certain countries are "too big to fail" and have therefore received special, perhaps easier, treatment from the Fund.[80] As a result, I have included the borrower's gross national product (*constant GNP*) at market prices in billions of constant 1995 U.S. dollars.[81] The coefficient on this variable should be negative if larger countries receive easier terms.

Given that this data set has time-series properties—in other words, it includes multiple over-time observations—there may be an over-time effect that is not being absorbed by the model. The terms of the Fund's Extended Fund Facility (EFF) with Mexico in 1982 may have influenced the Fund's stand-by arrangement (SBA) with Mexico in 1986 or the Fund's EFF with Brazil in 1983. One of the key assumptions in typical regression models is that all of the observations are independent. If a model is based on that assumption but the observations are actually dependent on each other, inefficient parameters and biased standard errors result. [82] In Gary King's words, the model should capture "the underlying process by which the random observations vary and covary over time. In a sense, the task of time series analysis is to model how history repeats itself or how it influences future events."[83] A final variable—a lagged dependent variable (number of binding conditions required by that borrower's previous Fund program), or *lagged Y*—is included to represent an alternative theory of change over time.[84] The implicit argument of the lagged-dependent variable is that a country's Fund loan agreement in year t determines or influences its Fund loan agreement in $t + 1$. If this variable is significant, then clearly there is an aspect of the "underlying process" that is not being captured by the explanatory variables in the model.

TESTING HYPOTHESIS I

The statistical analyses that follow unfortunately only test the competing arguments using the post-1970 cases in the Conditionality Data Set because many of the independent variables are only available after 1970. This is particularly unfortunate because the supplementary financier argument expects state influence to be greatest for those cases not used in the statistical analysis. Therefore, before proceeding to discuss the results of the statistical analyses, it is helpful to consider the relationships between the main independent variable (which is available for the pre-1970 period) and the dependent variable: the total number of binding conditions. When considering the entire 1952 to 1995 sample, there is basically no correlation (-0.0250 with $p = 0.7146$) between the *U.S. influence* proxy and the total number of binding conditions for a given Fund agreement. However, if one divides the sample into two groups, 1952–1970 and 1971–1995, a slightly different result emerges. U.S. supplementary financing (as measured by the *U.S. influence* variable) is positively correlated with the total number of binding conditions before 1970 (0.2882 with $p = 0.0059$) when the average number of binding conditions per arrangement was only 4. After 1970, when the average number of binding conditions skyrocketed to 9.3, U.S. supplementary financing was negatively correlated with the total number of binding conditions (although the correlation is not statistically significant, -0.1247 with $p = 0.1749$). In other words, the United States appears to have encouraged some conditionality in the early years, but pushed for less conditionality when the number of conditions truly "proliferated" after 1970. In the pre-1970 period, when the number of binding conditions remained relatively low (compared to its growth in later years) and when bilateral financing dominated, there was a positive and significant relationship. Later, when the real growth in the number of binding conditions—the change in conditionality that is the puzzle of this project—occurs, there is either a negative relationship or no significant relationship between *U.S. influence* and the number of binding conditions.

Table 5.2 tests competing arguments using the total number of binding conditions in a particular Fund loan agreement as the dependent variable (0 to 18; positive count). Because the dependent variable is a positive count, Poisson or negative binomial distribution regression analyses are implemented.[85] The Poisson distribution model is the most basic model for nonnegative count variables. However, the Poisson model has some restrictive assumptions—namely that the variance should equal the mean. Often the variance exceeds the mean for count variables. The negative binomial distribution model is also intended to be used with nonnegative count-dependent variables, but it relaxes some of the Poisson model's assumptions, including allowing the variance to exceed the mean (called overdispersion).[86]

Table 5.2 includes six different models. As with the many of the other tables that follow, the missing data problem becomes immediately apparent. There are 249 cases in the data set between 1952 and 1995. Of these 249, 221 have observations for the number of binding conditions. Of these 221, 131 are observations between 1970 and 1995.[87] In other words, 131 cases out of 249 possible is the highest number of cases possible with these equations. In reality, the missing data problem becomes much worse. For instance, equation

TABLE 5.2
Total Number of Binding Conditions

Variable	Model 1	Model 2	Model 3	Model 4	Model 5	Model 6
U.S. influence	-0.04 (0.02)*	—	-0.04 (0.02)*	—	-0.03 (0.02)	—
Creditor state	—	-0.68 (0.24)**	—	-0.63 (0.28)**	—	-0.618 (0.30)**
Reserves	0.02 (0.02)	0.03 (0.02)	0.02 (0.02)	0.03 (0.02)	0.02 (0.03)	0.03 (0.03)
GNP per capita	-0.00004 (0.00003)	-0.00006 (0.00003)**	-0.00003 (0.00003)	-0.00005 (0.00003)*	-0.00003 (0.00003)	-0.00005 (0.00003)
Regime	0.02 (0.01)**	0.02 (0.01)**	0.01 (0.01)*	0.01 (0.01)*	0.01 (0.01)	0.01 (0.01)
Tranche	0.001 (0.03)	0.001 (0.03)	-0.001 (0.03)	0.02 (0.03)	0.05 (0.05)	0.06 (0.05)
Constant GNP	0.0002 (0.0006)	-0.0003 (0.0006)	0.0002 (0.001)	-0.0004 (0.0007)	0.0002 (0.0007)	-0.0005 (0.0008)
Lagged Y	—	—	0.05 (0.01)**	0.05 (0.01)**	0.05 (0.01)**	0.04 (0.01)**
Salary increase	—	—	—	—	-1.5 (1.2)	-1.60 (1.16)
Constant	2.41 (0.09)**	2.69 (0.14)**	1.94 (0.16)**	2.21 (0.23)**	1.97 (0.18)**	2.30 (0.26)**
N	86	90	75	79	68	72
Log likelihood	-213.95	-222.91554	-172.26399	-180.46962	-154.45302	-162.47524
Mean log likelihood	-2.487768	-2.47683	-2.2968532	-2.284426	-2.2713679	-2.2566
Poisgof	0.5206	0.6332	0.9994	0.9999	0.9991	0.9999
Method	Poisson	Poisson	Poisson	Poisson	Poisson	Poisson

* p ≤ 0.1
** p < 0.05

5 has only 68 observations. Attempts to impute the missing variables, rather than resorting to line-item deletion, were unsuccessful because of the pattern of missingness. As a result of this high rate of missingness, results from the data analysis should be interpreted with some caution.

However, the large-N data analysis does lend support to the supplementary financier argument. For all but one of the models (model 5), the proxies representing creditor state influence (*U.S. influence* or *creditor state*) are negatively and significantly related to the dependent variable: the number of binding conditions included in a given Fund agreement. The more financing the United States provides in relation to the Fund loan and the more that a borrower's existing debt is owed to creditor states, rather than multilateral or private creditors, the fewer binding conditions will be included in a Fund agreement, holding several other variables constant. All of the equations include variables to control for the extent of the balance of payments problem (*reserves*), the level of development (*GNP per capita*), the level of democracy (*regime*), the size of the IMF loan in relation to the country's quota (*tranche*), and the size of the country's economy (*constant GNP*). In some specifications, *GNP per capita* and *regime* are significantly related to the total number of binding conditions. Countries that are more democratic tend to have more binding conditions, whereas more developed countries tend to have fewer binding conditions, holding other variables constant. Surprisingly, the other control variables are not significant in any of the specifications. Equations 3 through 6 add *lagged Y*. The coefficient on this variable is positive and significant in all specifications.

Equations 5 and 6 also include a variable meant to test the bureaucratic argument: *salary increase*. As mentioned previously, I have reservations about this metric. Nevertheless, according to Vaubel's argument, the coefficient on this variable should be positive and significant. In models 5 and 6, the coefficient is actually negative and insignificant, which contradicts this argument.

The mean log likelihood ratio suggests that model 6, which includes the bureaucratic proxy *salary increase*, in Table 5.2 has the best model fit.[88] In this model, the coefficient on *creditor state* is negative and significant, and the coefficient on *lagged Y* is positive and significant. This provides some support for the supplementary financier argument. As bilateral supplementary financing increases relatively, the number of binding conditions required by a Fund program decreases, holding other variables constant. The significance of the lagged dependent variable indicates, not surprisingly, that a borrower's previous Fund program influences its subsequent one.

The use of procedural conditions in Fund conditionality programs certainly changed from 1952 to 1995. Recall that Figure 4.1 showed the change in the average number of procedural conditions in Fund loan programs. Procedural conditions were incorporated in Fund loan programs during the 1952–1973 period, and their use actually dropped in absolute and relative terms during the period of 1974–1983. After 1983, the use of procedural conditions increased significantly. By 1991–1995, the average Fund conditional loan agreement included over two procedural conditions, on average nearly 20% of all binding conditions.

Hypothesis 2 deals with creditor state preferences over the design of Fund conditionality programs with respect to the type of binding conditions, namely procedural conditions versus targets. According to the supplementary financier argument, bilateral financiers prefer more targets and fewer procedural conditions. Is it true that countries that receive relatively more supplementary financing from creditor states tend to have Fund conditional loan arrangements with fewer procedural conditions?

Table 5.3 provides results from large-n analyses that test the supplementary financier's Hypothesis 2 against the alternatives. The dependent variable is the number of procedural binding conditions in a particular loan agreement, and all models in Table 5.3 are negative binomial regression analyses. The independent variables are the same as those included in Table 5.2's models except *lagged Y*, which is now the number of procedural binding conditions required by a borrower's previous program. The results in Table 5.3 are also somewhat similar. The creditor state interest proxies (*U.S. influence* and *creditor state*) are negatively and significantly related to the dependent variable for the first four models. For models 5 and 6, the coefficients on the creditor state proxies (*U.S. influence* and *creditor state*) are negative, with p values of 0.12 and 0.13, respectively. These results provide some support of the supplementary financier argument: as creditor state supplementary financing increases, the use of procedural conditions decreases. As with Table 5.2,

TABLE 5.3

Total Number of Procedural Binding Conditions

Variable	Model 1	Model 2	Model 3	Model 4	Model 5	Model 6
U.S. influence	-0.22 (0.10)**	—	-0.22 (0.10)**	—	-0.17 (0.11)	—
Creditor state	—	-1.40 (0.75)*	—	-1.73 (0.82)**	—	-1.34 (0.89)
Reserves	-0.01 (0.07)	0.04 (0.07)	-0.0004 (0.08)	0.03 (0.07)	-0.05 (0.09)	-0.02 (0.08)
GNP per capita	-0.0002 (0.0001)*	-0.0002 (0.0001)*	-0.0001 (0.0001)	-0.0001 (0.0001)	-0.0001 (0.0001)	-0.0002 (0.0001)
Regime	0.07 (0.02)**	0.06 (0.02)**	0.05 (0.02)**	0.04 (0.02)**	0.05 (0.03)**	0.05 (0.03)*
Tranche	-0.18 (0.12)	-0.17 (0.12)	-0.17 (0.12)	-0.15 (0.13)	-0.02 (0.18)	0.03 (0.17)
Constant GNP	0.002 (0.002)	0 (0.002)	0.002 (0.002)	-0.001 (0.002)	0.001 (0.002)	-0.0005 (0.002)
Lagged Y	—	—	0.19 (0.07)**	0.19 (0.06)**	0.16 (0.07)**	0.16 (0.07)**
Salary increase	—	—	—	—	-7.73 (4.19)*	-7.25 (3.97)*
Constant	1.04 (0.31)**	1.39 (0.45)**	.76 (0.35)**	1.26 (0.50)**	1.14 (0.48)**	1.48 (0.60)**
N	86	90	75	79	68	72
Log likelihood	-124.22384	-131.48847	-107.35204	-113.83554	-92.125777	-98.176671
Mean log likelihood	-1.4445	-1.460983	-1.4314	-1.44096	-1.35479	-1.36356

* p ≤ 0.1

** p < 0.05

the level of development (*GNP per capita*) and level of democracy (*regime*) variables are significant in some specifications, with the same implications as in Table 5.2. Countries that are more democratic tend to have more procedural binding conditions, whereas more development countries have fewer procedural binding conditions, holding other variables constant. The coefficient on the lagged dependent variable (*lagged Y*) is positive and significant in all models in which it was included, suggesting that a country's Fund program design at $t - 1$ influences the design of its Fund program at time t. In addition, the bureaucratic proxy (*salary increase*) is negative and significant, counter to what one would expect from the bureaucratic argument. As discussed previously, I have some reservations about the accuracy of this proxy.

In short, the findings in Tables 5.2 and 5.3 provide some initial support for the supplementary financier argument: as bilateral supplementary financing increases, Fund conditionality programs tend to require relatively fewer and relatively less stringent conditions. The realist argument is not supported: it predicted the coefficient on the bilateral influence variables to be positive and significant. Similarly, the bureaucratic argument is not supported by these results. In fact, counter to the bureaucratic argument, the models presented here suggest that as the Fund staff gain in power, the number of binding conditions and stringency of those conditions may actually decrease.

Case Study Analysis

The previous section established that when supplementary financing from creditor states relatively increases, Fund conditionality becomes less stringent, holding other variables constant. Borrowers that receive a good deal of financing from creditor states tend to have fewer conditions and less procedural conditions included in their Fund conditionality agreement. The implication here is that creditor states have pushed for these easier terms. This section focuses on one case of a Fund conditionality agreement—Brazil's 1965 SBA—in order to unpack whether creditor states are weakening the terms of Fund agreements, and if so, to uncover the mechanisms of that influence.

Creditor states have a number of opportunities to communicate their preferences over Fund conditionality to Fund staff and management, and thereby to influence Fund agreements. Country leaders, like U.S. Treasury officials, can simply contact Fund management and make their preferences known. Fund management often know country leaders well, maintain frequent contacts with them, and sometimes solicit their opinions on particular Fund agreements or other Fund activities.[89] Executive directors (EDs) can also communicate creditor state preferences. However, EDs often do not see draft agreements, particularly during the period under study, while they are in the process of being negotiated and constructed. Instead, EDs often receive a copy of the negotiated agreement only a few days before the scheduled Executive Board meeting during which they discuss and approve the agreement. As a result, EDs communicate their preferences about the agreement at the Executive Board meetings after the agreement is already a fait accompli and on the verge of being approved. These stated preferences are supposed to influence future Fund programs, but clearly they do not influence the program at hand. The exception to this rule arises when the ED represents a major creditor of the country, in which case they may be consulted earlier in the negotiation process and may be able to influence the terms of that agreement. A third avenue by which creditor states can communicate preferences about a particular Fund agreement is through Paris Club debt renegotiations.[90] The Paris Club began meeting in 1956, and the Fund has become "routinely" involved in these meetings since 1960.[91] These meetings provide an opportunity for the Fund staff and creditor representatives to discuss specifically how the Fund conditionality agreement will be tailored and how much supplementary financing and debt relief will be provided by creditor states.[92]

In this section, I discuss one case of a Fund conditionality agreement that does not seem to fit the predictions of the supplementary financier argument: Brazil's 1965 SBA. In 1965, Brazil received most of its supplementary financing from creditor states. The Brazil 1965 case received above-average (above the mean value for the Conditionality Data Set) amounts of bilateral and U.S. supplementary financing, according to the various measures of bilateral supplementary financing I collected (the proportion of total debt outstanding and disbursed, the proportion of total debt commitments, and the proportion of total debt disbursements that came from bilateral sources, as well as the United States' interest proxy discussed earlier). However, despite such high levels of bilateral supplementary financing, Brazil's 1965 SBA stood out as a particularly high conditionality program for that time. Thus, this case seems to defy the supplementary financier argument.

Brazil's 1965 SBA was chosen for exactly that reason: because it seems to contradict the predictions of the supplementary financier argument. Brazil received a relatively large proportion of its supplementary financing from creditor states, mainly from the United States, by several different measures; however, Brazil's conditionality was relatively stringent for its time. Did the United States and other creditor states push for more stringent terms in this case? In fact, and consistent with the supplementary financier argument, the United States actually pushed for (and received) easier conditionality terms for its ally relative to what Fund staff and other EDs considered appropriate for Brazil at the time.

By 1965, Brazil had developed somewhat of a reputation with the Fund staff and management for three reasons. First, the United States was actively involved in mediating the Fund's relations with Brazil. For instance, in a 1959 letter to André Meyer at Lazard Frères & Co., the Fund's managing director, Per Jacobsson, wrote that the Fund's negotiating tactics with Brazil had been "fully approved" by the U.S. ED.[93] In that year, however, Brazil ended up "bypassing the International Monetary Fund," which "insisted on greater austerity" and instead turned directly to the United States for financing.[94] The United States did not insist on a Fund program because of the specific political circumstances. According to a Fund assessment of the situation, there was "already considerable political agitation having in view the Presidential elections to take place in October, 1960. A refusal to help and consequent moratorium would strengthen anti-americanism which, in turn, might bring a leftist Government into power whereas otherwise the chances appear to favor the moderate Sao Paulo candidate."[95] Once Brazil did negotiate a SBA with the Fund in 1961, the U.S. ED made a grandiose statement in support of it at the Executive Board meeting, stating that "the Fund had few more important operations with which to deal. The success of the program would mean a great deal not only to Brazil but to the Western World as a whole and to the Fund."[96] The United States was clearly very involved in the Fund's relationship with Brazil during this period.

Second, Brazil was the largest and most consistent borrower with the Fund. In the words of the then head of the Western Hemisphere division, Jorge Del Canto, Brazil "has consistently been among the members which have made the greatest use of Fund resources."[97]

Third, Brazil had developed a reputation with the Fund staff as a deviant, or at least defiant, country. Before the 1965 SBA, Brazil had had two previous SBAs with the Fund, in 1958 and 1961. A November 1961 memo from Del Canto to the managing director and deputy managing director stated, "Brazil, an original member of the Fund, has consistently been among the members which have made the greatest use of Fund resources. Since April 1959 when the first purchase was made by Brazil, there have continuously been net drawings outstanding. This is a longer period than has ruled for any other member country."[98] Later the memo went on to review Brazil's bad history of reform. It stated: "In recent years when drawings have been made the Brazilian Government has on each occasion given assurance that the internal financial policies of the Government would be improved. The actual outcome has repeatedly diverged widely from the previous assurance.... This history of departure from undertakings is far worse than with any other member country in Latin America."[99] The recipient of the memo, who should have been either the managing director or deputy managing director, wrote (in longhand) after that sentence, " ... or elsewhere." As a result of these three factors—Brazil's history of borrowing, of being a deviant case according to Fund staff, and of having the United States mediate its relations with the Fund—the Fund staff were determined to protect themselves and negotiate an appropriately strict Fund program the next time.

Between 1960 and 1964, Brazil's economy slowed dramatically, and "capital inflows virtually ceased."[100] Per capita GDP growth fell from 6.6% in 1960 to 0 in 1964; inflation jumped from 26% in 1960 to 87% in 1964; foreign currency was scarce.[101] This economic disruption and President Goulart's "association with Communism" caused "housewives to protest in the streets."[102] On March 31, 1964, the popularly elected Brazilian President João Goulart was ousted by the Brazilian military. According to Cardoso and Fishlow, "the middle class welcomed the demise of a Goulart government that was both leftist and ineffectual."[103] This military coup led to a regime change and subsequently almost 20 years of military rule. It also kicked off a new period of economic growth, relative economic stability, and lower inflation, although with continued and widespread income inequality.[104]

Around June 1964, while the economy still stumbled, the new military government led by army Marshal Humberto Castelo Branco began talks with the International Monetary Fund and the United States about a loan agreement and stabilization program. Both initially thought the "political situation was so fluid" that a program could not yet be negotiated.[105] In October 1964, a delegation from Brazil visited the Fund in Washington, DC, and U.S. banks in New York. At this point, the Fund staff were skeptical of Brazil's commitment to reform. For instance, in a memo to Acting Managing Director Frank Southard Jr., Del Canto wrote, "There should be some clear-cut justification to see how far our money fulfills a useful purpose or if it is just throwing money into a bottomless pit. My own tentative view is that it will be difficult at this point, on the basis of the 'present' stage of their plans, to justify a major stand-by for Brazil." Del Canto advocated conditionality and reform and thought "the United States and other creditors . . . would like to see the Fund exact as many conditions as possible from Brazil, so as to facilitate their own actions." [106]

However, by mid-November, it seemed obvious that this estimation was incorrect. As a result of Brazil's history as a large borrower with unsustainable policies, the Fund staff and management were intent on demanding true (and strict) reform from Brazil in 1965. But analysis of the Fund archival files reveals that although the staff were hesitant about granting Brazil a program, the United States wanted Brazil to have an SBA that year. The United States strongly supported the new military government in Brazil—in fact the Brazilian military had received prior support of the coup, and the United States had even "dispatched warships to Brazil at the end of March in case they were needed." Goulart had been "far too radical" and closely associated with communism for the United States government. [107] According to E. Bradford Burns, "U.S. Ambassador to Brazil Lincoln Gordon . . . judged the military takeover 'the single most decisive victory for freedom in the mid-twentieth century.' If any further approval from Washington was needed, it came in the form of generous aid and loans which virtually inundated the new military government." [108] U.S. Assistant Secretary of State Thomas Mann called Frank Southard Jr. on November 19 and urgently sent one of his staff members over that day to show Southard a cable from the United States embassy in Brazil. [109] In short, the embassy wrote that the "Fund mission in Brazil has been raising difficulties about a stand-by arrangement," whereas the "U.S. Embassy . . . were strongly in favor of a stand-by arrangement." The United States and Brazil had already agreed to five conditions stated explicitly in this cable:

1. Quarterly budget targets;
2. No increase in the real return to coffee exporters so as to yield a maximum amount of revenue for the Treasury;

3. A flexible exchange rate policy with suitable assurances concerning its implementation;

4. No increase in Bank of Brazil credit unless offset in one way or another, to be specified;

5. Commitment to use the counterpart of U.S. aid, amounting to about Cr$200 to be applied to the budget deficit rather than to investment.[110]

The U.S. ambassador told the managing director to "instruct Mr. Del Canto to negotiate a stand-by arrangement as agreed."[111] Mann took a milder tack. According to a memorandum Southard wrote for the Fund archival files, Mann "thought the real question was whether the Fund and the U.S. should take a chance on the stand-by now or wait until January. The U.S. was fully convinced that we should *not* wait."[112]

After the United States exerted pressure, negotiations proceeded in a brisker fashion. On December 5, "negotiations for a stand-by were completed . . . when the President and Cabinet approved the letter of intentions negotiated between the mission and Ministers Bulhoes and Campos."[113] According to Jorge Marshall et al., "The effective negotiations on the economic policy put in practice by the government, however, were apparently not carried out so much by the IMF as by certain U.S. agencies, like U.S. AID and the Export-Import Bank. During this period, the Fund's role seems to have been more formal than effective."[114] The general perception was that Brazil had gotten a good deal. An article in the Brazilian paper *O Estado de Sao Paulo* stated that other Latin American countries were "jealous and frustrated" with Brazil because "they think, and with reason, that the Government of President Johnson, as well as the International Monetary Fund, made concessions which they had not made before to any other country of the continent, to help to obtain the monetary stabilization and the increase in development." The article went on to describe the negotiations between the Castelo Branco government and the International Monetary Fund. According to the article, the Fund wanted to wait for more reforms and possibly agree to a stand-by by mid-February or early March, but the Brazilian government rejected this plan and presented another that was so "convincing . . . that the International Monetary Fund changed its position in connection with Brazil. As a matter of fact, besides the drawing, the 'stand-by' credit was also approved."[115]

Even after these negotiations, U.S. pressure appears to have continued. On December 17, the U.S. ED, William Dale, wrote the Fund's managing director to urge an easing of one requirement: treating drawing on a U.S. loan (or borrowing from the United States) as a "liability for the purpose of the exchange test."[116] This request came after the stand-by had already been agreed and the letter of intent had been signed by the Brazilians, so in the end was not changed.[117] Del Canto's December 30, 1964, memo also conveys "the tremendous strain under which the staff and secretaries have been working for weeks and days to turn out our long Brazilian report at such short notice."[118]

The Brazilian SBA was accompanied by large amounts of U.S. aid, as well as the rescheduling of official debt by Paris Club creditors through the Hague Club framework.[119] Despite Fund staff efforts to negotiate stricter standards and delay negotiations until Brazil had proven itself more committed to reform, the United States pushed through the program with relatively easier terms. The SBA was still strict by 1965 standards, with 12 binding conditions; the average that year was 5 binding conditions. However, despite this number of binding conditions, the agreement was perceived as easier than it might have been in the absence of U.S. pressure. During the Executive Board meeting when the agreement was passed, several EDs expressed concerns. Ulrich Beelitz, the ED from Germany, "agreed to the proposed stand-by, although he has some doubts. . . . He wondered whether the Fund should allow a high proportion of the stand-by to be drawn immediately after the Board decision in a case that involved so many uncertainties that no one could predict, let alone guarantee, the satisfactory implementation of the stabilization program."[120] John Kirbyshire, the alternative ED from the UK, approved the program but thought that the "Brazilian authorities still seemed to be relying too much on the generosity of creditors—who were perhaps not quite as generous as the Brazilian authorities appeared to think"; he was "taken aback" to find certain policies described in the letter not included as binding conditions.[121] In addition to the loan itself, the Fund also agreed to reschedule repayment of Brazil's "repurchases" or principal repayments, which some EDs also opposed.[122] As late as 1966, the alternate EDs from Argentina and Guatemala continued to express "disappointment" about "sympathetic and understanding" treatment of Brazil versus Argentina.[123] By contrast, the U.S. ED, William Dale, considered the program negotiated between the Fund and the Brazilian authorities a "careful and technically very tight program" and he complemented "the [Brazilian] Government [which] has shown determination and courage in this beginning."[124]

Conclusion

When creditor states try to influence the terms of Fund conditionality agreements, they are overwhelmingly trying to intervene on behalf of an ally and ease the stringency of the Fund agreement. In this chapter, I have discussed in depth this assumption that creditor states prefer relatively weaker conditionality agreements. Quantitative analyses indicate that when countries receive relatively more supplementary financing from creditor states in general or the United States in particular, their Fund loan agreement tends to have relatively fewer binding conditions and fewer procedural binding conditions. The case of Brazil's 1965 stand-by agreement demonstrates how the United States pushed for weaker terms for its ally in one instance.

Although this evidence demonstrates how powerful creditor states influence Fund agreements, it refutes realist conventional wisdom. Creditor states are able to influence Fund loan agreements when they are the dominant supplementary financier, and they tend to push for weaker conditionality in those cases. By contrast, realists argue that powerful states have driven the changes in Fund conditionality and push for more stringent conditionality. Thus powerful creditor states have not been the impetus behind the broad changes in Fund conditionality that we have observed over the last 50 years, as realists would argue. Instead, private financial institutions and multilateral organizations—the subjects of the next two chapters—have pushed for many of the broad changes in Fund conditionality that we observe.

CHAPTER SIX

Private Financial Institutions as Supplementary Financiers

Introduction

There are three types of supplementary financiers: creditor states, private financial institutions (PFIs), and multilateral organizations.[1] This chapter focuses on PFIs. They are of particular interest because they lack the institutionalized mechanisms of influence that states and other multilateral organizations have at their disposal. Scholars often consider PFIs' interests to be subservient to, or subsumed by, state interests, rather than in competition with them.[2] As a result, PFIs are a hard case and provide a good test of the supplementary financier argument.

This chapter begins with a discussion of PFI interests (in providing supplementary financing) and then derives their preferences over the design of Fund conditional loan agreements. I argue that private financial institutions lend for profit and prefer Fund loan agreements with terms that help them increase the likelihood that their lending will be profitable. Next, I present descriptive statistics on the dependent variable—the inclusion of "bank-friendly" conditions—and the changes in private supplementary financing. The last two sections provide empirical testing of the supplementary financier argument. The penultimate section tests whether countries are more likely to have Fund conditional loan agreements with bank-friendly conditions when private financial institutions are organized through debt restructuring. The final section unpacks the mechanisms of private financial institution influence over Fund conditionality by focusing on two case studies of Fund loan agreements.

Interests and Preferences

PFIs provide financing to Fund borrowers in order to make a profit.[3] They extend loans to and make investments in countries when they expect a positive return, and they want Fund programs to help ensure their profitable return. For most of the period under investigation, the main PFI supplementary financiers were commercial banks, and they wanted Fund loan agreements to increase the probability that their loans would be paid back.[4]

This interest may manifest itself in different preferences regarding the terms of Fund agreements. In other words, in the interest of profit, PFIs may want borrowers to implement various kinds of reforms—and to have these commitments to reform included in the borrower's Fund conditionality agreement—that they believe will increase the likelihood of loan profitability.[5] For instance, several scholars argue that investment in export industries may increase the likelihood of sovereign debt repayment.[6] As Boot and Kanatas state, the "export-revenue generating capacity of a sovereign may be positively linked to the degree of enforceability of its debt agreements."[7] If true, then presumably PFIs would prefer sovereigns to commit a portion of their investment to the tradable sector. Claessens and Diwan specifically address how Fund conditional loan programs can "provide incentives and sanctions that make credible a debtor's promises to invest."[8] Ultimately, however, investment or investment in export industries is important because it increases the likelihood of economic growth (which in turn increases the likelihood of debt repayment). This goal—of economic growth—is one that all types of supplementary financiers (creditor states, PFIs, and multilateral organizations), the borrowing country, and the IMF may share.

For the purpose of isolating PFI influence on Fund conditionality agreements, I have focused on a narrow set of conditions that I have labeled "bank-friendly conditions." Instead of committing a borrower to implement certain policies (for example, that encourage growth), these conditions specify that a country must pay back a commercial bank creditor as a condition of its Fund loan. This type of condition seemed to best isolate PFI influence, as opposed to other types of conditions that could more easily appear to be in the interest of other actors, particularly creditor states or multilateral organizations.

Creditor states and multilateral organizations have legitimate mechanisms to coordinate their demands and influence the Fund, for instance through the Executive Board or joint Fund-Bank missions, respectively. As a result, their influence on Fund programs should be directly proportional to their relative contribution of supplementary financing. PFIs, by contrast, do not have legitimate, established mechanisms of influence. Officially, they are not supposed to influence the content of Fund programs at all. As a result, PFI influence should not be directly proportional to their relative contribution of supplementary financing. Instead, PFI influence hinges on their ability to generate a credible threat that substantial financing will be lost if Fund activities do not conform to their preferences.

Often, however, PFIs cannot credibly generate this threat for two related reasons. First, when there are multiple PFIs involved in negotiations with a potential Fund borrower, they face a collective action problem. The PFIs may all benefit from a Fund conditionality agreement with "bank-friendly" conditions, but individually, they may not want to commit to withhold financing if the bank-friendly condition is omitted and provide financing if the condition is included in the borrower's Fund agreement. These constraints and commitments are themselves costly. PFIs also may not want to engage in costly negotiations with the Fund, and may not agree on how much financing should be provided or withheld if the conditions are included or omitted, respectively.[9] PFIs will be able to overcome this collective action problem when a single financier dominates the group—or, more often, when they get organized.[10] Previous scholars have studied when PFI organization is more or less likely, and what forms it is likely to take. For instance, Charles Lipson has studied how and when private creditors organize themselves, for instance through syndicate lending and during debt rescheduling negotiations.[11] For the purposes of this book, PFI organization of some sort is necessary so that PFIs can coordinate their demands on the Fund and generate the threat in the first place.

Second and relatedly, in order for this generated threat to be credible, the PFIs' ex post incentives must support enforcement of the threat. As North and Weingast have argued, "While parties may have strong incentives to strike a bargain, their incentives after the fact are not always compatible with maintaining the agreement."[12] Under certain circumstances, PFIs may prefer the Fund to include a bank-friendly condition in its agreement, but the inclusion or exclusion of this condition will not change the PFIs' incentives enough to induce them to provide or withhold the necessary supplementary financing, respectively. Given that PFIs are less likely to expend the energy to lobby the Fund in the first instance, we are more concerned about the second instance: when PFIs would be willing to provide supplementary financing even if the Fund agreement did not include a bank-friendly condition. The threat to withhold financing must be ex post incentive compatible in order to be credible. Unless PFIs are disinterested enough to walk away from a potential financing opportunity, their threat will not be credible, and the Fund has no incentive to change the terms of its agreement. In order to operationalize PFI influence, I use a variable (*private*) that captures both the idea of PFI organization and the willingness to withhold supplementary financing: whether or not PFIs are engaged in private debt renegotiations around the time of the Fund loan negotiations. Further discussion of why this is an appropriate proxy and of its potential biases is provided in the testing section that follows.

An alternative view of commercial bank influence on the Fund is provided by Oatley and by Broz and Hawes.[13] Neither considers commercial bank influence on the terms of Fund conditionality. Instead, both consider commercial bank influence on the size of a Fund loan. For instance, Oatley finds that Fund borrowers with higher indebtedness to commercial banks, particularly U.S., German, Swiss, and British banks, receive larger loans from the Fund. For Oatley, however, commercial banks are domestic political actors and influence developed country preferences over the size of Fund loan agreements. He contends that commercial banks influence Fund agreements through their home governments and executive directors.[14] Similarly, Broz and Hawes assume U.S. commercial banks' influence runs through the U.S. Congress to the U.S. executive director and then to the Fund itself.[15]

Neither provides any evidence to support their particular causal story or the idea that commercial banks influence the Fund through state representatives.[16] In fact, Oatley's finding that U.S., German, Swiss, and British banks seem to have greater influence than Japanese and French banks casts doubt on this avenue of influence because the Japanese and French EDs should have greater influence on the Fund's Executive Board (by virtue of their larger voting share) than should the ED representing Switzerland.

Both Oatley and Broz and Hawes may demonstrate commercial bank influence over the size of Fund loans, but they merely theorize about, without providing evidence of, the mechanisms of that influence. The assumptions used here are notably different. Although commercial banks may sometimes lobby their home governments to try to influence Fund loan agreements, I argue that—particularly with respect to Fund conditionality, rather than loan size—state representatives are not commercial banks' main avenue of influence. States often have different preferences over Fund agreements than banks, as demonstrated in Chapter 5. But even if states were easily coopted by domestic interests including banks, this might not be the most effective way for banks to influence the Fund for a variety of reasons (including competition with other domestic interests, individual EDs' quite imperfect control of the Fund, and so on). A much more effective and less costly avenue of influence travels directly between the PFIs themselves and Fund staff and management.

In the end, however, the question of whether and how PFIs influence Fund conditionality agreements is an empirical one. This chapter employs both large-N and small-N empirical work to demonstrate not only that PFIs influence Fund conditionality, but also how they do it. The supplementary financier suggests that PFIs will be able to influence the terms of Fund conditionality arrangements when they can generate a credible threat to withhold necessary supplementary financing if their demands are not met. The PFI threat will only be credible under certain conditions: if they are organized, and if the threat is ex post incentive compatible. The supplementary financier argument thus generates the following testable hypothesis:

HYPOTHESIS 3   *If PFIs are organized and can credibly threaten to with-hold/provide financing from/for a particular country, then that country's*

Fund program should be systematically more likely to include "bank-friendly" conditions, holding other variables constant.

Longitudinal Changes in Private Financing and Bank-Friendly Conditions

CHANGES IN FINANCING

Private external financing increased dramatically in the late 1960s and 1970s. It is this increase, the subsequent cycles of private financing to Fund borrowers, and their effects on which this chapter focuses. But private external financing did not begin in the late 1960s; it was also common in the 19th and 20th centuries before World War II. This section will briefly review the dominant trends in private external financing, both before World War II and after it. In short, during the 19th century and until Word War I, external financing was dominated by private actors, mainly individual bondholders and the banks that served as underwriters of these bond issues from Britain, as well as Germany and France. After World War I, the United States became a more important player, both in terms of private and official external financing flows. Official flows generally became more important during and immediately after the two world wars. However, during the 1960s, and particularly during the 1970s and 1980s, the funding stream shifted and came not only from states, but also from banks, either through new loans or reschedulings. Banks, flush with petrodollars, dramatically increased their lending to developing countries. After the debt crisis of the early 1980s, commercial banks reduced their exposure to developing countries relatively. During the 1990s, private investors became more active through equity, bond, and foreign direct investments.

From the mid-19th century until 1913, external financing increased steeply and was generally dominated by private investors from Britain, Germany, and France. The increase in private external financing from Europe was dramatic. Total European net overseas private long-term assets increased a whopping 2,025% between 1855 and 1913, from $1.7 billion to $36.1 billion (in constant 1913 U.S. dollars).[17]

The British dominated international private investment in the 19th century and continued to lead the pack until World War I.[18] German and

French private investors became more active in the early 20th century, investing particularly in Eastern and Central Europe and the Middle East.[19] However, by 1914, 44% of international foreign investment still came from the United Kingdom (whereas 20% came from France, 13% from Germany, and 8% from the United States).[20] The main source of this financing was the British public, which invested broadly in international bonds. Between 1873 and 1913, an average of 5% of Britain's annual gross product was invested abroad.[21] British investment was truly global, impacting six of the seven continents.[22]

Much of the British investment focused on lending to private actors (55%) involved in infrastructure development, particularly railway companies. For example, between 1860 and 1876, 59% of securities issued in London for private companies operating abroad were for railway companies (in Europe, the United States, Latin America, or the colonial territories).[23]

After World War II, there were several changes in the external financing landscape. First, after World War I, the United States emerged as a net creditor country and became the main source of new global capital as European lending decreased. Consequently, the center of financial activity shifted from London to New York. Second, capital flow became more common between European countries and between the United States and Europe, rather than flows between the core and the periphery.[24] Third, official flows increased relative to private flows. Major sources of official lending included the U.S. Allied war loans and the British and French loans to other European governments.[25] In addition, private issues were increasingly used to serve state goals and interests. For instance, the financing for the Dawes and Young loans to Germany and the League of Nations loans to Austria, Hungary, Greece, Bulgaria, Estonia, and Danzig were actually raised in the private capital markets.[26] Fourth, lending increasingly went to governments and government entities, rather than to private firms, as these reconstruction loans attest. For instance, of the $9.4 million new capital issues from New York from 1920 to 1931, 80% went to other governments; the other 20% went to corporations but were still government-controlled or guaranteed.[27] This contrasts with 1870–1914, when the majority of external financing went to the private sector, rather than the public sector. Finally, there was a significant decrease in annual real investment abroad between 1913 and 1930.[28] In the late 1920s, the number of foreign issues in New York declined dramatically as private investors shifted their attention to the domestic stock market.[29] As a result of the decreased flow of financing (due to the above-mentioned shift in U.S. investor preferences) and the decrease in export earnings (due to the relative closure of the U.S. market with the 1930 Smoot-Hawley Tariff Act), countries faced increasing balance of payments deficits and began defaulting on their external debt obligations in the early 1930s.[30]

In summary, external financing in the 19th century and until 1914 was mainly provided by private investors from Britain, France, and Germany and was directed to a truly global mix of countries, often to private companies involved in infrastructure building. After World War I, the United States became a net creditor country, European lending decreased, real investment abroad declined in general, and the lending that continued to occur increasingly went to the public, rather than to the private, sector.

After World War II, bilateral official financing dominated the external financing landscape, particularly from the 1940s to the 1960s. As discussed in Chapter 5, the external financing came mainly from the U.S. government, particularly the U.S. Treasury and Export-Import Bank. However, during the 1960s, 1970s, and 1980s, the funding stream shifted and came not only from states, but also from banks, either through new loans or reschedulings. During the 1960s, commercial banks began providing direct loans to developing countries. However, after the oil price increases of 1973, the commercial banks became much more active in financial intermediation between oil producing (surplus) and oil consuming (deficit) countries. As a result, there was a massive increase in international private lending to governments, mainly in direct bank credits, but also in bond issues.[31]

Table 6.1 and Figures 5.2 and 6.1 depict the post–World War II changes in the sources of external financing from a few different angles. For instance, Table 6.1 compares net foreign aid to net private investment in developing countries, according to the Organisation for Economic Co-operation and Development's (OECD) Development Cooperation and Development Assistance. Net private investment increased in the 1966–1970 time period and quickly surpassed ODA until the 1986–1989 time period.

Figure 5.2 represents the total disbursements of long-term debt for all developing countries and is based on World Bank (rather than OECD) data. The four series in this figure include public or publicly guaranteed (PPG) debt, which is loaned by other states (bilateral), international organizations

TABLE 6.1

Volume of Aid Compared with Private Financial Flows to the Third World

Net Financial Flows, Current Billions	1950–1955	1956–1960	1961–1965	1966–1970	1971–1975	1976–1980	1981–1985	1986–1989	Total 1961–1989
Net foreign aid (ODA)	11.7	20.3	30.1	32.7	50.7	98.4	139.2	173.1	524.2
Net private investment	—	13.5	12.1	26.3	51.4	158.6	164.8	108.0	521.2
FDI (multinationals)	—	—	9.8	13.3	32.4	50.0	51.7	69.0	226.2
Aid (constant billions)	79	115	146	144	145	170	208	184	1146

SOURCE: David Halloran Lumsdaine, *Moral Vision in International Politics* (Princeton, NJ: Princeton University Press, 1993). © 1993 Princeton University Press. Reprinted by permission of Princeton University Press.

NOTE: Lumsdaine (1993; 34) documents his sources as OECD, *Development Cooperation and Development Assistance*, various years: 1961, p. 19; 1964, pp. 106–9; 1967, pp. 184–85; 1970, pp. 172–73; 1974, p. 232; 1977, p. 188; 1978, p. 216; 1982, p. 195; 1982, p. 213; 1985, p. 334, 336; 1986, p. 284; 1990, pp. 264, 267–68; 1991, pp. 197–98. According to Lumsdaine, "Table entries are in billions of dollars, all current save the last line which is in 1988 (billions of) dollars. ODA figures before 1960 include other official flows, but these are relatively small. The constant figures are in 1988 dollars, computed using a GNP deflator."

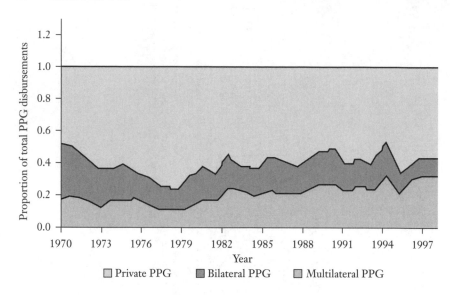

Figure 6.1. Disbursements of public or publicly guaranteed debt to middle-income countries, 1970–1998, by source of financing
SOURCE: From World Bank (2000).

(multilateral), private financial institutions (private), and private nonguaranteed debt (which is loaned from the private sector to the private sector). In compiling its data, the World Bank does not include certain Fund credits in its multilateral PPG series; for this figure, I added these Fund credits so that the multilateral series reflected in Figure 5.2 does include IMF credits. Focusing on the changes in private financing in particular, Figure 5.2 indicates that from 1973 to 1982, disbursements of PPG external debt from the private sector (commercial bank loans to the public sector) increased rapidly; they stabilized from 1983 to 1991, then began increasing again in 1992. Private nonguaranteed debt (from the private sector to the private sector) increased more gradually from 1970 to 1982, dropped off between 1982 and 1988, and increased dramatically from 1988 (US$8.4 billion) to 1997 (US$128.4 billion, not adjusted for inflation).

Low- and middle-income countries have experienced somewhat different trends in external financing in the postwar period. Private financing has dominated official financing, particularly for middle-income countries, as indicated in Figure 6.1. Over 50% of the total disbursements of PPG external debt came from private creditors by the early 1970s; by 1979, it peaked at 77% of the total disbursements of PPG external debt; after 1979, the relative amount of private PPG debt disbursements declined relatively but stayed at about 50% for all years between 1972 and 1998, except 1995. Disbursements of PPG external debt from multilateral sources ranged between 10% and 32% of total PPG debt disbursements, reaching their highest values in the late 1980s and 1990s. Bilateral PPG external debt drops from a peak of 32% in 1970 to a low of 11% in 1997.

For low-income countries, official rather than private disbursements dominated, and today multilateral financing plays a relatively much larger role. (See Figure 7.1 for low-income countries.) Bilateral PPG external debt dropped more or less steadily from a peak of 71% of total PPG debt disbursements in 1971 to 18% in 1998. In 1970, multilateral PPG external debt is only 16% of total debt disbursements but climbs quickly, hovering in the 30% range in the 1980s and the 40% and 50% range in the 1990s. Disbursements of multilateral PPG external debt to low-income countries reached its peak of 59% in 1995 and 1996. Private PPG external debt, which occupies such a large share of the total debt disbursements for middle-income countries, reached its relative peak for low-income countries at 40% in 1978, remaining in the low 30% range for the 1980s and dropping off in the early 1990s. As a result of these different disbursement trends for low and middle-income countries, they also have different trends regarding long-term debt disbursed and outstanding. Over the last few decades, middle-income countries have been saddled with mainly private debt, whereas low-income countries mainly have official debt outstanding.

CHANGES IN THE DEPENDENT VARIABLE

PFIs provide supplementary financing to borrowing member states because they hope to make a profit from that loan or investment. For PFIs, Fund conditionality agreements are useful because they may increase the probability of a profitable return. This study focuses on the one change in the terms of Fund conditional loan arrangements that seems to best isolate the influence of PFIs: the inclusion of a certain class of conditions that seem to be clearly serving the interests of PFIs. These conditions, labeled "bank-friendly conditions," provide PFIs with more direct assurances that their commercial bank loans

TABLE 6.2

Examples of Bank-Friendly Conditions

1	The borrowing country is required to set aside certain fiscal revenues to match or "complement" international loans with fiscal revenues.*
2	A percentage of the Fund loan must be set aside for debt reduction payments or replenishment of reserves.
3	The country must make debt service payments, as agreed with commercial banks and/or official creditors.
4	The country must limit financial intermediation by national banks and/or move financial intermediation to the private sector.
5	The government must meet a target for reducing government's external payments arrears.

* For example, Haiti: EBS/66/218, September 7, 1966, 12, IMF Archives.

will be repaid. Bank-friendly conditions specify that the borrowing country has to pay back a commercial bank creditor as a condition of its Fund loan. As a result, these conditions make it more costly for a borrower to default on a bank loan, thereby increasing the likelihood of repayment.

Table 6.2 lists the five types of bank-friendly conditions from the sampled Fund conditional loan arrangements. One example is from Ghana's 1983 stand-by arrangement (SBA). The arrangement included "irrevocable instructions" that the stand-by loan be deposited directly in a Bank of Ghana account at the Bank of England; the Bank of England would follow irrevocable instructions that these deposits would then be directly transferred to the Standard Chartered Bank to repay a short-term bridging loan. In other words, Fund financing was being directly funneled to a commercial bank creditor, rather than to Ghana itself.[32]

Argentina's 1992 Extended Fund Facility included "set asides to support future debt-reduction operations with Argentina's commercial bank creditor," and if Argentina "incurs any new external payments arrears after June 30, 1992," then its loan would be suspended.[33] Sixty-one arrangements in the sample (or 25%) include a bank-friendly condition as binding. Interestingly, all 61 include only one bank-friendly condition as binding. As a result, the dependent variable is binary: whether or not a given conditionality agreement includes a bank-friendly binding condition.

The use of bank-friendly conditions increased dramatically over the 1952 to 1995 period. Before the 1973 oil crisis, when private commercial bank lending to middle- and low-income countries was still relatively rare, only

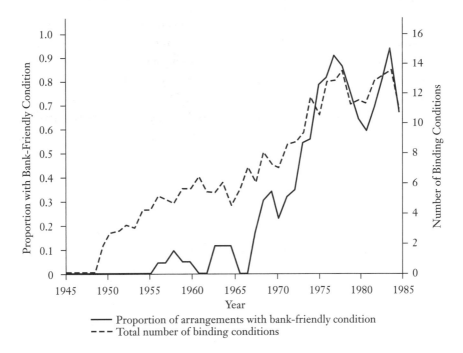

Figure 6.2. Change in number of binding conditions and use of bank-friendly conditions
SOURCE: From the Conditionality Data Set.

3% of sampled Fund conditional loan arrangements (or two arrangements) required that a bank-friendly condition be met. Between the oil crisis and the debt crisis (from about 1974 until 1982), when commercial bank lending to developing countries surged, 20% of sampled Fund loan agreements included at least one bank-friendly condition. After the debt crisis, when private supplementary financing was scarce and discriminating, over 70% of Fund loan agreements included a bank-friendly condition. A total of 79% of sampled arrangements between 1983 and 1990 required a bank-friendly condition, whereas 73% of sampled arrangements between 1991 and 1995 required a bank-friendly condition. The increase in bank-friendly conditions is one facet of the broader changes in Fund conditionality, including the increase in the total number of binding conditions and the changes in the types of binding conditions. Figure 6.2 provides a portrait of the increase in the use of bank-friendly conditions, as compared to the overall increase in the number of binding conditions over the 1952 to 1995 period for the 230 cases for which data was available from the Conditionality Data Set. The measure of bank-friendly conditions is a three-year moving average of the proportion of the sampled arrangements in a given year that required a bank-friendly condition as binding; it varies between 0 and 1. The measure of the number of binding conditions is the average number of binding conditions required by all sampled arrangements started in a given year; it varies between 0 and 13.5.

Large-N Econometric Analysis

The longitudinal increase in private supplementary financing is not perfectly co-temporaneous with the increase in the use of bank-friendly conditions. Private supplementary financing increased dramatically in the early 1970s, while the use of bank-friendly conditions increased most steeply in the late 1970s and early 1980s. Does this pattern cast doubt on the supplementary financier argument? As suggested earlier by Hypothesis 3, the supplementary financier argument suggests that PFIs will be most likely to influence the terms of Fund conditional loan agreements when they are organized and can credibly threaten to withhold (or provide) financing from (or for) a particular borrowing country. In order to test Hypothesis 3 directly, this section presents results from large-N multivariate analyses that test whether private financial institutions seem to have influence Fund conditionality arrangements in the predicted ways, when controlling for several other relevant variables. In the subsequent section, I discuss the mechanisms of PFI influence in more detail, including a brief discussion of two cases.

INDEPENDENT VARIABLES

According to the supplementary financier argument, PFIs prefer Fund conditional loan arrangements to include bank-friendly conditions. We should expect PFIs to exercise leverage over the Fund when they are an important source of supplementary financing for the borrowing country and are organized enough to articulate their preferences and credibly threaten to withhold financing.

The amount of private financing or proportion of external financing that comes from private sources may appear to be the most obvious proxy for private influence; however, it does not capture the logic of the supplementary financier argument.[34] One could imagine PFIs providing (relatively and absolutely) abundant financing to borrowers and yet exercising little or no leverage over the Fund—for instance, during most of the "petrodollar recycling" period when PFIs were less organized (despite syndicated lending) and could certainly not credibly threaten to withhold financing given that the sovereign loans were considered so lucrative. In other words, the supplementary financier argument does not predict a stable over-time relationship between the amount of private financing and their leverage over the Fund.[35]

In order to test the supplementary financier argument, I instead use a proxy for private influence (*private influence*) which captures the idea that PFIs would be able to exercise leverage when they are organized and can credibly threaten to withhold financing: a binary variable that is coded 1 when the borrowing country restructured their private debt in that year or the previous year.[36] Private debt restructuring is a key moment when PFIs may be able to organize themselves, develop a coherent bargaining strategy, and articulate their preferences to Fund representatives. Scholarly attention has turned to private debt restructuring as an important form of commercial bank cooperation before.[37] Admittedly, this is only one of the possible ways that PFIs could organize themselves and credibly threaten to withhold borrower financing if their preferred terms are not included in the Fund program. PFIs may be able to influence Fund conditionality in other situations not captured by this proxy that may result in a negative bias (against the hypothesized relationship). The supplementary financier argument predicts that the coefficient on the private influence variable should be positive and significant.

A plausible alternative hypothesis is that Fund activity—including the design of Fund conditionality agreements—is driven externally by powerful states. Realist scholars have argued that powerful states, most often the United States, use international organizations like the Fund as tools to achieve their foreign policy goals. For instance, Strom Thacker argues that the United States' political preferences and the international balance of power are the "underlying causes of the IMF's behavior."[38] This seems particularly plausible in the case of the IMF, whose weighted voting system institutionalizes the greater influence of powerful states, particularly the United States.

In order to test this argument and control for the influence of powerful states, the *U.S. influence* variable (which was introduced and also used in Chapter 5) is included as a proxy for U.S. influence. It is the total amount of

U.S. loans and grants to the given borrowing country in the year of the Fund arrangement, divided by (and normalized by) the amount of the IMF loan agreement.[39] If we expect, as realists do, that changes in Fund conditionality including the introduction of new conditions like bank-friendly conditions have been driven by powerful states, then the coefficient on this variable should be positive.

The supplementary financier also considers the potential influence of powerful creditor states. However, it contends that the United States and other powerful states have not been the driving force behind the introduction of new conditions and the increases in Fund conditionality; instead, they have actually pushed for reductions in Fund conditionality and worked against many of the observed changes in Fund conditionality. The supplementary financier argument therefore predicts that the coefficient on the *U.S. influence* variable should be negative, whereas the realist argument predicts it should be positive.

Another plausible alternative hypothesis is that Fund conditionality and the changes in Fund conditionality have been driven by the Fund's bureaucracy. The *salary increase* variable is the proportional increase in the average staff salary since the previous year and mimics a proxy for bureaucratic power and autonomy used in Roland Vaubel's work on the Fund.[40] The logic is that as Fund bureaucratic power and autonomy increase (indicated in an increase in average salaries that year), it is more likely to insert "discretionary" conditions—like bank-friendly conditions—that serve to further "increase its power."[41] Thus, according to the bureaucratic argument as articulated by Vaubel, the coefficient on this variable should be positive and significant.

Several other independent variables are included in the statistical analyses that follow. The *reserves* variable controls for the severity of the borrower's balance-of-payments problem; it is the ratio of foreign reserves to imports in the year that the country began its Fund conditional loan agreement and should be negatively related to the dependent variable.[42]

The *GNP per capita* variable is in constant 1995 dollars and the predicted coefficient is negative.[43] The *regime* is a regime-type variable that ranges from −10 (full autocracy) to +10 (full democracy).[44] Some would expect this coefficient to be positive (if democracies have systematically higher conditionality programs because they demand conditionality to tie their hands), and others would expect it to be negative (if democracies have systematically lower conditionality programs because they resist tougher conditions out of fear of voter retribution).[45] The *tranche* variable is the amount of the Fund loan, divided by the amount of the country's Fund quota. According to Fund official policy, larger loans require more "justification," and therefore the predicted relationship between this variable and the presence of bank-friendly conditions is positive.[46] The *constant GNP* variable is the borrower's gross national product (GNP) at market prices in billions of constant 1995 U.S. dollars.[47] The coefficient on this variable should be negative if larger countries receive easier terms, as some have argued.[48] A more detailed discussion of these variables and the hypotheses underpinning them is included in Chapter 5.

Finally, as discussed previously in Chapter 5, this data set has time-series properties, and there may be an over-time effect that is not being absorbed by the model. In Chapter 5 (and in Chapter 7), a lagged dependent variable is included in the analyses. The implicit hypothesis underlying the lagged dependent variable is that the number of binding conditions (or procedural binding conditions) in a country's program in year $t - 1$ should influence the number of binding conditions (or procedural binding conditions) in year t. So one might expect the terms of Mexico's 1982 Extended Fund Facility (EFF) to have influenced the terms of Mexico's 1986 SBA. In this chapter, a more general control for the effect of time is used: a simple linear time trend called *year*. The year is coded 0 in 1952 and 43 in 1995. As with the lagged dependent variable, if *year* is significant, then clearly there is an aspect of the "underlying process" that is not being captured by the explanatory variables in the model. Despite the fact that the results presented use *year* instead of a *lagged Y*, I did also run these models using the lagged-dependent variable. The same basic results hold, although the magnitude of the coefficients change. These results are presented in Appendix 4. Because the model fit is generally better using *year* than *lagged Y*, this chapter presents the analyses including only *year*.

RESULTS

Do private financial institutions systematically influence the terms of Fund conditional loan arrangements? The *private influence* independent variable and bank-friendly condition dependent variable are positively correlated; the simple pairwise correlation is 0.359 with a p value of 0.000. This positive

TABLE 6.3
Change in the Inclusion of Bank-Friendly Conditions (Logit)

Variable	Model 1	Model 2	Model 3	Percentage missing
Private influence	1.57 (0.70)**	5.89 (2.35)**	6.00 (2.14)**	0%
U.S. influence	−0.04 (0.09)	−0.47 (0.28)*	−0.06 (0.14)	13%
Salary increase	−8.56 (6.36)	−11.46 (8.75)	−8.62 (8.08)	8%
Reserves	—	.16 (0.24)	—	53%
GNP per capita	—	−0.0001 (0.0004)	—	21%
Regime	0.03 (0.04)	0.07 (0.08)	0.05 (0.06)	2%
Tranche	−0.26 (0.26)	−0.35 (0.38)	−0.24 (0.34)	3%
Constant GNP		−0.02 (0.01)	−0.02 (0.01)**	19%
Year	0.23 (0.04)**	0.18 (0.08)**	0.21 (0.04)**	0%
Constant	−6.15 (1.26)**	−3.31 (3.08)	−4.73 (1.33)**	—
N	201	76	154	
Log likelihood	−55.17	−29.49	−41.01	
Mean log likelihood	−0.275	−0.388	−0.266	
Pseudo R^2	0.4777	0.4400	0.5405	
Null model	78.1%	51.3%	73.4%	
(modal outcome)	(157 when y = 0)	(39 when y = 1)	(113 when y = 0)	
PCP	89.6%	86.8%	90.3%	—

* $p \leq 0.1$.
** $p < 0.05$.

and significant relationship lends initial support to the argument that PFIs have influenced the terms of Fund conditional loan arrangements. The multivariate results offer stronger confirmation.

Table 6.3 provides estimations of three logit models that test whether or not organized PFIs increase the likelihood of the inclusion of bank-friendly conditions in Fund loan agreements.[49] There are some severe missing data problems with three of the economic independent variables: *reserves, GNP per capita*, and *constant GNP*.[50] As a result, Model 1 omits those independent variables plagued by the highest rates of missingness in order to establish whether the predicted relationship between the private influence variable and the presence of bank-friendly conditions exists for the bulk of the sample. In Model 1, the coefficient on *private influence* is positive and significant, as is the coefficient on *year*. None of the other variables is significant. The impact of private financier influence on the probability of having a bank-friendly condition is strong. Holding other variables in the model at their means, an increase in the *private influence* variable from 0 (its minimum) to 1 (its maximum) results in an increase in the likelihood that the Fund conditional loan arrangement will require a bank-friendly condition (Y = 1) from 7% to 25%.[51]

Model 2 includes the three economic variables mentioned above, and the number of cases drops to 76. The coefficients on *GNP per capita* and *reserves* are not significant. The coefficient on *constant GNP* is negative and nearly meets the significance criteria with a *p* value of 0.102. In other words, larger countries (measured by GNP) are less likely to be required to meet a bank-friendly condition, holding other variables constant. Most of the coefficients on the other independent variables change in magnitude, but not sign or significance, from Model 1. One exception is the *U.S. influence* variable, which is significant in this specification. As *U.S. influence* (measured by U.S. relative financing) increases, the likelihood of a country being required to meet a bank-friendly condition decreases. This negative coefficient conflicts with the predictions of the realist argument and is consistent with the predictions of the supplementary financier argument that powerful states push for weaker conditionality.[52] When the U.S. exercises its influence on a particular Fund program, the probability of a bank-friendly condition being included decreases. This suggests that the impetus for this expansion of Fund conditionality might not have originated from the United States, as realists would contend.

Model 3 omits only *reserves* and *GNP per capita*, the two variables that have the highest rates of missingness but are not significantly related to the dependent variable, and retains the *constant GNP*.[53] Model 3 appears to have the best model fit, with the highest mean log-likelihood (Mean L-L) ratio, percent correctly predicted (PCP), and pseudo R^2. The percent correctly predicted is the percentage of predicted outcomes that equal the actual outcomes, when predicted probabilities greater than 0.5 are rounded to 1 and less than or equal to 0.5 are rounded to 0.[54] Model 3's percent correctly predicted (90.3%) is usefully compared to the null model's percent correctly predicted (73.4%).

The results from Model 3 support the conclusion that PFIs have been successful at influencing the terms of Fund conditional loan arrangements. The influence of PFIs is even more striking in Models 2 and 3 than it was in Model 1. Comparative statics elucidate this. For a hypothetical loan agreement with a hypothetical country where all other independent variables in the model are held at their means, if one increases the value of the *private influence* variable from 0 (its minimum) to 1 (its maximum), the probability that the Fund loan agreement requires a bank-friendly binding condition increases from 30% to 99% in Model 2 and from only 5% to 96% in Model 3.

Model 3 also casts doubt on some of the alternative arguments, which focus on powerful states and bureaucratic actors. Neither the *U.S. influence* nor the *salary increase* variables—measured by U.S. relative financing and the increase in average Fund salaries, respectively—are in the direction predicted by these alternative arguments or are significant. The *tranche* variable is also not in the predicted direction and is also not significant. The other significant variable in Models 3 is the *constant GNP*, which suggests that larger countries do receive less stringent arrangements from the Fund, and the *year* tracking variable, which suggests that some other over-time change process is not captured by the model.

In short, these results lend support to the supplementary financier argument and cast doubt on the realist and bureaucratic alternative arguments. There is a strong relationship between the *private influence* variable and the bank-friendly dependent variable. The next section clarifies how that relationship works.

Mechanisms

The previous section suggests that private financial institutions systematically influence the terms of Fund conditional loan arrangements. It identifies a relationship between variables. This result provides some support for the supplementary financier argument, which predicts that PFIs should be able to influence Fund conditionality agreements when they are organized and therefore can articulate their interests and threaten to withhold financing.

PFIs do not have access to the legitimate channels of influence that other supplementary financiers (creditor states and multilateral organizations) often do. Therefore, it is not obvious how they exercise their influence. In order to clarify how PFIs influence Fund loan agreements, I first discuss the mechanism highlighted in the previous section—how PFIs influence Fund arrangements during private debt restructuring—and one case when a country's debt was restructured and its conditionality program included a bank-friendly condition. Then I discuss one case when a country's private

TABLE 6.4
Private Debt Restructuring and the Inclusion of Bank-Friendly Conditions

Private Debt Restructuring	INCLUSION OF BANK-FRIENDLY?	
	No	Yes
No	158 (Quadrant A)	41 (Quadrant B)
Yes	9 (Quadrant C)	20 (Quadrant D)

SOURCE: Data from the Conditionality Data Set.

debt was not restructured, but a bank-friendly binding condition was included in the country's Fund program.

INFLUENCE DURING PRIVATE DEBT RESTRUCTURING

When PFIs are organized during debt restructuring, they are able to exercise leverage over the Fund. Of the 29 cases that had their private debt restructured in that or the previous year, 69% included a bank-friendly condition as compared to 27% of the total cases from the Conditionality Data Set (Table 6.4).

This finding seems to contradict received wisdom, which points instead to the Fund's influence over the banks during these meetings. During debt restructuring negotiations, the Fund could threaten to "sabotage any agreement between creditors and the debtor" and thereby "provide residual coordination for the banks . . . to provide new credits to the impoverished debtor."[55] The accepted interpretation has thus been that the Fund is often the strongman in debt renegotiations, demanding new credits from and exercising leverage over the banks. The underlying reasoning behind this interpretation has been that default—or no restructuring agreement—would be the most costly option for banks, but presumably not for the Fund. The Fund could therefore more credibly threaten to walk away from an agreement than could the banks.

This assumption is curious. How credible would a Fund threat to "sabotage any agreement between creditors and debtor" really be? The Fund has certainly been able to exercise leverage over some banks, providing a focal point solution to the "bankers' dilemma" and helping them achieve their collective self-interest. But the banks are also often able to exercise leverage,

and they are most poised to do so when they are organized via creditor committees that can articulate common preferences and a threat to withhold
financing from several—often hundreds—of banks.

In addition to this influence gained by organization, PFI organization via
debt restructuring in particular gave PFIs enhanced leverage between 1983
and 1989 due to the Fund's formal policies on lending into arrears and
financing assurances. The Fund's policy, through much of this period, of not
lending to countries with external (including private) payments arrears and
at times requiring financing assurances from PFIs gave these PFIs renegotiating debt in arrears a "de facto veto over Fund lending," according to one
Executive Board decision.[56] If the banks did not agree to renegotiate outstanding debt or provide financing assurances, the Fund program would either not be approved or would be automatically suspended.[57] The general
Fund policy of not lending to countries with external payments arrears began informally through Fund arrangements in the 1960s and was formalized
by the Executive Board in 1970. This policy was established with a nod to
PFI interests. It stated that external payments arrears were undesirable because they "harm[ed] . . . a country's international financial relationships because of the uncertainty they generate[d]" and that this uncertainty could in
turn have "pronounced adverse effects on the creditworthiness of the debtor
country."[58] The policy strengthened PFIs' hand in securing timely payment
from borrowers, but it was not until 1983 that the Fund's formal policies allowed banks to have virtual veto power over many Fund programs.

In the early 1980s, the Fund's practice changed so that Fund programs
not only required the elimination or reduction of existing payments arrears,
but also explicit "financing assurances" from PFIs. The Executive Board's
April 1983 decision sanctioned the Fund's increasingly active role in private
and official multilateral debt renegotiations, and formalized the Fund policy
of requiring financing assurances from private and official supplementary
financiers.[59] Again, these financing assurances have generally been interpreted as examples of Fund leverage over the banks. However, these financing assurances enhanced the banks' influence over the Fund; the banks could
effectively hold a Fund program's negotiations hostage when renegotiating
its own debt. Fund programs required certain financing assurances. Therefore, if the banks did not agree to provide financing, the Fund program
would not be approved or would be automatically suspended.[60]

Since 1989, and in light of the Brady Plan and the growing international consensus supporting debt reduction, the Executive Board has revised its policies on external arrears three times in order to loosen PFI control over the approval of Fund programs during these critical junctures. In 1989, the policy was first revised to "tolerate" private, not official, arrears.[61] As James Boughton, assistant director of the Fund's Policy Development and Review Department, wrote, "The basic policy then [1983–1989] in effect specified that the Fund would approve arrangements only when it had received firm assurances that the member's adjustment program would be fully financed. . . . The staff . . . concluded that other creditors should no longer be allowed to determine whether an arrangement would be approved."[62] The heyday of the PFIs' enhanced influence (for the period under study, 1952–1995) over Fund conditionality arrangements was therefore the 1983 to 1989 period.[63] The Conditionality Data Set bears this out: 17 of the 20 cases in Table 6.4's quadrant D (when a bank-friendly condition was required as binding and a country's private debt had been restructured) occurred during this period.[64] Two more formal revisions of the Fund's arrears policy were passed in 1998 and 1999, both intended to reduce PFI influence further. The 1998 decision extended the 1989 policy of sanctioned lending into private arrears to nonbank private creditors (for example, bondholders) and nonsovereign arrears. The 1999 decision relaxed the criteria when the Fund could lend into private arrears.[65]

PFIs were thus effective at influencing Fund conditionality programs during private debt restructuring both because they were organized via ad hoc creditor committees, able to articulate common preferences and credibly threaten to jointly withhold financing, and because of their enhanced influence due to the "financing assurances" policy between 1983 and 1989.

MEXICO'S 1982 EXTENDED FUND FACILITY AGREEMENT

Meetings between the Fund's management or staff and representatives from commercial banks provided an opportunity for the Fund to communicate how much financing the banks needed to provide given the design of the program, and for the banks to communicate the terms of the Fund program needed for them to commit their supplementary financing. Probably the most famous meeting between the Fund's management and bankers was the

November 1982 meeting between the Fund's managing director, Jacques de Larosière, and international bankers preceding Mexico's 1982 EFF loan agreement.

Mexico faced an enormous external debt burden, reduced export earnings, and pressure on its already devalued currency, and it was on the brink of defaulting on its commercial debts. A complicated rescue package was negotiated. The United States and the Bank for International Settlements offered initial bridging loans to allow time to negotiate a Fund agreement. The Fund program itself was designed with two primary ingredients to ensure a balance: a condition that the fiscal deficit be reduced (from about 16.5% of GDP in 1982 to 8.5% of GDP in 1983) and an assumption of $2 billion in official supplementary financing and $5 billion in private supplementary financing (new medium-term credits) in 1983.[66] The Fund loan itself was $3.75 billion (plus a $220 million unconditional first credit tranche loan). This supplementary financing assumption was crucial, allowing the Fund and Mexico to agree to (what was thought to be) a politically feasible demand contraction.

Many other scholars have discussed the dramatic negotiations preceding this Fund loan agreement.[67] Most focus on de Larosière's influence over the commercial banks, or as Kraft put it, the Fund's "imposing a forced loan on major private banks."[68] On November 16, 1982, de Larosière met in New York with a group of representatives from 17 major commercial banks and explained the dilemmas of the Mexican crisis, including Mexico's need for about $8.25 billion, of which only $1.3 billion could come from the IMF and $2 billion from other official sources.[69] Famously, he demanded that the banks increase their financing to Mexico by $5 billion (that is, new loans) in 1983, "roll over existing short-term credits," develop an agreement to reschedule Mexico's medium- and long-term debt, and "'clean-up' $1/2 billion in private sector interest arrears that would be outstanding by the end of 1982," or else the Fund would not agree to its loan program with Mexico.[70] Scholars have focused on the Fund's influence on these banks. As Lipson wrote, "Never before had the Fund intervened so directly in the affairs of commercial lenders."[71]

The banks were in a notoriously weak bargaining position, given that many U.S. and Japanese banks were heavily exposed in Mexico.[72] However, the Fund also had a lot riding on a resolution of the Mexican crisis, which many thought threatened to destabilize the international financial system. The credibility of de Larosière's November 16 threat is therefore questionable. The Fund not only pressured the banks to provide fresh financing, it also bent over backward to accommodate the banks' concerns, as it would in future negotiations. The commercial bankers, particularly the ones on the Advisory Committee, did not want Mexico to default, and therefore they were willing to provide financing. However, they wanted the Fund to provide them with more direct assurances that private arrears would be paid down. (This, as you might recall, is one of the bank-friendly conditions.) At the November 16 meeting, the bankers expressed the concern that "the authorities could do more to solve the problems of private sector arrears to banks. In some cases, companies that could afford to meet their interest payments were being blocked by regulations prohibiting them from using foreign exchange for that purpose." De Larosière "was reluctant to put the IMF in the middle of the effort to settle private sector arrears, [but] he promised to speak to the Mexican officials about it."[73]

The initial Fund loan agreement with Mexico had already been drafted and signed by the Mexican authorities on November 10, before de Larosière's meeting with the bankers. The letter of intent did discuss Mexico's current external debt, its projected debt servicing requirements, and its need for foreign financing, but its discussion of private sector arrears to PFIs was vague and brief, indicating only that Mexico hoped to get banks to postpone private external credit repayments. Clearly the original agreement reached between the Fund and the Mexican authorities had not included provisions for the reduction of private sector arrears to PFIs that the bankers demanded. Fund staffers returned to Mexico from December 13 to 17, 1982, before the commercial bankers secured the required financing. They discussed additional conditions for the Fund program with the Mexican authorities and addressed the bankers' concerns.

On December 21, after the Fund staff returned from Mexico, the staff sent an update to the Executive Board, notifying them of modifications to the Fund agreement and indicating that the bankers' demands had been met. It stated that "the Mexican Government established special procedures for the settlement of arrears on interest payments due by Mexican private borrowers to commercial banks abroad."[74] These procedures allowed private borrowers to deposit their interest payments in local currency in PFI accounts established with the Bank of Mexico, and then the bank would begin paying PFIs these interest payments in foreign currency starting January 31, 1983.

Two days after this memo was sent, the banks raised the "critical mass" of the $5 billion in new money, and the Executive Board approved Mexico's EFF agreement. It included 10 binding conditions. The seventh stated that Mexico would not borrow from the Fund if a "counterpart deposit scheme, without exchange rate guarantee, [had not been] . . . set up to provide for the identification and orderly reduction of arrears" by December 31, 1983.[75]

Mexico's 1982 EFF is just one example, and an unlikely one given the received wisdom about these negotiations, of PFI influence on the terms of Fund conditional loan arrangements. PFIs were able to insert a binding condition in the Fund agreement that was of particular interest to them. In later years, as banks became more reluctant to reschedule and the Fund maintained the policy of requiring financing assurances, their leverage over the Fund became even stronger.

ALTERNATIVE MECHANISMS OF INFLUENCE AND TURKEY'S
1978 STAND-BY ARRANGEMENT

Sixty-seven percent of the cases of Fund agreements with bank-friendly binding conditions in the Conditionality Data Set (41 cases) did not have their private debt restructured in that or the previous year (Table 6.4, quadrant B). Either another mechanism of PFI influence is at work, or another factor is contributing to the inclusion of this condition. In this section, I discuss one of these 41 cases in order to clarify why the bank-friendly conditions are included, and if PFIs exercise influence in other ways: Turkey's 1978 SBA.

Turkey's 1978 SBA is a useful case for a few reasons. First, Turkey is a strategically important country, and one in which certain powerful creditor states took a keen interest at this time. As a result, we might expect powerful states' influence to eclipse PFI influence, particularly for this case. However, at this time, Turkey and the Fund were dependent on private sources of supplementary financing for Turkey. By 1978, Turkey already owed private creditors over $6 billion.[76] Turkey received a large (but rapidly decreasing) chunk of its supplementary financing—24.5% of Turkey's PPG debt commitments in 1978—from private sources.[77] As a result, there is also good reason to believe that PFIs might also be successful in exercising leverage, if they could organize themselves. Second, this case is one of the earlier cases in Table 6.4's quadrant B (in the group of agreements with bank-friendly binding conditions that did not have their private debt restructured in that or the previous year). One might expect PFI pressure on the Fund to be more overt and transparent in earlier cases, when they may have been communicating their preferences about Fund conditionality agreements for the first time. In later cases, Fund staff may be able to anticipate PFI preferences, and thus their influence may be less observable. Finally, this case was selected for practical reasons. The Fund files for this case include documents that helped me recreate the negotiation process, whereas other case files were relatively bare.

In the wake of the oil crisis of 1973–1974, Turkey's current account swung sharply from a surplus of $534 million in 1973 to a deficit of $3.4 billion in 1977. Most of this deficit, about 81%, had been financed by foreign borrowing; much of it, about 54% in 1977, by short-term credits.[78] In 1977, PFIs began curtailing net lending, and Turkey plunged into a debt crisis; arrears began to accumulate, growth dropped sharply from 8.9% to 4.9% that year, and inflation climbed from 15.6% to 24.1%.[79] Turkey approached the IMF for a loan program in 1977, and a Fund mission visited Ankara in September of that year.[80]

The PFIs were organized in their dealings with Turkey and the Fund, even if they did not successfully renegotiate debt in 1978. In fact, one banker was quoted at that time as stating, "The requirements of this situation sparked an effort of cooperation I haven't seen before in country lending."[81] By December 1977, representatives from several exposed commercial banks were meeting on Wednesdays in New York to address the mounting Turkish debt crisis.[82] In March and April 1978, eight commercial banks organized as a coordinating committee, representing about 220 PFIs in total, to negotiate new credits and reschedulings of existing short-term debt with Turkey.[83] These negotiations did not bear fruit until the summer of 1979 (when a different SBA was in place), but the PFIs were still quite organized during the negotiations of Turkey's 1978 SBA.

The PFIs were also directly in contact with the Fund during these negotiations. For instance, executives from Chase Manhattan Bank contacted Lord Alan Whittome, the head of the Fund's European division responsible for constructing Turkey's SBA, about the pending Fund program. Whittome kept in contact with official and private supplementary financiers during this negotiation period and considered PFI financing particularly crucial.[84] The Chase executives served as representatives for a number of commercial banks and told Whittome that

> they have talked to banks in a number of countries and throughout the United States. They are reasonably sure that net new lending totaling $1 billion could be available in four equal tranches over a 12-month period provided a stand-by arrangement with the Fund was concluded and *was thought to be adequate*. (My informant said that he had met some fears that given our experience in Egypt we might now be content to take a too lenient attitude.)[85]

The Chase representatives also indicated through several additional phone calls and contacts that the PFIs "would not come to any agreement with the Turks prior to a *satisfactory* arrangement with the Fund."[86] Thus the PFIs organized themselves and indicated that an "adequate" Fund program was necessary in order to ensure that their financing be forthcoming.

From December 11 to 20, 1977, a Fund mission returned to Turkey to negotiate the 1978 arrangement. On December 16, in the middle of that mission visit, "a meeting of the major U.S., German and Swiss banks to determine the banks' attitudes vis-à-vis Turkey" was held.[87] The timing of this meeting suggests that it was planned to assess and influence Turkey's 1978 SBA; however, details of the meeting are unknown.

The resulting two-year SBA was ultimately approved in April 1978.[88] It required eight binding conditions, including a bank-friendly condition that specified that Turkey must devise a schedule to pay down existing arrears by November 1, 1978, and must not allow any new arrears to "arise."[89] In turn, the commercial banks "made disbursement of any part of the new loan conditional upon a program being prepared for dealing with arrears."[90] However, Turkey had trouble meeting this condition. In September 1978, the Fund waived this and other conditions as a result of noncompliance.[91] By November 1978, Turkey had not devised a schedule to pay down its arrears and the Fund considered suspending the next installment of its loan, but the Fund staff did not want to provoke a further withdrawal of private financing. An internal memo discussed the "need to avoid any impression that there has been any break in our discussions with the Turks in order not to give the commercial banks a heaven sent excuse to delay further their agreement both to the rescheduling of $3 billion of bank debt and the provision of a new loan of (hopefully) around $½ billion."[92] The PFIs continued to drag their feet regarding both reschedulings and new loans, while the Fund and Turkey waited anxiously for the promised infusion of private financing. In December 1978, Whittome continued to try to convince the PFIs to dispense the promised supplementary financing to Turkey.[93] He wrote that the Fund had "been fairly constantly involved in talks with the banks and I have deliberately much exceeded the lines laid down by the Board by encouraging individual banks to think sympathetically." However, Turkey did not establish a schedule for paying down arrears on schedule, as was required by the 1978 SBA and demanded by the PFIs, and private financing was not forthcoming.[94] This stand-by was eventually canceled in 1979.

Turkey's 1978 SBA provides an example of an agreement that was not correctly predicted by the private influence proxy alone, but that does fit the broader logic of the supplementary financier argument. PFIs organized themselves to coordinate their provision of financing to Turkey and also to coordinate their demands on the Fund. The Fund agreement included a bank-friendly binding condition that addressed the PFIs' main concern: arrears. However, this condition was never met, and the private financing never came.

The postscript to this SBA is equally interesting. A new Turkish SBA was approved in July 1979. This agreement, like Mexico's 1983 EFF, is known for being heavily influenced by big creditor countries (particularly the United States and Germany) concerned about Turkey's recent flirtings with the Soviet Union.[95] However, Fund negotiators were also keenly interested in addressing the concerns of the PFIs. Staff-generated instructions to the Fund's April 1979 mission to Turkey stated explicitly, "It is worth noting also that a satisfactory settlement of the issue of overdue suppliers' credits is regarded as a condition for the disbursement of any new loan by foreign commercial banks. A schedule, with the status of a performance criteria [or binding condition], will need to be established for the gradual elimination of nonguaranteed arrears."[96] Although the negotiating and drafting process of the 1979 arrangement was long and contentious, the final agreement did include a bank-friendly condition addressing the PFIs' concerns and did result in a nearly concurrent pledge of supplementary financing from the PFIs, including a $407 million syndicated loan and rescheduling of $2,698 million in debt by August 1979.[97] In 1979, 68.7% of Turkey's PPG debt commitments were from PFIs.[98]

Conclusion

This chapter tests Hypothesis 3: that private financial institutions should influence Fund conditionality agreements when they are organized and can credibly threaten to withhold financing. The chapter begins by discussing PFI interests—in profit—and their preferences over the design of Fund conditionality agreements, particularly the inclusion of certain conditions like bank-friendly conditions that increase the likelihood that banks will be paid back and make a profit off their loans. Next, I discuss the trends in private external financing, historically and today. The longitudinal trends in private supplementary financing do not track perfectly with the inclusion of bank-friendly conditions in Fund agreements. This finding does not necessarily discredit the supplementary financier argument, however, which actually predicts that (particularly in the case of PFIs, which do not have legitimate mechanisms of influence) PFIs will influence Fund conditionality agreements when they are organized and can credibly threaten to withhold financing, not simply when they provide it.

In fact, the chapter presents evidence that PFIs do influence Fund conditionality in predicted ways. The large-N empirical work (using the Conditionality Data Set [Appendix 1]) suggests that PFIs have been successful at influencing the terms of Fund conditional loan arrangements and casts doubt on the realist and bureaucratic alternative arguments. Two case studies—Mexico's 1982 EFF and Turkey's 1978 SBA—demonstrate how PFIs have influenced the terms of conditionality agreements in practice. In the case of Mexico's 1982 EFF, an initial agreement was brokered between the Fund and Mexican representatives, and then changed to include a condition the organized commercial bankers demanded. In the case of Turkey's 1978 SBA, PFIs were also very organized (although not in the way coded by the private influence proxy) and seem to have influenced not only the design but also the trajectory of the stand-by agreement.

CHAPTER SEVEN

Multilateral Organizations as Supplementary Financiers

Introduction

One of the most dramatic and recent changes in the external financing of developing countries has been the increase in financing from multilateral organizations. One of the implications of this increase has been a change in the nature of Fund conditionality. When other multilateral organizations provide financing that supplements a Fund loan, they demand certain conditions—often detailed, policy-oriented conditions—that serve their own interests and mandates.

This chapter focuses on the influence of multilateral organizations and particularly on the influence of the World Bank (the one multilateral organization that overwhelmingly dominates supplementary financing) on International Monetary Fund conditionality. The chapter begins by describing the changes in external and supplementary financing provided by multilateral organizations, then discusses the interests and preferences of the World Bank and other multilateral development organizations in more detail. Three types of evidence are used to demonstrate the influence of other multilateral organizations on IMF conditionality. First, simple descriptive statistics show that Fund conditionality has changed in certain predicted ways as multilateral supplementary financing increased over time. Second, large-N statistical analyses demonstrate that when countries receive more supplementary financing from other multilateral organizations, their Fund conditionality agreements tend to have more conditions and more detailed, procedural conditions (versus simple targets), holding other variables constant. Finally, a discussion of the mechanisms of influence and two illustrative country case studies—Ghana and Bangladesh—reveal how multilateral organizations like the World Bank have influenced individual Fund agreements.

Independent Variable: Multilateral Financing After World War II

Supplementary financing is often crucial for the short-run success of individual Fund programs given that the Fund provides only a fraction of the amount of money necessary for a borrowing country to balance its payments and implement the Fund-designed program successfully. Consequently, supplementary financiers are able to exercise leverage over the Fund to include certain conditions that Fund conditionality programs in order for their financing to be forthcoming. In recent years, there have been some significant changes in the provision of supplementary financing by other multilateral organizations that has led to increased multilateral influence over the design of Fund programs.

Since the end of World War II and particularly since the early 1980s, there has been a steady increase (both absolute and relative to other types of financiers, particularly creditor states) in financing from multilateral organizations for all developing countries. Figure 5.2 shows that disbursements of multilateral public or publicly guaranteed (PPG) external debt climbed past bilateral PPG debt disbursements in 1983 and exceeded private non-guaranteed (PNG) disbursements from 1983 to 1992 and again in 1998.

The trend for middle- and low-income developing countries is somewhat different, however. Figures 6.1 and 7.1 display the shifts in the provision of PPG debt for middle- and low-income countries, respectively. For middle-income countries, the disbursements of multilateral external debt are only a

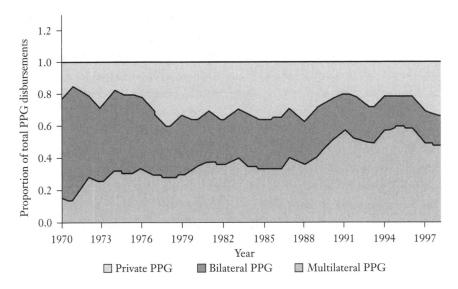

Figure 7.1. Disbursements of public or publicly guaranteed debt to low-income countries, 1970–1998, by source of financing
   SOURCE: From World Bank (2000).

small proportion of total PPG external debt disbursements, while they are a much larger share of total PPG external debt disbursements for low-income countries. In other words, multilateral financing is much more important for low-income countries than for middle-income countries, relatively. For both groups, the share of multilateral disbursements increases after 1982, but much more significantly so for low-income countries.

These figures obscure at least two trends that are important for the purposes of this chapter. First, these figures provide data on the general external financing of low- and middle-income countries. Interestingly, they actually underestimate the importance of multilateral supplementary financing (financing that supplements a Fund loan). The share of multilateral disbursements for those countries entering into a Fund conditional loan arrangement is on average larger than that of the general developing country population. Second, these figures provide general data on multilateral (versus bilateral and private) financing, but do not reveal which multilateral organizations (or states or private financial institutions) are providing the financing. Just as creditor state financing has been dominated (particularly in the immediate post–World War II period) by U.S. financing, so the multilateral supplementary financing today is dominated by the World Bank. Of the financing from multilateral organizations that supplements Fund loans, the majority comes from the World Bank's International Bank for Reconstruction and Development (IBRD) or International Development Association (IDA). In fact, between 1970 and 1995, the World Bank provided between 58% and 81% of PPG multilateral debt disbursements.[1]

In short, several trends in multilateral financing should be noted. First, multilateral external financing increased absolutely and relatively since the early 1980s. Second, this increase has been particularly significant for low-income (versus middle-income) countries. Third, multilateral supplementary financing has increased even faster than multilateral external financing. And finally, the bulk of this multilateral supplementary financing has come from the World Bank.

Assumptions: Multilateral Organizations' Interests and Preferences

Because the lion's share of multilateral supplementary financing comes from the World Bank, I take the Bank's policy interests as representing multilateral supplementary financiers' interests (mainly other multilateral development banks) at large. This section will therefore mainly focus on the World Bank's interests in providing supplementary financing and hence their preferences over Fund conditionality.

Multilateral organizations, like the World Bank, are considered actors unto themselves, not simply empty shells implementing state preferences.[2] Multilateral development banks, like the World Bank, are interested in certain policy ends, and they loan in order to encourage the implementation or maintenance of these policies. This depiction of multilateral development banks may appear inconsistent with the general argument advanced here about the International Monetary Fund. However, the International Monetary Fund is also assumed to be an actor with interests—a bureaucratic actor interested in the short-term success of its programs and its future bargaining leverage with borrowers. Supplementary financiers are able to influence the Fund explicitly because of these organizational interests.

The World Bank and IMF have different interests in lending because of their different initial mandates.[3] Although their activities have certainly

changed since those early days, these initial mandates still inform their activities, organizational development, and hiring practices. Despite their frequent pairing and joint founding in 1944 at the Bretton Woods conference,
the World Bank and International Monetary Fund were established to serve
two different missions.[4] While the Fund was established to help maintain and
monitor a system of stable exchange rates, the World Bank was established
to address the broad issues of reconstruction and development. In particular, the original World Bank organization, the IBRD, "was supposed to be a
financial intermediary providing finance for productive projects, primarily
for reconstruction purposes."[5]

As stated in a World Bank history, "From the outset, the Bank's subject
matter covered a broader space than that of the Fund, and over the decades, it
expanded."[6] New organizations were later established as part of the World
Bank Group. The IDA was created in 1960 as a concessionary window to facilitate lending to poorer countries; the International Finance Corporation,
International Center for Settlement of Investment Disputes, and Multilateral
Investment Guarantee Agency were also established as part of the World Bank
Group.[7] According to Ibrahim Shihata, these five organizations were and are
united under a "common objective, the encouragement of the transfer of resources to their developing member countries in pursuit of economic growth
and the alleviation of poverty."[8] The most important organizations for our
purposes are, and the focus here is on, the two public lending arms: the IBRD
and the IDA. The mandate to address developmental concerns quickly took
center stage, particularly for these two organizations, focusing World Bank
interests on poverty alleviation and economic growth broadly defined.[9]

As a result of these distinct mandates, the Fund and Bank differ consider-
ably.[10] In the early years, while the Fund was maintaining the Bretton Woods
exchange rate system by (among other things) providing short-term loans
to offset temporary payments imbalances, the Bank was focused on project
lending.[11] Typical project loans helped support infrastructure and development projects, like building roads, dams, and water-treatment facilities.
Through this project lending, and particularly after the Bank's reorganiza-
tion in 1952, the Bank became involved in specific sectoral reforms and began widely hiring "sectoral specialists."[12] As a result, Fund and Bank staff
differed from a very early stage; Fund staff were almost exclusively economics PhDs, whereas Bank staff included engineers, agriculturalists, and other

sector-specific specialists with particular preferences about microeconomic policy.[13] Bank projects focused on (and many continue to focus on) specific sectoral reforms from agriculture, energy, finance, and power to telecommunications, transportation, and sanitation.[14]

Starting in the 1980s, the Bank became explicitly involved in program or economy-wide, rather than narrow project, lending. The new lending vehicles—called structural adjustment loans (SALs) and sectoral adjustment loans (SECALs)—focused on fostering growth by encouraging policy reforms.[15] The Fund and Bank began working together on structural adjustment lending in the mid-1980s through the Structural Adjustment Facility (SAF), later the Enhanced Structural Adjustment Facility (ESAF) and now the Poverty Reduction and Growth Facility (PRGF). However, the Bank's goals were always explicitly broader than the Fund's. Their structural adjustment lending was supposed to not only support policies that led to growth, but also "to protect the poor against adjustment shocks to their jobs and incomes, and . . . to add to the macro adjustment targets an assortment of related matters that spelled out the quality of life for the poor and disadvantaged, among others."[16]

The Bank's focus has historically, and continues to be, focused on microeconomic, supply-side reforms and encouraging policies that meet a variety of (sometimes conflicting) goals including poverty alleviation, environmental preservation, and social sector development.[17] As a result, the Fund and Bank tend to differ in their preferences over the design of Fund programs. Although both the Bank and the Fund share a preference for restoring a country's payments balance and creditworthiness, Bank staff often want SALs to serve a wider range of goals.[18] The Bank staff are typically more holistic, concerned with the long run and interested in specific, supply-side, microeconomic reforms. By contrast, the Fund is often interested in short-run stability, rather than long-run development, and has historically been more interested in encouraging broad, macroeconomic reforms while leaving microeconomic choices up to the borrower.[19]

In short, the Fund and Bank were founded with different mandates. Although their activities and foci have certainly changed since those founding years, these initial mandates have influenced their development. The Fund's and Bank's lending was different from the start: sectoral and development-oriented versus revolving loans to offset short-term payments imbalances. The Fund employed, and continues to employ, macroeconomists, whereas the Bank began by employing sectoral specialists and has expanded to employ a variety of specialists in not only sectors but also substantive areas like gender equity and the environment.[20] Cumulatively, these differences have resulted in different interests in providing financing and different preferences over the design of Fund programs.

Multilateral organizations have been a major source of supplementary financing since the early 1980s. Most multilateral supplementary financing comes from the World Bank; as a result, this discussion has focused on the World Bank's interests and preferences. However, the assumptions generated from the World Bank should be roughly applicable to the regional development banks. According to Anne Krueger, the other multilateral development banks—including the Inter-American Development Bank, the Asian Development Bank, the African Development Bank, and the European Bank for Reconstruction and Development—"were modeled closely on the World Bank" and can be viewed as a "testimonial to the success of the Bank."[21]

In short, multilateral organizations finance for policy ends. They deal intensively with the Fund's borrowing member states and have specific policy preferences that sometimes differ from the Fund's. The main multilateral organization providing supplementary financing for developing countries is the World Bank. The World Bank, for instance, has specific policy preferences regarding development, poverty alleviation, private sector development, and institution building (among others), which are not necessarily the same as the Fund's. In practice, this means that multilateral organizations often prefer Fund conditional loan arrangements to include procedural conditions—specific, detailed directives that specify how policies should be implemented—related to their specific policy preferences. They also often prefer more conditions that address developmental concerns comprehensively from multiple angles. Thus two hypotheses are generated from the interests and preferences of multilateral organizations:

HYPOTHESIS 4   *If a country receives relatively more (less) supplementary financing from multilateral organizations, then its Fund loan arrangement should include relatively more (less) binding conditions.*

HYPOTHESIS 5   *If a country receives relatively more (less) supplementary financing from multilateral organizations, then its Fund loan arrangement should include relatively more (less) procedural conditions versus targets.*

TABLE 7.1

Change in the Number and Proportion of Procedural Conditions in Fund Conditional Loan Arrangements, 1952–1995

Variable	1952–1973	1974–1982	1983–1990	1991–1995
Average no. of procedural conditions per agreement	0.8	0.2	2.0	2.3
Average proportion of procedures to total no. of binding conditions	0.13	0.02	0.16	0.18

SOURCE: Data from the Conditionality Data Set.

Descriptive Statistics

The broad longitudinal trends conform with these hypotheses. As you will recall from Figures 5.2, 6.2, and 7.1, multilateral supplementary financing increased particularly after 1983. Similarly, the use of procedural conditions in Fund conditionality agreements jumped after 1983. For instance, Table 7.1 indicates that between 1974 and 1982, an average Fund conditionality agreement included only 0.2 procedural binding conditions. Just 2% of all binding conditions included in Fund agreements were procedural (as opposed to targets) during this period. By contrast, from 1983 to 1990, an average Fund conditionality agreement included two procedural binding conditions. Sixteen percent of all binding conditions were procedural from 1983 to 1990.

Large-N Econometric Analysis

The longitudinal increase in multilateral supplementary financing appears to be roughly concurrent with certain changes in conditionality, including an increase in the number of binding conditions and a change in the type of binding conditions. However, these concurrent trends do not convincingly demonstrate that increases in multilateral supplementary financing caused these changes in conditionality. In order to try to establish a causal relationship and test Hypotheses 4 and 5, this section presents results from large-N multivariate analyses to determine whether multilateral organizations seem to have influenced Fund conditionality arrangements in the predicted ways,

TABLE 7.2
Cross-Tabulation of Relative Financing (Commitments) and
Number of Binding Conditions

Binding Conditions	More Bilateral than Multilateral	More Multilateral than Bilateral
Low no. of binding conditions	25 obs (6.2 mean) 62.5%	34 obs (6.7 mean) 41%
High no. of binding conditions	15 obs (10.9 mean) 37.5%	48 obs (12.3 mean) 59%
Column summary	40 obs (7.98 mean) 100%	82 obs (9.98 mean) 100%

SOURCE: Data from World Bank (1999) and the Conditionality Data Set.

when controlling for several other relevant variables. In the subsequent section, I discuss the mechanisms of multilateral influence in more detail, including a brief discussion of two selected country cases.

TESTING HYPOTHESIS 4

As you will recall, the supplementary financier argument suggests that multilateral financiers prefer both more binding conditions (Hypothesis 4) and more procedural binding conditions (Hypothesis 5). An initial look at the data lends credence to Hypothesis 4. Table 7.2 cross-tabulates the source of a country's loan commitments and the number of binding conditions in its Fund conditional loan arrangement. The left-hand column includes cases when the country received more PPG loan commitments from bilateral sources than from multilateral sources, whereas the right-hand column includes cases when the country received more PPG loan commitments from multilateral sources than from bilateral sources in the year of their Fund loan agreement. A low number of binding conditions is defined here as less than 10 binding conditions, the median value of the total number of binding conditions for post-1970 coded arrangements. The median value for post-1970 arrangements is used because debt commitments data are only available after 1970; therefore, only post-1970 cases are included in the Table 7.2 cross-tabulation. The table indicates that when countries receive more of their debt commitments from multilateral sources than from bilateral sources, they are more likely to have a high number of binding conditions. When countries receive more of their debt commitments from bilateral sources, they are more likely to have a low number of binding conditions in their Fund conditional loan agreements.

TABLE 7.3
Total Number of Binding Conditions as the Dependent Variable

Variable	Model 1	Model 2	Model 3
Creditor state	−0.362 (0.219)*	−0.535 (0.311)*	−0.500 (0.274)*
Multilateral	0.571 (0.269)**	0.409 (0.354)	0.512 (0.333)
Reserves	—	0.019 (0.026)	0.019 (0.024)
GNP per capita	−0.00001 (0.00002)	−0.00004 (0.00004)	−0.00004 (0.00003)
Regime	—	0.010 (0.007)	0.011 (0.006)*
Tranche	0.056 (0.030)*	0.058 (0.046)	0.020 (0.033)
Constant GNP	—	−0.0003 (0.0008)	—
Lagged Y	0.066 (0.010)**	0.039 (0.013)**	0.044 (0.012)**
Salary increase	—	−1.444 (1.175)	—
Constant	1.61 (0.189)**	2.16 (0.286)**	2.03 (0.239)**
N	108	72	79
MLL	−2.342	−2.247	−2.271
Method	Poisson	Poisson	Poisson

* $p \leqslant 0.1$
** $p < 0.05$

Table 7.3 presents the results from several large-n analyses, testing Hypotheses 1 and 4. The dependent variable is the total number of binding conditions in a particular Fund loan agreement (0 to 18; positive count). The key proxy for creditor state influence (*creditor state*) is the ratio of bilateral PPG debt outstanding and disbursed (DOD) to the total amount of PPG DOD; *creditor state* was also utilized in the Chapter 5 analyses and is discussed further in that chapter. Similarly, the proxy for multilateral supplementary financier influence (*multilateral*) is the ratio of multilateral PPG DOD to the total amount of PPG DOD. Models were also run using alternative proxies—for example, the ratio of bilateral or multilateral debt disbursements to total disbursements and the log of this ratio—with similar results. The other independent variables included in the models have been introduced in Chapter 5 (and to a lesser extent Chapter 6). All of the models include variables to control for the level of development (constant *GNP per capita*), the size of the Fund loan (*tranche*), and the number of binding conditions included in the previous loan for that borrowing country (*lagged Y*). The lagged dependent variable (*lagged Y*) is meant to capture change over time. Model 2 also includes variables to control for the extent of the balance of payments problem (*reserves*), the level of democracy (Polity IV *regime*-type variable), the size of the country's economy (*constant GNP* in billions of U.S.

dollars), and a bureaucratic proxy (*salary increase*).[22] For a fuller discussion of these variables, refer to those chapters.

As with previous chapters, the statistical analyses presented here only test the competing arguments using post-1970 cases from the Conditionality Data Set (Appendix 1) because the main independent variables (measuring the relative amount of supplementary financing from creditor states and multilateral organizations) are only available since 1970. This results in a severe missing data problem. There are 249 cases in the Conditionality Data Set between 1952 and 1995. Of these 249, 221 have observations for the number of binding conditions. Of these 221, 131 are observations between 1970 and 1995.[23] For many of the economic variables, data is only available since 1970. As a result, 131 cases out of 249 possible is the highest number of cases possible for most of these equations. (Through additional research I have found values for the main multilateral and bilateral influence proxies. As a result, I have data for 135 cases instead of 131.) In reality, the missing data problem becomes much worse. For instance, Model 2 has only 72 observations. Attempts to impute these values, rather than resorting to line-item deletion, were unsuccessful because of the pattern of missingness. Consequently, the results should be interpreted with some caution. However, the central results should not be compromised because there is ample variation in the multilateral supplementary financing proxy for the post-1970 cases.

Table 7.3 includes three different models. Because the dependent variable is a positive count variable, Poisson or negative binomial regression analyses are implemented, as indicated.[24] The large-N data analysis provides modest support for Hypotheses 1 and 4. For all three models, the proxy representing the creditor state influence is negatively and significantly related to the total number of binding conditions included in a particular Fund agreement. In other words, the more a country receives its supplementary financing from other states (rather than private financial institutions or multilateral organizations), the fewer binding conditions should be included in its Fund agreement, holding other variables constant. This result is consistent with the findings from Chapter 5. In addition for all three models, the proxy representing multilateral influence is positively related to the total number of binding conditions included in a particular Fund agreement, but it is only significant in Model 1 (which has the highest N of 108).[25] The only variables, other than those representing the influence of creditor states and multilateral organizations, that are significantly related to the dependent variable are the *lagged Y* (whose coefficient is positive and significant for all specifications) as well as *tranche* and *regime*, both of which are significant for a single model. Surprisingly, all other control variables are not significant in any of the specifications.

Model 3 omits the *constant GNP*, which is both highly insignificant and highly correlated with another variable (constant *GNP per capita*) and the bureaucratic proxy (*salary increase*). The bureaucratic proxy is omitted from Model 3 because I believe, despite Vaubel's arguments, that this is a flawed proxy of bureaucratic influence. Many of the increases in staff salaries are proposed according to a formula meant to mimic market and inflation increases.[26] Alternative proxies for bureaucratic influence are equally, if not more, problematic.[27]

The mean log likelihood ratio suggests that Model 2 has the best model fit, despite its low N.[28] In this model, the coefficient on the creditor state interests' proxy is negative and significant, the coefficient on the multilateral supplementary financier proxy is positive but not significant at 0.10, and the coefficient on the lagged dependent variable is positive and significant. This provides modest support for the supplementary financier argument.

TESTING HYPOTHESIS 5

Since 1983, there has been a dramatic increase in the use of procedural conditions. Scholars have suggested several different explanations—a change in the borrowing clientele, a bureaucratic bid for more power—for this qualitative shift. The supplementary financier argument suggests, by contrast, that other multilateral organizations like the World Bank have pushed the Fund to include these procedural conditions. It predicts that bilateral supplementary financiers should prefer (and push for) relatively more targets, while multilateral financiers should prefer (and push for) more procedural conditions.

Table 7.4 takes a first cut at assessing this argument. Countries that receive more bilateral than multilateral debt commitments in the year of their Fund agreement are less likely to have a procedural condition included in their Fund loan agreement than are countries which receive more multilateral debt commitments than bilateral debt commitments. Moreover, of the

TABLE 7.4
*Comparing Supplementary Financing Commitments
and Use of Procedural Conditions*

Variable	More Bilateral than Multilateral	More Multilateral than Bilateral
No procedural conditions	22 obs (55%)	30 obs (37%)
One or more procedural conditions	18 obs (45%) (mean 1.56)	52 obs(63%) (mean 2.31)
Column totals	40 obs (100%) (mean 0.7)	82 obs (100%) (mean 1.46)

SOURCE: Data from the Conditionality Data Set.

countries that do have at least one procedural condition included in their Fund loan agreement, the countries that receive more multilateral debt commitments than bilateral debt commitments are also more likely to have more procedural conditions (2.31) than those countries that receive more bilateral than multilateral debt commitments (1.56).

For the models in Table 7.5, the dependent variable is a count variable: the number of procedural binding conditions included in a Fund program. Table 7.5 presents three models that test Hypotheses 2 and 5. The supplementary financier argument predicts that states or bilateral supplementary financiers will prefer and push for relatively fewer procedural conditions, which offer borrowers less political room for maneuver, whereas multilateral supplementary financiers (again, the main one being the World Bank) will prefer and push for relatively more procedural conditions. The independent variables in Models 1 through 3 are the same as those used in Table 7.3 (and have been introduced in Chapters 5 and 6), with the measures of creditor state and multilateral organization influence being the ratio of bilateral or multilateral DOD over the total DOD, respectively. For Models 4 and 5, the ratios of bilateral or multilateral debt disbursements (DIS) *to* total PPG and PNG loan disbursements (*creditor state DIS* and *multilateral DIS*) are used as alternative proxies for creditor state and multilateral organization influence.[29] According to all five models, the more supplementary financing a borrower receives from multilateral sources, the more likely it is to have procedural binding conditions in its Fund conditionality agreement, holding other variables constant. The multilateral influence variable is both in the predicted direction and significant. The coefficient on the bilateral variable is negative, as expected, but only significant in one specification.

TABLE 7.5
Change in the Use of Procedural Conditions

Variable	Model 1	Model 2	Model 3	Model 4	Model 5
Creditor state	−0.937 (0.437)**	−0.917 (0.892)	−1.152 (0.768)	—	—
Multilateral	1.761 (0.529)**	1.95 (0.99)**	2.449 (0.878)**	—	—
Creditor state DIS	—	—	—	−0.39 (0.74)	−0.13 (0.83)
Multilateral DIS	—	—	—	1.61 (0.60)**	1.75 (0.68)**
Reserves	—	−0.060 (0.078)	−0.007 (0.068)	.02 (0.07)	.02 (0.07)
GNP per capita	—	−0.0001 (0.0001)	−0.00003 (0.00008)	−0.00001 (0.00008)	.00001 (0.00008)
Regime	—	0.048 (0.023)**	0.042 (0.017)**	0.05 (0.02)**	0.04 (0.02)**
Tranche	—	0.022 (0.164)	—	−0.003 (0.09)	−0.01 (0.09)
Constant GNP	—	0.001 (0.002)	—	—	—
Lagged Y	—	0.148 (0.056)**	0.172 (0.049)**	—	0.08 (0.07)
Salary Increase	—	−6.682 (3.930)*	—	—	—
Constant	0.121 (0.231)	0.695 (0.700)	0.117 (0.527)	−0.14 (0.55)	−0.33 (0.59)
Method	Poisson	Poisson	Poisson	NB	NB
N	135	72	79	92	81
MLL	−1.563	−1.342	−1.4149	−1.431	−1.439

NOTE: DIS = debt disbursements, according to the World Bank's definition; MLL = mean log likelihood; NB = negative binomial regression analysis.

* $p \leq 0.1$

** $p < 0.05$

The model with the best fit, according to the mean log likelihood ratio, is Model 2. According to this model, Hypothesis 5, which concerns the positive influence of multilateral financiers on the number of procedural conditions, is supported; the coefficient on the multilateral influence variable is both positive and significant. Although the coefficient on the bilateral influence variable is negative, as predicted, it is not significant. The other significant variables in this equation are *regime*, the *lagged Y* variable, and *salary increase*, the bureaucratic proxy. As countries become more democratic, they tend to have more procedural conditions, holding other variables constant. Greater increases in staff salaries tend to be associated with relatively fewer procedural conditions, in contradiction to the bureaucratic argument. (However, as stated previously, I have strong reservations about this proxy, and as a result, I discount this finding.) And predictably, the number of procedural conditions included in a borrower's previous Fund agreement influences the number of procedural conditions in the borrower's current Fund agreement. The constant *GNP per capita*, *tranche*, *reserves*-to-imports ratio, and *constant GNP* variables were not significant.

Mechanisms of Influence

As opposed to the influence of the other supplementary financiers, multilateral influence on Fund conditionality programs is quite formal, institutionalized, public, and even accepted (at least by upper management; Fund staff still complain). In this section, I discuss the history of Fund and Bank cooperation and friction, and the development of institutionalized cooperation between the two organizations in the 1980s. Institutionalized cooperation between the Bank and Fund should not be misunderstood as a convergence of interests and preferences, however. Evidence of continued resistance to the cooperation and predictable differences of opinion on Fund conditionality are presented. Finally, this section and the chapter end with two country cases—Ghana and Bangladesh—that illustrate how the Bank has influenced individual Fund conditionality agreements.

Cooperation between the Bank and Fund in designing Fund programs is quite common now, but this has not always been the case. According to Jacques Polak, cooperation between the organizations was somewhat rare and based on idiosyncratic factors from the 1950s to the 1970s.[30] In fact, in 1966, the organizations tried to clearly delineate their "respective areas of primary responsibility" with the Bank responsible for "the composition and appropriateness of development programs and project evaluation, including development priorities," while the Fund was responsible for "exchange rates and restrictive systems . . . adjustment of temporary balance of payments disequilibria, and . . . evaluating and assisting members to work out financial stabilization programs."[31] The organizations agreed to consult—to exchange information before and after missions, and to share documents—in order to "avoid inconsistent advice." In 1970, the Bank's president and the Fund's managing director reiterated the 1966 "understandings" about cooperation through a joint memorandum.[32] However, Bank and Fund coordination beyond that remained quite limited until the early 1980s. After all, the two organizations were still involved in relatively separate activities. Although both organizations often lent to the same countries, the Bank was lending to support educational institutions and irrigation systems, while the Fund was lending for 12 short months to help a country stabilize its currency. The purposes and foci were distinct and different. As a result, cooperation was limited.

In the early 1980s, however, this changed. Starting in the 1970s, the Bank and Fund's areas of activity had begun to converge.[33] For instance, in 1974 the Fund established the Extended Fund Facility, which represented its first foray into medium-term lending to address slow growth. In 1980, the Bank began structural adjustment lending, or "balance of payments (rather than project-related) loans linked with broad understandings on the borrowing country's general economic policies" for SALs or sectoral policies (for example, the banking sector) for SECALs.[34] Coordination and cooperation began slowly in the early 1980s when, according to Jacques Polak, staff transfers between the organizations increased; Fund staff papers to their Executive Board included a section on borrower relations with the World Bank; staff members from one organization were invited to observe and sometimes comment at board meetings for the sister organization; staff members from one organization were invited on missions of the other; and draft papers were exchanged for comments before final versions were submitted to their respective boards.[35] This coordination is discussed explicitly in a series of reports to the organizations' boards. For instance, one Fund staff report stated with neutrality: "In several countries, lending activities of the two institutions were closely coordinated in support of the policy advice given by each other.

In such instances, Fund-supported programs incorporated essential elements of the structural reforms supported by the Bank, which helped strengthen the program design." [36]

Coordination and cooperation became more institutionalized and formal in the late 1980s. The Fund's SAF, which provided three-year concessional loans to low-income countries, was established in 1986 and by design involved collaboration with Bank staff and its board. [37] In the initial debates about this facility, the U.S. executive director actually proposed negotiating Bank and Fund structural adjustment programs "jointly." [38] Although the final proposal did not go that far, it did stipulate that the Bank and Fund staff would develop a policy framework paper (PFP), which summarizes the borrower's economic problems and the content of the proposed policy program (along with the Letter of Intent and Fund staff report) and is "developed in close collaboration of the applicant country and the staffs of the Fund and the Bank." Bank staff would often accompany the Fund mission to the prospective borrowing country during negotiations. [39] The resultant PFP would first be "reviewed" by the Bank's Executive Board and then, along with two additional documents, approved by the Fund's Executive Board. [40] In 1986, the SAF was reformed and replaced with the Enhanced Structural Adjustment Facility (ESAF). [41] The ESAF program was intended to provide concessional loans to the same set of low-income countries, but required somewhat higher conditionality and more frequent loan disbursals than the SAF. [42] The World Bank and IMF worked closely through these programs. As Boughton has written:

> Much more systematic collaboration [between the World Bank and IMF] developed in the second half of the decade through the SAF and the ESAF. . . . The primary vehicle for collaboration under those facilities was the PFP, designed as a framework for medium-term programs of policy reform agreed among the country, the Bank, and the Fund. Most PFPs included a section on the social implications of the adjustment program, and some also included a discussion of mitigating measures and requirements for social safety nets. [43]

In 1999, the ESAF was in turn renamed the Poverty Reduction and Growth Facility (PRGF). These three Fund lending facilities—the SAF, ESAF, and PRGF—mimic Bank lending in that they are longer term (10-year lending limits) with low-interest, concessional loans.

However, the problem of duplication and conflict did rear its head. The two organizations butted heads publicly over several programs in the late 1980s, including Bank programs with Argentina and Turkey in 1988 and a Fund program with Côte D'Ivoire in 1989.[44] By 1989, the managing directors of the two organizations agreed to a particular division of labor and responsibilities in order to ameliorate this conflict.[45] According to Jacques Polak, the Brady Plan, proposed by then U.S. Secretary of Treasury Nicholas Brady, also detailed a division of responsibilities: "the negotiation of stabilization packages fell again clearly to the Fund; the Bank, at the same time, continued to play its major role in the design of structural reforms in such areas as tax policy and administration . . . the reform of public enterprises, social security, trade, financial sectors, and, in more recent years, privatization."[46] Both the Brady Plan and the 1989 Memorandum reemphasized the original division of labor between the Fund and Bank established at Bretton Woods. According to one former Bank vice president, the post-1989 division of labor

> allowed the Bank, in consultation with the Fund to take the lead in the institutional underpinnings of macroeconomic policy: tax administration, a new public finance law to control expenditures, privatization of public enterprises, civil service reform to downsize public employment, [and] a new Charter for the monetary authority establishing limited powers of money creation and lending to the Government. The Fund, in consultation with the Bank, took the lead in discussions on short-term targets and the general architecture of the macropolicy framework. . . . Collaboration was genuine—including joint missions, advance readings of drafted policy positions and mission briefs, and frequent staff consultations on short- and medium-term projections.[47]

However, many observers still consider their activities to have converged too much and call for a return to their original (narrower) mandates.[48]

In short, the Bank has several institutionalized avenues to influence Fund programs and Fund conditionality. Their staffs are permanently located across the street with an underground tunnel connecting their two buildings; frequent opportunities for informal contact present themselves. But the formal contact has proved more fruitful. Bank participation and approval is required for SAF, ESAF, and PRGF PFPs. Increasingly Bank staff participate in Fund missions to borrowing countries (during which Fund programs are negotiated), or Bank missions are scheduled concurrently. According to

Boughton, "Bank staff participated in 39 Fund missions" from 1979 to 1983 and 102 from 1985 to 1989.[49] The Fund has also outsourced much of its expertise to the Bank, relying on Bank assessments of appropriate conditions for certain structural areas where the Fund does not have particular expertise.

One should not mistake this close cooperation as a convergence of preferences, however. Evidence suggests that despite this cooperation, Fund and Bank staff continue to have different preferences about the design of Fund programs, and thus that the inclusion of certain policy-oriented conditions is the result of Bank pressure. Jacques Polak summarizes the differences in the following way:

> Although some convergence has occurred over the years, the Bank's practices on conditionality differ considerably from those of the Fund. In its pure form, Fund conditionality stipulates a limited number (rarely more than ten) of monitorable indicators of performance. . . . The Bank's conditions are far more numerous, averaging fifty-six per SAL in a recent year (1989). . . . Even with the widening of the Fund's interests in structural aspects, the bread and butter of Fund missions remains the crucially important issues of macroeconomic management, such as monetary policy, overall fiscal policy, and the exchange rate. . . . The subjects with which the Bank has to deal are not so neatly concentrated. It has to pay attention to a much wider array of issues, stretching over many sectors and institutions; it also has a longer planning horizon and its contacts in the government need to be much more widely dispersed than the Fund's.[50]

Moreover, according to Polak, these differences in preferences over Fund program design "are not random or personal, but institutional."[51]

Disagreements are often hidden from public view. However, analyses of World Bank files (by Carol Lancaster) and interviews with Fund staff members (by the author) suggest that these disagreements over program design are common and run along predictable lines. For instance, Carol Lancaster identifies the sources of tension for Bank staff with uncommon clarity. She writes:

> Bank files suggest that periodically, at senior levels of Banks management, there was real frustration with the Fund's approach to economic reform. There were problems. First, the Fund's mission was different from that of

the Bank. Stabilization—closing the balance of payments gap—could be achieved through relatively short-term demand management approaches: reductions in the levels of credit, devaluation, increased taxation, and reductions in government expenditures. These . . . did not address the more difficult and longer-term need to stimulate new growth. . . . The Bank recognized the need for stabilization but was concerned that it not be implemented in a way that blocked growth. Much of the frustration with the Fund centered on the policy framework papers that each adjusting government was supposed to draft and negotiate with the Fund and the Bank. (The reality, according the Bank and Fund staff, was that the Fund wrote the first draft and negotiated it with the Bank and the government.) . . . Other complaints concerned Bank staff's being left out of key meetings with African government officials on monetary, fiscal, and macroeconomic issues.[52]

Interviews conducted with Fund staffers revealed mirror frustrations. According to one longtime Fund staff member, the content of Fund conditionality is now broader and resembles World Bank-sponsored programs more. This staff member stated that many of the newer conditions now included in Fund programs "are unobserved [which] makes them very difficult to measure . . . and also, in a sense, takes the rigor away from the process." This staff member considered there to be predictable differences between the two organizations. As he stated, "it was very clear that the Fund was rigorous and the Bank was fluffy. This extension of the conditionality of the Fund over a very large range, it is inevitable that it must get fluffier too." According to this staffer, these changes in Fund conditionality occurred mainly during Michel Camdessus's tenure as managing director, from January 1987 to 2000/2001. Again, he stated: "It's the widening of the Fund's objective to, quote, high-quality growth, which led to a widening of conditionality . . . a widening of the conditions which played a role into the acceptability of the program."[53]

Whether or not Bank conditionality is "fluffier" than Fund conditionality is a point of debate, but Bank conditionality does have certain distinctive features that differ systematically from Fund conditionality, and that reflect the difference between Fund and Bank preferences. For instance, according to Kapur et al., 65% to 81% of the conditions required by World Bank SALs between 1980 and 1991 were "supply-side, growth-oriented policies" (versus typical Fund conditions described by Kapur et al. as "absorption-reduction" and "switching" conditions).[54]

In order to illustrate in greater detail how the World Bank has influenced the design of Fund conditionality programs, two country cases will be discussed: Ghana and Bangladesh.

GHANA

Under the military government of Flight Lieutenant Jerry Rawlings and the financial leadership of Kwesi Botchwey, Ghana turned to both the World Bank and International Monetary Fund for assistance in the early 1980s.[55] This period marked a turning point for Ghana: a civilian government was replaced with a military one, while an economic downturn was reversed.[56] Two Economic Recovery Programs were implemented from 1983 to 1986 and from 1987 to 1991, and a period of robust economic growth soon followed.[57] As a result, Ghana in the 1980s is often offered as an example of successful reform; both the Fund and World Bank have laid claim to this success.[58]

For the Fund, these Ghanaian programs were particularly noteworthy. According to James Boughton, Ghana was "perhaps the most well-publicized example of the use of structural adjustment facilities to promote programs that protect the interests of the disadvantaged."[59] Not coincidentally, the Fund's programs during this period were also heavily influenced by the World Bank. Starting with Ghana's 1984 stand-by arrangement (SBA), Fund press releases explicitly acknowledged the World Bank's influence over the design of its loan programs for Ghana.[60] Concurrently, multilateral supplementary financing commitments to Ghana surpassed bilateral supplementary financing commitments. According to the Ghanaian government, 52% of the aid commitments in 1983 came from multilateral organizations, with 74% of the multilateral aid commitments coming from the World Bank that year. In 1984, 71% of aid commitments came from multilateral organizations, with 42% of those multilateral commitments coming from the World Bank alone.[61]

Fund programs in the late 1980s, particularly the 1987 SAF and the 1988 ESAF, were designed with explicit World Bank participation. And both the 1987 SAF and 1988 ESAF loans bear the distinctive marks of World Bank influence. In total, these SAF and ESAF programs are more focused on longer-term structural reforms than the standard SBA or Ghana's earlier Fund programs. For instance, compare Ghana's 1983 SBA with the 1987

SAF and 1988 ESAF. Ghana's 1983 SBA included eight conditions; all eight of these conditions were relatively standard Fund conditions. For instance, the 1983 SBA included what I call the Fund's four basic conditions; between 1983 and 1990, 98% of the cases in the Conditionality Data Set included all four basic conditions. These four conditions require Ghana to agree not to "(i) impose or intensify restrictions on payments and transfers for current international transactions, or (ii) introduce new, or modify existing, multiple currency practices . . ., or (iii) conclude bilateral payments agreements which are inconsistent with Article VIII, or (iv) impose or intensify import restrictions for balance of payments reasons."[62] In addition, there were binding conditions limiting the "net claims on the Government by the banking system," the "contracting of new nonconcessional public and publicly guaranteed external debt," the amount of external payments arrears, and setting the cedi exchange rate. By 1983, all of these conditions were standard fare for a Fund conditionality agreement.

The 1987 SAF included binding conditions pertaining to typical areas of Fund concern, including the net domestic assets of the banking system, the net claims on the government by the banking system, net foreign assets of the Bank of Ghana, amount of external payments arrears, and limits on new nonconcessional external loans. However, it also included conditions and structural benchmarks that reflected typical World Bank concerns—for example, by focusing on specific, sectoral policies, and poverty alleviation measures. One condition limited the "bank financing of the operations of the Cocoa Board"; other structural benchmarks required Ghana to sell or liquidate various state enterprises and adopt a public investment program, among others. The official Fund press release announcing the 1987 SAF identified three main objectives of the program: to decrease inflation, generate a balance of payments surplus which would allow Ghana to pay down its external payments arrears, and "achieve an annual rate of growth of real GDP of the order of 5 percent, which would improve real per capita income by about 2 percent per annum."[63] The 1987 SAF PFP was "largely drafted by Fund and World Bank staff" and was "approved" by the Bank's Executive Board before being passed by the Fund's, both formal and institutionalized mechanisms of Bank influence on Fund conditionality.[64]

Ghana's 1988 ESAF included even more binding conditions and procedural binding conditions, as Table 7.6 indicates. At the beginning of the Fund

TABLE 7.6
Ghana's Fund Conditionality Agreements

Year	Agreement Type	No. of BCs	No. of procedural BCs
1966	SBA	4	0
1967	SBA	5	0
1968	SBA	3	0
1969	SBA	3	0
1979	SBA	9	1
1983	SBA	NA	NA
1984	SBA	10	1
1986	SBA	12	1
1987	EFF	12	1
1987	SAF	14	3
1988	ESAF	16	5
1995	ESAF	NA	NA

SOURCE: Data from the Conditionality Data Set.

NOTE: SBA = stand-by arrangement; BC = binding condition; EFF = Extended Fund Facility; ESAF = Enhanced Structural Adjustment Facility; NA = not available; SAF = Structural Adjustment Facility.

Executive Board Meeting that approved this loan program, the managing director read the reactions of the World Bank's executive directors, as is typical for ESAF programs.[65] For instance, World Bank executive directors had commented on the Ghanaian "Government's efforts to reduce the size of the state-owned enterprise sector" and noted that "with the support of technical assistance financed by the World Bank, the program is expected to accelerate in the coming years."[66] In total, the 1988 ESAF program included 16 binding conditions, over 30% of which were procedural, like the abolition of Ghana's import licensing system.[67] In 1988, Ghana also committed to a group of poverty alleviation reforms designed by the World Bank called the Program to Mitigate the Social Costs of Adjustment (or PAMSCAD).[68] The ESAF program was also designed to help support PAMSCAD and its poverty alleviation measures. According to Boughton, "In support of PAMSCAD and the government's more general efforts to improve social policies, the Fund's assistance via the ESAF was designed not only to ensure the viability of macroeconomic policies, but also to support the establishment of a 'Special Efficiency Fund' for the retraining, relocation, and redeployment of public employees displaced by the restructuring of the economy."

By 1995, the Fund's focus had broadened a great deal. In its first midterm review of the 1995 ESAF (in November 1995), the Fund mission traveled to

Accra at the same time as a parallel World Bank mission in order to evaluate its lending program. The Fund staff singled out five main issues for discussion during their review. Two of these were traditional Fund concerns: lowering inflation and controlling the fiscal balance. Three were newer areas of concern: controlling pay increases to civil servants, deregulating the marketing and pricing of petroleum, and liberalizing cocoa trade and "removing the Cocoa Board's monopoly over crop exports."[69]

In short, Ghana's conditionality programs changed dramatically during the 1980s and 1990s, as multilateral supplementary financing came to play a more important role. Starting with Ghana's 1984 SBA, but particularly with the later SAF and ESAF programs, the World Bank was able to insert conditions to suit its interests and preferences. Fund programs designed in conjunction with the Bank included not only standard conditions like credit targets, but also newer conditions that reflected Bank preferences, like specific investment programs and reform of the cocoa industry.

BANGLADESH

Before 1987, all of Bangladesh's Fund conditionality programs were relatively similar. Each required from seven to nine binding conditions, and no procedural conditions. (See Table 7.7 for summary statistics of Bangladesh's Fund conditionality programs from 1975 to 1990.) As late as 1985, the Fund's historian James Boughton described the division of labor between the World Bank and IMF with respect to Bangladesh as traditional, with "the Fund again focused primarily on macroeconomic stabilization, while the World Bank made several loans to Bangladesh aimed at financing essential imports and promoting structural reforms."[70] In fact, by the mid-1980s, the World Bank had already developed a long history of advising Bangladesh, dating back to the 1960s period of Pakistani rule, and a reputation as the preeminent source of development advice and aid in that country.[71] Recent Bank loans included a rural development loan for $100 million in 1983, a $40 million loan to support primary education in 1980, and population control loans in 1979 and 1986, among others.[72]

Bangladesh's 1987 SAF, designed "jointly" with World Bank staff, marked a significant change.[73] The number of binding conditions jumped to 16, with 5 of those being procedural binding conditions. SAF programs were designed

TABLE 7.7
Bangladesh's Fund Conditionality Agreements

Year	Agreement Type	No. of BCs	No. of Procedural BCs
1974	SBA	NA	NA
1975	SBA	7	0
1979	SBA	7	0
1980	EFF	8	0
1983	SBA	8	0
1985	SBA	9	0
1987	SAF	16	5
1990	ESAF	11	3

SOURCE: Data from the Conditionality Data Set.

NOTE: SBA = stand-by arrangement; BC = binding condition; EFF = Extended Fund Facility; ESAF = Enhanced Structural Adjustment Facility; NA = not available; SAF = Structural Adjustment Facility.

in annual increments. For the first year, the SAF agreement included the four "basic" conditions and other typical Fund conditions, such as limits on external public debt, the government deficit, the net domestic assets, and net credit to the central government. In addition, Bangladesh's 1987 SAF required it to commit to specific policy-oriented measures that the World Bank preferred. For instance, Bangladesh was supposed to "undertake a detailed technical study of the tax structure and administration; and implement measures to increase tax collection, and improve enforcement of taxes." It was also supposed to "improve [public] project implementation through revised contract award procedures; and Granting greater operational autonomy to implementing agencies." The 1987 SAF also required Bangladesh to implement financial sector reform with four specific agricultural credit reforms and three specific reforms pertaining to industrial credit. These sector-specific policy reforms bear the stamp of the World Bank's influence, not the Fund's.[74] According to James Boughton, "many of these reforms were structured specifically to minimize any adverse impacts on the poorest groups in the economy," and the PFP "noted the government's intention to better enable small farmers to restructure loans if necessary after bad harvests, to phase in the elimination of food subsidies gradually, and to use the revenues from the elimination of subsidies for social programs targeted directly at the poor."[75]

Bangladesh's history of Fund programs, like Ghana's history, reflects the influence of the World Bank on Fund conditionality. Before formal World

Bank participation in the design of Bangladesh's and Ghana's Fund programs, Fund conditionality remained focused on conditions of traditional concern, like credit targets and exchange rates. Once the World Bank began formally participating in the design of their Fund programs, Fund conditionality for Bangladesh and Ghana changed dramatically. The number of binding conditions increased, as did the use of procedural conditions. These procedural conditions reflected the traditional concerns not of the International Monetary Fund, but of the main source of supplementary financing: the World Bank.

Conclusion

In sum, this chapter demonstrates how multilateral supplementary financiers, namely the World Bank, have influenced Fund conditionality. The World Bank, like other supplementary financiers, provides financing to supplement Fund loans for certain reasons. Given that the World Bank is interested in providing financing to encourage certain specific microeconomic policy reform, it has tried to influence the design of Fund programs to incorporate these conditions. This chapter has presented various types of evidence that supports this conclusion. Longitudinally, we observe predicted changes in Fund conditionality at the same time that multilateral supplementary financing has increased. Large-N analyses show that when countries receive more multilateral supplementary financing, holding other variables constant, their Fund programs tend to have more binding conditions and more procedural binding conditions. Interview and other evidence suggests that despite formalized cooperation, World Bank and IMF staff preferences over Fund program design continue to differ. Finally, individual cases demonstrate how Fund programs have changed as World Bank staff have become formally involved in program design.

CHAPTER EIGHT

Conclusion

Summary of Findings

In this book, I advance a relatively simple argument: many of the controversial changes in the terms of Fund conditionality agreements reflect the interests and preferences of supplementary financiers. The Fund often provides only a fraction of the amount of financing that a borrowing country needs in order to balance its payments that year and implement the Fund's recommended program. Both the Fund and the borrower rely (often explicitly) on outside financing to supplement the Fund's financing. This reliance gives the supplementary financiers some leverage over the design of Fund programs. The supplementary financiers in turn want to influence the design of Fund programs because these programs help them ensure borrowers are using their financing in the ways they prefer. The change in the terms of Fund programs results, at least partly, from the fact that supplementary financiers are not a uniform bunch. Supplementary financiers include three types of actors—creditor states, private financial institutions, and multilateral organizations—and each type of supplementary financier has systematically different preferences regarding how Fund programs should be designed. Consequently, as the sources of state financing and supplementary financing have shifted over the last 50 years, so have the demands on the Fund and the terms of Fund conditionality agreements.

The book presents a range of evidence to support this argument. Because limited data were available before I started this project on the terms of Fund conditionality programs, I constructed the first time-series cross-sectional data set of the terms of Fund conditionality agreements from the Fund loan agreements themselves: the Conditionality Data Set. By using this data set, I was able to retell the history of Fund conditionality and how the terms of these agreements have changed for certain borrowers over the last 50 years in Chapter 3. In Chapter 4, I assess whether the pattern of changes in Fund conditionality conforms with the observable implications of the two most prominent conventional wisdoms—realism and bureaucratic theory—or with the observable implications of the supplementary financier argument. The history and descriptive statistics cast doubt on the conventional wisdoms. Both powerful state representatives and Fund staff have actually opposed many of the changes in the Fund conditionality we observe. The patterns of conditionality change do not reflect Executive Board directives or powerful states' stated preferences, as realists might expect. The patterns of program uniformity and diversity do not mimic the patterns we would expect to observe if the IMF's rationalized bureaucratic culture was the crucial driving force behind Fund conditionality change. However, the history and new descriptive statistics about Fund conditionality change do provide initial support for the supplementary financier argument: changes in Fund conditionality do conform broadly to global changes in the provision of supplementary financing.

In Chapters 5 through 7, I used the Conditionality Data Set to see whether relatively more financing from creditor states resulted in fewer binding conditions and less stringent binding conditions; whether bank-friendly conditions were more likely to be included in Fund loan agreements for borrowers when their private financiers were organized through debt conferences; and whether Fund conditionality agreements tended to have relatively more conditions and more detailed, procedural conditions when relatively more supplementary financing came from multilateral sources, holding other variables constant. Generally, the results from large-N statistical analyses provided strong support for the supplementary financier argument. When Fund borrowers receive relatively more supplementary financing from creditor states in general, or the United States in particular, their Fund programs tend to require relatively fewer binding conditions and also relatively fewer of the detailed, procedural binding conditions. When a country's private creditors were organized via a debt conference before a Fund loan agreement was concluded, their Fund agreement was much more likely to require a "bank-friendly" binding condition than if these private creditors were unorganized. Finally, when a Fund borrower received relatively more of its supplementary financing from other multilateral organizations, like the World Bank, its Fund agreement tended to require them to meet more binding conditions and also more detailed procedural binding conditions. For each of these chapters, individual country cases helped connect the causal chain, clarifying how creditor states, private financial institutions, and multilateral organizations have been able to communicate their preferences and influence the Fund. In addition, throughout all of the chapters, archival (and often interview) evidence was used to help give context to the debates within the Fund about the increase in Fund conditionality, among other things.

Despite its simplicity, this argument has provoked a surprising array of responses. Strong opponents of the IMF and longtime staffers at the IMF have both responded to this argument and the evidence to substantiate it with satisfaction. The influence of supplementary financiers can vindicate Fund critics who argue the Fund caters to the interests of international capital at the expense of borrowing country interests. Conversely, IMF staffers have told me that the argument supports their impression that the Fund is being unduly influenced, and that consequently the expansions and failures of Fund conditionality are no fault of their own. Scholars of international organizations have often expressed surprise that the evidence supports this argument, which goes against the dominant conventional wisdom that either powerful states or bureaucrats have masterminded these changes. Meanwhile, a former high-level member of the Fund's management team was puzzled that anyone would be surprised that the Fund is influenced by creditor states, private financial institutions, and other multilateral organizations. Of course the Fund listened to supplementary financiers and responded to their preferences, this individual argued; otherwise, how would the Fund be able to reestablish market confidence?[1]

Broader Implications

This argument and these findings have important implications both for the specific debates about IMF conditionality and for our broader understanding of international organizations. The specific debates about IMF conditionality have centered on whether the Fund's conditionality in its current form is appropriate. Many question whether it is right for an international organization to dictate policies to a borrowing country, particularly when these policies may disproportionately hurt the poor.[2] Others question whether a lender of last resort should get its hands dirty with thorny questions of development. These questions are terribly important. Policy decisions impacting citizens around the globe hinge on their answers. However, the questions are also normative, and hence one's answer depends on one's individual values. The positive argument advanced here cannot provide answers to such questions, but it does suggest that critics should reconceive the Fund and thus reframe their criticisms in order to effect change.

The International Monetary Fund is neither an all-powerful bureaucracy imposing its will, nor an apolitical technocratic organization neatly fulfilling its mission immune from outside influences. Instead, the International Monetary Fund is an organization comprising, I believe, well-intentioned economists who want to help right the economic wrongs they perceive in countries with spiraling deficits, plunging currencies, glacial growth, and massive debt. Their own concerns—for better or for worse, depending on one's own predilections—are relatively narrow. They advise countries to implement certain policies or meet certain targets because they believe they will resolve the countries' economic woes. Often they do not only suggest these policies, but (as has been the focus of this book) they design explicit incentive systems whereby borrowers must meet targets or implement policies in order to receive the next installment of their loan from the Fund. But as political scientists know well, countries are not perfect laboratories, and these reforms may not yield the expected results. Some, like Joseph Stiglitz, suggest that the Fund's advice is outdated and often wrongheaded. However, even assuming that the advice is perfectly crafted to yield the best economic results, hurricanes and earthquakes, military coups and civil wars, interest rate hikes and plunging commodity prices, among so many other factors, can upend even the most "well-designed" Fund program. Because above all else, Fund staff and management want their program to help turn this economy around, they know the real silver bullet is external financing. The Fund's loan is often not even large enough to cover this year's balance of payments deficit—the most immediate concern—much less the other costs associated with the new recommended policies and future years of reform. Outside financing is absolutely necessary for Fund program success. As a result, the Fund is open to, and Fund conditionality programs bear the marks of, this influence.

The IMF should be understood as neither an all-powerful dictator of policies, nor a technocratic lender of last resort, but rather as a facilitator of financing to borrowing member states. Many of the conditions actually originate as demands from supplementary financiers, and the borrowers agree to these conditions in order to receive both Fund and supplementary financing. The Fund's mission is not the narrow resolving of short-term balance-of-payments problems by mustering its own resources and sage advice, as it perhaps was initially envisioned in the Fund's Articles of Agreement. Instead, the Fund helps maintain economic stability by encouraging flows of supplementary financing.

According to this new understanding of Fund activities and Fund purpose, is the expansion of Fund conditionality right or wrong, or simply practical? One's conclusions about which actors *should* be influencing the Fund's activities depend on what one thinks the Fund *should* be doing. The normative answer is not obvious. Protesters in the streets can rightly point to the findings presented in this book as evidence of the International Monetary Fund as a tool of international capital. Fund staffers and management can rightly point to the finding presented here as evidence of the constraints within which they function in order to help borrowers regain market confidence. However, a debate of the appropriateness of Fund conditionality in its current form should begin by recognizing the important, if controversial, role the Fund truly plays in the international system for borrowers and creditors alike. Before advocating changes in Fund conditionality, one should assess whether these changes would prevent the Fund from fulfilling its role as a facilitator of financing. Some may judge that the costs associated with Fund conditionality—costs to democracy and economic costs disproportionately borne by the poor—far outweigh the benefits of facilitated financing.

But the true benefits of Fund conditionality, which include not only (often unfulfilled) promises of growth, but also promises of financing, should be weighed accordingly.

One of the most serious costs associated with the expansions of Fund conditionality is its constraint on democracy, at both domestic and international levels. At the domestic level, many countries have participated in Fund conditionality programs continuously for years, if not decades. As the Conditionality Data Set has revealed, the range of policies covered by these conditionality programs has expanded. Binding conditions now concern not only fiscal deficit targets, but wage and price controls and other policies that intimately impact people's lives. In this book, I have argued that many of the conditions actually originate as demands from supplementary financiers, and the borrowers agree to these conditions in order to receive the Fund and supplementary financing. Thus supplementary financiers are defining policies for borrowing countries. Even though borrowing country politicians (often finance ministers or treasury secretaries) accept the terms of these Fund conditionality agreements in return for promises of financing, the fact that borrowing country policies are being defined by supplementary financiers, rather than its citizens, exacerbates the infringement on democracy. In some ways, this is a familiar story of constraints. Supplementary financiers constrain the Fund, which in turn constrains borrowing country politicians. However, the result, disturbingly, is that supplementary financiers, not necessarily citizens in borrowing countries, are constraining borrowing country politicians. As a result, democratic institutions atrophy and citizens lose relative control over a broad range of economic, and increasingly political and social, policies that impact them directly. This may be just one of the many avenues by which citizens' control of their government has waned due to "globalization" (for lack of a better word), but it is nonetheless a significant one for many of the Fund's frequent borrowers.

The argument presented here not only suggests that the IMF may be contributing to the weakening of borrowing countries' democratic institutions, but also raises questions about the role of democracy in the International Monetary Fund itself. To the extent that Fund activities are not being determined by its membership or by the decision-making rules in the Executive Board and Board of Governors, then the influence of supplementary financiers also points to a failure of democracy at the international level.

Major changes in the Fund's activities—the expansion of Fund conditionality in new policy areas and in ways that have increased the organization's power and influence over borrowers—have neither been dictated by the Fund's member states nor approved by either of its two governing bodies. This empirical finding—that states have not been the primary drivers of the substantial changes in this international organization's activities—suggests that international organizations may be facing an even greater "democratic deficit" than previously thought.

Thus one of the central implications of this study for students of international organizations is that state control of international organizations can vary and is often elusive. States continue to play an important role in controlling international organizations. In the case of the Fund, the Executive Board is the final veto player, deciding whether a Fund program should be approved or denied. Similarly, states provide the Fund's financing and influence its activities in myriad other ways. However, states' preferences are not necessarily decisive in defining the contours of international organizational activity. Instead of arguing provocatively that state influence over the Fund is moribund, I am suggesting that state influence should be conceived as variable. For many international relations scholars, states are assumed to be the primary actors in world politics and their influence—as a group   is treated as constant. This study provides one way of thinking about how state influence varies (on the basis of creditor states' contribution of supplementary financing), a way of predicting when state influence will be greatest and what to expect the material consequences of that influence to be (less stringent conditionality). Recent scholarship has suggested alternative ways of conceiving of how state influence over international organizations may vary.[3] One productive avenue for future scholarship would be to compare several international organizations and thus arrive at generalizable conclusions about these variations in state control over international organizations.

International organizations may not be perfectly controlled by states, but they also may not be perfectly defining their activities. The general thrust of this project is to question both of the dominant approaches to studying international organizations, which either assume that international organizations are simply doing states' bidding, or—in my mind equally problematic—that international organizations are simply doing what they want on the basis of some notion of bureaucratic interest or culture. This book suggests that both of these approaches should be rigorously tested and attention paid to the idea that nonstate as well as state actors may be influencing international organizations, shifting their incentives and appealing to their interests. This book does not "disprove" the dominant alternative arguments or argue that they have no relevance in explaining changes in IMF activity. Certainly powerful states and bureaucrats exercise some influence over the Fund and its conditionality. However, the book does suggest at least two things about these alternative arguments. First, the explanatory power of these arguments is greatly exaggerated and, under scrutiny, often does not appear to be supported by empirical data. And second, the supplementary financier argument not only introduces a new category of actors—supplementary financiers—but also suggests different ways of understanding how powerful states and bureaucratic actors exercise influence over IMF conditionality in particular, and international organizational activity more generally. Actors may be influencing international organizations through informal means and backdoor channels, rather than the formal areas of influence on which scholars have often focused.

The International Monetary Fund is influenced by states and by nonstate supplementary financiers, like private financial institutions. And yet their influence is not random at all. There is a clear logic behind these diverse actors' influence on the Fund. Supplementary financiers appeal to the Fund's own interests—in designing successful loan programs and in maintaining their bargaining leverage with borrowers—and therefore we can predict when creditor states or private financial institutions or multilateral organizations should be able to influence the Fund and also when we should observe the stamp of their influence on Fund conditionality agreements. Many elements of international relations work this way. Multiple actors influence outcomes, and yet there is a logic to understanding which actors should influence outcomes at any given time. Our challenge as scholars is to identify why actors exercise influence and then which actors should be able to exercise influence and impact outcomes. Our world does not consist of single types of actors or of single causal arrows. Our theories should simplify and clarify, but they should also recognize and attempt to unpack this diversity.

Reference Matter

Conditionality Data Set, Other Data Sources, Archival Sources, and Interview Evidence

CONDITIONALITY DATA SET

In order to measure conditionality, I built a data set with 249 cases of IMF conditional loan arrangements (stand-by arrangements, EFF, SAF, and ESAF) from 20 countries between 1952 and 1995. An observation is a unique conditional loan arrangement—in other words, a unique country loan-year. True random sampling, although methodologically preferable, was not possible given the organization and resources of the Fund archives. The Fund archives organize documents by country; staff time to pull, vet, and declassify documents is minimized by requesting a number of agreements from a single country, rather than single agreements from multiple countries. Consequently, I selected representative countries and then—data and access permitting—included all relevant agreements for that country between 1952 (when conditionality began) and 1995 (after which many arrangements remained classified at the time I gathered the data). This type of case selection does have certain methodological advantages. For instance, one can test how previous arrangements influence current ones. The 249 cases came from the following 20 countries: Argentina, Bangladesh, Bolivia, Brazil, Central African Republic, Côte D'Ivoire, El Salvador, Ghana, Haiti, Korea, Mali, Mexico, Morocco, Niger, Philippines, Romania, South Africa, Turkey, the United Kingdom, and Yugoslavia.

Despite the atypical case selection method, the 249 cases are generally representative, both by region and arrangement type. Table A1.1 compares the Conditionality Data Set with the entire population of 759 stand-by, EFF, SAF, and ESAF loan agreements between 1952 and 1991. The sample very closely approximates (within three percentage points) the proportion of

TABLE A1.1

Comparing Sample with Universe of Arrangements, by Region and Arrangement Type

	UNIVERSE		SAMPLE	
	n	%	n	%*
Region				
Africa	269	35	67	27
Asia	115	15	46	18
Europe	41	5	33	13
Middle East	12	2	—	—
Western Hemisphere	286	38	92	37
Developed	36	5	11	4
Arrangement type				
Stand-by	664	87	221	87
EFF	41	5	14	6
SAF	35	5	7	3
ESAF	19	3	8	3
Missing	—	—	3	1

SOURCE: The Conditionality Data Set; and International Monetary Fund Annual Reports, 1952–1992.

NOTE: "Universe" includes all stand-by, EFF, SAF, and ESAF arrangements 1952–1991 (N = 759). The sample includes 262 arrangements between 1952–1995 and 2000. EFF = Extended Fund Facility; ESAF = Enhanced Structural Adjustment Facility; SAF = Structural Adjustment Facility.

* Data are rounded and may not add to 100.

cases from all regions except Africa, which is underrepresented, and Europe, which is overrepresented in comparison to the 1952–1991 universe. The sample is also generally representative with respect to arrangement type. The European overrepresentation is warranted given that the "universe" comprises only cases between 1952 and 1991, whereas the sample comprises cases between 1952 and 1995. Since 1991, the Fund has seen an absolute and proportional increase in European agreements, particularly from the former Soviet Union and Eastern Europe. The Middle East is excluded from the sample as a result of the nature of the sampling method; including all arrangements for a single Middle Eastern country would have overrepresented the Middle East more than it is currently underrepresented (0% versus 2%).[1]

The Conditionality Data Set codes each loan agreement according to its terms as stated in the original loan agreement, including the letter of intent, attachments, and the resulting press release. A typical loan agreement contains a letter from the borrowing country's finance minister requesting a loan and detailing an extensive policy program concerning many different sectors of the economy and government. The arrangement itself, often a second document, generally outlines more policy proposals and the program's schedule of reviews, and often in the penultimate paragraph specifies which conditions are binding. Binding conditions trigger the suspension of the Fund loan if they are violated. Most arrangements have many other conditions that are also listed in the policy program but are not binding; in other words, there are no specified consequences if they are violated.[2] Each case was coded according to 31 separate criteria questions and 52 different binding conditions. The data set contains information on a variety of program terms other than binding conditions, including provisions for phasing, reviews, and consultations.

OTHER DATA SOURCES

For additional information on independent variables included in the Conditionality Data Set that were either imported from other data sets (e.g., World Bank 2000) or were constructed from secondary sources, see Chapters 5 through 7.

IMF ARCHIVAL SOURCES

Archival documents cited in this book come primarily from the general or country-specific "1760" or stand by arrangement files at the International Monetary Fund archives in Washington, DC. I also consulted numerous other types of files at the IMF Archives, including but not limited to the subject and country files for the EFF, SAF, and ESAF programs, specific mission (810) files, and files pertaining to Debt Renegotiation and Multilateral Aid (S1190–1196) and relations with private banks.

Documents are identified by their date and with as much additional identifying information as possible. For instance, if the document is a "Board document," then it is identified by its EBM (Executive Board Meeting), EBS, or SM code number, date and page number, when available, and the repository where is was found. Other documents are identified by their author, date, page number, title or brief description (where applicable and available), and the repository where it was found.

INTERVIEWS

I conducted 16 interviews between September 1999 and May 2002 in Washington, DC; San Francisco, California; and New York, New York. Each interviewee was asked a list of open-ended questions about the process of constructing, influencing, and revising Fund conditionality programs, about the role of being an executive director or staff member (depending on the interviewee), and about the role of the Fund in the international system. From this starting point, conversations veered in different directions depending on the interviewee. Interviewees largely preferred to remain anonymous; as a result, references to these interviews are general. The interviews conducted and consulted by the author are as follows:

Interview 1: Executive director or member(s) of Executive Director's office, September 14, 1999.

Interview 2: Executive director or member(s) of Executive Director's office, February 8, 2000.

Interview 3: Executive director or member(s) of Executive Director's office, February 8, 2000.

Interview 4: High-level Fund staff member, February 9, 2000.

Interview 5: Executive director or member(s) of Executive Director's office, February 10, 2000.

Interview 6: High-level Fund staff member, February 10, 2000.

Interview 7: Executive director or member(s) of Executive Director's office, February 10, 2000.

Interview 8: Executive director or member(s) of Executive Director's office, February 11, 2000.

Interview 9: Executive director or member(s) of Executive Director's office, February 11, 2000.

Interview 10: Executive director or member(s) of Executive Director's office, February 14, 2000.

Interview 11: Executive director or member(s) of Executive Director's office, February 15, 2000.

Interview 12: Executive director or member(s) of Executive Director's office, February 15, 2000.

Interview 13: Executive director or member(s) of Executive Director's office, February 17, 2000.

Interview 14: High-level Fund staff member, August 30, 2000.

Interview 15: Commercial bank executive, October 3, 2000.

Interview 16: Former high-level fund manager, May 28, 2002.

Article I from the International Monetary Fund's Articles of Agreement

1. To promote international monetary cooperation through a permanent institution which provides the machinery for consultation and collaboration on international monetary problems.

2. To facilitate the expansion and balanced growth of international trade, and to contribute thereby to the promotion and maintenance of high levels of employment and real income and to the development of the productive resources of all members as primary objectives of economic policy.

3. To promote exchange stability, to maintain orderly exchange arrangements among members, and to avoid competitive exchange depreciation.

4. To assist in the establishment of a multilateral system of payments in respect of current transactions between members and the elimination of foreign exchange restrictions which hamper the growth of world trade.

5. To give confidence to members by making the Fund's resources available to them under adequate safeguards, thus providing them with the opportunity to correct maladjustments in their balance of payments without resorting to measures destructive of national or international prosperity.

6. In accordance with the above, to shorten the duration and lessen the degree of disequilibrium in the international balance of payments of members.

Source: Horsefield (1969b), 1:187–88.

Basic Facts about Selected Fund Facilities and Arrangements[3]

- STAND-BY ARRANGEMENTS (SBAs): Established in 1952; originally lasted six months, now last approximately one to three years; repayments to be made between three to five years; loans are at market rate; drawings and reviews made quarterly; focus problem is short term balance of payments deficits.
- *FIRST CREDIT TRANCHE*: Generally no longer utilized; low conditionality; borrower is "required to show reasonable efforts to overcome its balance of payments difficulties;" no performance criteria.[4]
- *UPPER CREDIT TRANCHE*: Higher conditionality than first credit tranche; member required to provide "substantial justification" and a "strong and viable program" in order to draw from upper credit tranches; funds paid in installments subject to binding conditions or performance criteria; these conditions have changed over time.[5]
- COMPENSATORY FINANCING FACILITY: Established in 1963; could draw up to 100% of quota; "floated" alongside, and therefore did not count against, regular tranche purchases; focus problem was a fall in export earnings for primary product producers; no/low conditionality. Remodeled in 1983 as a high-conditionality facility.[6] Re-named *Compensatory Financing and Contingency Facility* and reformed in 1988; now requires reform programs.
- 1974 OIL FACILITY: June 1974 to December 1974 only; no performance criteria; no phasing; floated alongside, and therefore did not count against, regular tranche purchases; no necessary program of action; main problem was payments imbalances from oil price increases.

- 1975 Oil Facility: January 1975 to May 1976 only; program of action was necessary; main problem was again payments imbalances from oil price increases.
- Extended Fund Facility(EFF): Established in 1974; arrangements last for three to four years and are considered "medium-term"; repayments are to be made between 4.5 and 10 years; the loans are made at market rate; drawings and reviews are made quarterly; the main problem to be solved is structural balance of payments problems and chronic low growth; three-year program of action is specified at the beginning of program and revised each year; performance criteria (or binding conditions) are applied.
- Structural Adjustment Facility(SAF): Established in 1986; lasts for three years and are considered "medium-term" programs; repayments to be made between 5.5 and 10 years; loans at a nominal interest rate of 0.05% per annum; disbursed one installment per year; for low income countries only; focus problem is the "protracted balance of payments difficulties;" program of action with yearly-targets specified in policy framework paper written by country representative, often with IMF or World Bank guidance; country's progress is evaluated quarterly; in cooperation with World Bank. The SAF is often considered to have demanded weaker conditionality than the ESAF.[7] All SAF resources were disbursed by December 1995.
- Enhanced Structural Adjustment Facility(ESAF): Established in December 1987; lasts for three years, but can be extended to four; repayment to be made between 5.5 and 10 years; loans made at a nominal interest rate of 0.05% per annum; semiannual drawing conditional on results of semiannual reviews; in cooperation with the World Bank; higher conditionality than SAF. Renamed in 1999, see PRGF.
- Systemic Transformation Facility: Established in 1993 and expired in 1995; was created to deal primarily with the economic transitions of the former Soviet Union and Eastern Europe.
- Supplementary Reserve Facility. Established in reaction to the 1997–98 Asian financial crisis for countries facing larger balance of payments crises due to "sudden and disrupting loss of market confidence;" loans made for one year and repaid in 2.5; high and increasing interest rates encourage quick repayment.

- POVERTY REDUCTION AND GROWTH FACILITY. (PRGF) The ESAF renamed in November 1999 to give it a "more explicit antipoverty focus." Three-year poverty reduction program required; 0.5% interest per annum; repayable over 10 years with a 5.5-year grace period for principal repayments.

TABLE A4.1
Change in the Inclusion of Bank-Friendly Conditions (Logit)

Variable	Model 1T	Model 2T	Model 3T
Private influence	1.98 (0.76)**	3.50 (1.94)*	3.97 (1.62)**
U.S. influence	−0.14 (0.12)	−0.67 (0.32)*	−0.26 (0.18)
Salary increase	−5.20 (6.87)	−11.15 (10.27)	0.17 (8.48)
Reserves	—	−0.04 (0.28)	—
GNP per capita	—	−0.0002 (0.0004)	—
Regime	0.01 (0.04)	0.14 (0.08)*	0.06 (0.06)
Tranche	0.05 (0.30)	−0.24 (0.44)	0.14 (0.38)
Constant GNP	—	−0.009 (0.008)	−0.01 (0.005)*
Lagged Y	3.30 (0.55)**	2.59 (0.91)**	3.09 (0.68)**
Constant	−1.92 (0.53)**	1.99 (1.37)	−1.28 (0.68)*
N	178	71	141
Log likelihood	−56.73	−25.38	−42.10
Mean log likelihood	−0.3187	−0.3574	−0.2986
Pseudo R^2	0.4167	0.4825	0.4937

* $p \leq$ o.i.
** $p <$ o.o5

Notes

CHAPTER ONE

1. IMF (2002c) 102.

2. International Financial Institution Advisory Commission (2000).

3. See, e.g., "If belt-tightening fails, what next?" *Business Week*, February 7, 1977, 42; Alan Cowell, "The IMF's imbroglio in Africa," *New York Times*, March 14, 1982, A4; Kenneth S. Smith, "World Bank, IMF: Do they help or hurt Third World?" *U.S. News and World Report*, April 29, 1985, 43; Cragg Hines, "Dispute erupts over the IMF's role in Asia's economic collapse," *Houston Chronicle*, November 15, 1998, 23; Stiglitz (2003, 119).

4. See Willett (2001) for a summary and analysis of the left and right critiques; see also Overseas Development Council (2000), Council on Foreign Relations (1999), and Stiglitz (2003) for some noteworthy critiques.

5. This consensus continues to be opposed by a minority. For instance, Tony Killick (1992) welcomes some of these structural conditions, such as addressing concerns of income inequality. There is a definite conflict between those who argue that the Fund should limit conditionality and protect state sovereignty and those who argue that the Fund does not pay enough attention to issues of, for example, income inequality and environmental degradation, and should include such conditions in their programs (e.g., Killick 1992).

6. Joseph Kahn, "The IMF will revamp its lending: A plan to build up cash ready for emergencies," *New York Times*, September 16, 2000, B1.

7. Stiglitz (2003), esp. 34–35 and chap. 3; see also Vreeland (2002).

8. The term *domestic sovereignty* was coined by Krasner (1999).

9. De Gregorio et al. (1999, 77).

10. International Financial Institution Advisory Commission (2000).

11. Gourevitch (1978).

12. Although the academic literature on the Fund itself—particularly the determinant of its activity, rather than the consequences of them—has been surprisingly

spare. Noteworthy contributions include Stone (2002), Vreeland (2003), and Martin (2000).

13. For example, Krasner (1993); Mearsheimer (1994–1995).

14. The academic literature has just begun to address the politics of Fund lending in a serious, empirical way. Earlier scholars assumed that Fund activity was dictated by the United States. Kapstein (1994, 96, and chap. 4) uses the two virtually interchangeably. Some examples from the media include the following: In 1982 the *New York Times* reported with regard to a loan agreement with Tanzania, "The fear is that the United States will use its influence to harden the terms of I.M.F. conditionality, particularly in those countries that need help but do not represent strategic importance to Washington nor share Washington's political affinities" (Alan Cowell, "The IMF's imbroglio in Africa," *New York Times*, March 14, 1982, A4). The *Financial Times* also credited changes in conditionality policy to the Reagan administration's preferences (Luard 1982).

15. Thacker (1999); Kapur (2001) advances a similar argument.

16. Barro and Lee (2001), 1, 11–12, 18–19.

17. Dreher and Jensen (2003). This draft is not particularly explicit as to how they measure number of conditions, although it appears to be a simple sum of conditions listed by the Fund through documents on its Web site.

18. Kahler (1990); chap. 5 addresses Kahler's argument directly.

19. Stiglitz (2002), 80.

20. Oatley (2002).

21. Most IOs are actually created by other IOs now. See Shanks et al. (1996).

22. Gold (1972), 195–97.

23. Dell (1981), 12; de Vries (1986), 504. See Chapters 3 and 4 for more details about the different Conditionality Guidelines.

24. See Chapter 3 for a more detailed discussion. In fact, in 1978, the year before this decision, U.S. Congress members complained about the stringency of the Fund's conditions and instructed the U.S. representative on the Executive Board to vote accordingly. "IMF and the United States: Congressional conditionality," *Economist*, February 18, 1978, 85.

25. Lipson (1986), 229; James (1996), 333.

26. Joseph Kahn, "Treasury secretary offers a new vision for the IMF: Less long-term lending and more candor," *New York Times*, December 15, 1999, C3. Other U.S. government, academic, and media leaders—including the *New York Times*, the IFIAC Commission, and the Joint Economic Committee of the U.S. Congress—rallied around the Clinton administration's proposal that the Fund restrict its lending to short-term emergency financing, rather than longer-term developmental loans focused on poverty reduction and economic growth, which make up the bulk of its current activities. The IFIAC Commission advocated this unanimously (3 of 59) ("A focused role for the IMF," *New York Times*, December 20, 1999, A38).

27. "U.S. Treasury secretary urges new vision for IMF," April 25, 2004. U.S. Department of State, Consulate General of the United States, Mumbai, India, http://mumbai.usconsulate.gov/.

28. For a comparison of these literatures, see Moe (1991) and Barnett and Finnemore (1999).

29. Moe (1984), Niskanen (1971). Martin (2000) argues that states strategically delegate authority to the Fund's bureaucracy when it serves their interests.

30. Quotes from Vaubel (1996), 195; see also Vaubel (1986, 1991).

31. George Shultz (1995, 5), quoted in Goldstein (2000, 2).

32. Barnett and Finnemore (1999), 707. See also Meyer and Rowan (1977, 341, 348, 352); Finnemore (1996), 330; Ascher (1983).

33. Barnett and Finnemore (1999), 707.

34. Stiglitz (2002) includes an interesting argument (if inconsistent with some of the rest of his arguments) regarding the Fund's neoliberal ideology and narrow, outdated economic training.

35. Barnett and Finnemore (1999), 710–15.

36. Barnett and Finnemore (2004); Kuhn (1996).

37. In other words, because their activities are largely hidden from domestic interest groups, it depresses domestic interest group activism. The recent push for Fund transparency in the 1990s has resulted in increased domestic interest group activism.

38. Barnett and Finnemore (2004). For a rationalist view on the importance of agenda-setting powers and how these powers give the agent a degree of autonomy, see Romer and Rosenthal (1978).

39. Key observers at the Fund have also frequently argued that staff have a great deal of independence. As early as 1969, the Fund's historian, Keith Horsefield, wrote that the increasing staff independence and influence was "undeniable," even a "revolution." Horsefield (1969), 470–73. See also Southard (1979).

40. See, e.g., Goldstein (1996) and Milner (1997).

41. Vreeland (2002); see also Przeworski and Vreeland (2000).

42. Kapur (2001) argues that the shift in clientele reduced the risk to creditor countries of pushing for increases in conditionality.

43. For example, IMF (2001a), 2.

44. Polak (1999); Guitián (1981), 24.

45. For instance, Polak (1994, 8) contends that the Fund's changing "clientele" led "the Fund in the 1970s [to begin] to tailor its credit facilities to the specific needs of developing countries."

46. Vreeland (2001) is concerned with borrower demand for Fund programs. He argues that governments with more veto players (which also tend to be more democratic by his measure) are more likely to enter Fund programs because they need conditionality to help them overcome domestic opposition and enact their preferred policies. If we accept that Fund conditionality is variable, an extension to this

argument is that democracies may demand higher conditionality programs than authoritarian governments with fewer veto players.

47. See Stiglitz (2002).

48. By "best explained," I mean that the supplementary financier argument explains more of the change in Fund conditionality than do alternative arguments. See Chapter 2 for more on this topic.

CHAPTER TWO

1. For the first, see Keohane and Nye (1972, 1977). For the second, see Keohane (1984). Scholarship on the influence of transnational actors has exploded since the end of the Cold War; see Risse (2002).

2. Keohane (1984), 91, chap. 6.

3. Ibid.; Stein (1982). As Krasner (1993, 239) points out, the assumption is that outcomes are currently Pareto suboptimal, so that a new outcome can be devised whereby "at least one actor can gain without compromising the utility of others."

4. Abbott and Snidal (1998).

5. von Furstenberg (1987), 122.

6. For the Fund's purposes as laid out in the Articles of Agreement, see Horsefield (1969), 188–89, and Appendix 2.

7. Cohen (1983); Lipson (1981). See also Lipson (1985, 1986).

8. Clark (1998), 182, cited in Kapur (2001), 33. On Fund homogeneity, see Clark (1996).

9. Chwieroth (2003, 9) codes and considers "the importance of professional training in [certain] economics departments as a key mechanism through which economic norms and ideas are instilled in actors."

10. Interestingly, the managing director has not always been credentialed.

11. The Fund's reputation has been bruised in recent years, not only by press accounts of program failure, but also by empirical and popular literature that has questioned the effectiveness of Fund programs. See Stone (2002, 43–45) for a summary of the empirical literature on the relationship between Fund programs and growth; and Stiglitz (2003) for a popular account.

12. IMF (2000b), 259.

13. These financing gaps are due to both objective limits in the amount the Fund can lend to individual countries and a Fund philosophy that they should not provide all of the financing a country needs to balance its payments. The Fund's financing is supposed to "supplement" financing from private and official lenders; see Masson and Mussa (1995), 23.

14. Memo from Robicheck to Brand, February 17, 1960.

15. Current account data is taken from the World Development Indicators. This is the percentage of cases for which current account data were available in the Conditionality Data Set (Appendix 1).

16. See the Conditionality Data Set (Appendix 1).

17. The Fund advises countries to implement supply-side measures as well.

18. Polak (1991), 15.

19. EBS/60/32, March 29, 1960, IMF Archives.

20. EBS/58/76, Suppl. 2, December 18, 1958, IMF Archives. This was a binding condition.

21. Capital inflow is both a stated goal of the Fund program and an internal measure of the success of Fund programs, which further compounds its reliance on supplementary financiers. See Schadler et al. (1995).

22. Lipson (1986, 232) makes a similar point.

23. Memo from Jorge Del Canto, December 2, 1963, 3, IMF Archives.

24. S1760, 1970–75, IMF Archives. In fact, Sir Joseph Gold proposed that the Fund issue "certificates" instead of "symbolic" Fund programs. Memo from Gold to the Managing Director, December 3, 1970, IMF Archives. As Gold wrote, "Over the past years, there have been cases in which members have requested and received stand-by arrangements for reasons other than the need for financial assistance from the Fund. The reasons that prompted the request for the stand-by arrangement [included] . . . the desire to convince foreign creditors of the creditworthiness of the member and its ability to repay its indebtedness." This idea of the certificate was never approved, however, because staff feared that it would be difficult to ensure the standards of the certificate if the Fund was not financially invested. See, e.g., S1760, 1970–75, Memo from Richard Goode to the Managing Director regarding symbolic stand-by arrangements, December 17, 1970, IMF Archives.

25. McCauley (1986); Goreux (1989). See Marchesi and Thomas (1999) for a recent formalization of this argument.

26. For instance, Edwards (2000); Bird and Rowlands (1997); Faini et al. (1991).

27. Einhorn (1979); Polak (1991), 58; Schadler et al. (1995), 14.

28. Much of the empirical literature considers only private catalysis. Rowlands (2001) also includes official flows.

29. Lipson (1986).

30. Marchesi and Thomas (1999) for the first; Masson and Mussa (1995, 25) for the second.

31. In some ways, this mimics the law merchant's function in Europe in the Middle Ages. Milgrom et al. (1990).

32. Sachs (1989), 259; Diwan and Rodrik (1992); Dhonte (1997); Crawford (1987); Marchesi and Thomas (1999).

33. A notorious example is private banks' attempt to impose conditionality without the Fund in Peru in 1976. As Cohen (1983, 332) has written, "banks, as private institutions, simply did not have the legal or political leverage to dictate policy directly to a sovereign government." See Lipson (1981), 623.

34. Rodrik (1995) argues that the Fund may be more likely to influence borrowers as a result of the advantage of being "less politicized."

35. Fearon (1997); Kahler (1992), 111; North and Weingast (1989); Root (1989).

36. Milgrom et al. (1989), 808.

37. See, e.g., Waltz (1986), 85; Keohane (1984), esp. chaps. 5–6. Another prominent interest-based approach has different ontological assumptions: the main actors are domestic, and thus states' international policies serve these domestic actors' interests; e.g., Milner (1997); Moravcsik (1997).

38. Scholars are mainly divided between those who view foreign aid as motivated by humanitarian concern (e.g., Lumsdaine 1993) and those who view foreign aid as motivated by state political interests (e.g., Schraeder et al. 1998). The dominant approaches to understanding states' foreign policies in international relations are interest-based and conceive of those interests as political, and I side with that interpretation. See, e.g., Waltz (1986), 85; Keohane (1984), esp. chaps. 5–6.

39. When states get involved in influencing the terms of Fund conditionality arrangements, they also usually push for weaker conditionality than the staff. This is a prediction of the argument and also is borne out by evidence. See Finch (1989); De Gregorio et al. (1999).

40. I thank Tom Willett for this suggestion.

41. This assumption was induced through secondary source materials and interviews. For a concurrent perspective from a former Fund staffer and representative from Citibank and First Boston Corporation, see Friedman (1983), 120–21.

42. Kapstein (1994). See also Eichengreen and Portes (1989), 13, 18–19, 39; Krasner (1999), 128, 130, 132; Lindert and Morton (1989), 51; Spiro (1999); Wellons (1987). By contrast, Fishlow (1987), 46–56, argued that most British investments were made largely for profit motives, whereas German and French investments were more politicized. Feis (1974) also argued that British investments were political instruments.

43. In the 1990s, banks are increasingly earning their income from nonlending activities. See Adams et al. (1998), 181–82. Here I focus on the traditional case that applies to most of the time period under study.

44. Dorfman (1994).

45. Ibid., 10.

46. Interview 15 by the author, October 2000. This is often the case with sovereign loans, which are often not very profitable relative to private-sector transactions. Banks have very little bargaining leverage over sovereigns. As the Bank of America credit booklet states, "lending to sovereign governments is different. The fact that they 'don't go bankrupt' is simply one aspect of the fact that it is very hard to enforce a loan agreement which they refuse to honor" (Dorfman 1994).

47. World Bank (1999). These percentages are of IDA and IBRD PPG debt disbursements divided by all multilateral PPG debt disbursements. The multilateral PPG series excludes most IMF disbursements, which makes this an appropriate metric of *supplementary* (to the Fund's loan) multilateral external financing. See Chapter 5 for a more detailed discussion of this data source.

48. Kapur et al. (1997), 2.

49. World Bank (2001).

50. Cohen (1983, 326–27) has a slightly different interpretation.

51. Ibid., 315–16. However, after the debt crisis in the early 1980s, private creditors reduced and official creditors increased their exposure to the developing world. See Goreux (1989), 153.

52. This shift in financing need not be unidirectional. There have been cycles of public-private financing.

53. Interview 14 with author, August 2000.

CHAPTER THREE

1. For some other definitions of conditionality see, e.g., Joseph Gold, the former general counsel and legal director of the IMF, who wrote that "conditionality refers . . . to the policies that the Fund wishes to see a member follow in order that it can use the Fund's resources in accordance with the purposes and provisions of the Articles" (Gold 1979, 2). By contrast, Graham Bird defines conditionality as the "monetary model" of balance of payments—or the particular package of policies that the IMF has been promoting recently. Bird (1996), 490–91.

2. The contract itself is a product of bargaining between the IMF and national representatives (and other outside actors, like supplementary financiers). However, using the word *contract* is misleading in two respects. First, because the status quo is no longer an option, this appears to be circumstantial coercion, rather than a contract. (See Krasner 1999, chap. 3, where he defines coercion as the elimination of the status quo by one of the parties, rather than by exogenous events.) Second, the conditionality arrangements, as will be discussed later, are not legal agreements and explicitly avoid legal "contractual" language.

3. For some significant contributions to this literature, see IMF (2001a, 2001b, 2002a, 2002b); Goldstein (2000); Ahmed et al. (2001); International Financial Institution Advisory Commission (2000).

4. Notable examples of this early literature include Dell (1981); Guitián (1975, 1981); Polak (1991); Williamson (1983); Horsefield (1969). For an excellent recent history, see Boughton (2001), chap. 13.

5. Ivanova et al. (2003, 5); the MONA database includes arrangements since 1992 and is missing 18 agreements from that first year.

6. See, e.g., Ivanova et al. (2003) and Goldstein (2000). Goldstein (2000, 37–38, 42) also discusses other data sources, including an unpublished 1987 report.

7. See Drake (1994); Pauly (1997).

8. Dell (1981) writes that before Bretton Woods, all other member states except the United States wished "to place strict limitations on the Fund's responsibilities vis-à-vis the economic policies of its members."

9. Dell (1981), 1–3.

10. Moggridge (1980), 143, quoted in Dell (1981), 2.

11. Moggridge (1980), 25:404, quoted in Dell (1981), 1.

12. This is wording from the Bretton Woods agreement itself.

13. Dell (1981), 6.

14. Ibid., 6–7.

15. James (1996), 53–56.

16. Articles of Agreement, Article V, Section 3 (i) and (ii), in Horsefield (1969b), 191; also Dell (1981), 3.

17. Horsefield and Lovasy (1969), 2:390.

18. Gold (1979).

19. For the exact wording of Article I, see Appendix 2, i–vi; or Horsefield (1969b), 187–88.

20. de Vries (1986), 14–20, esp. 15–16.

21. Ibid., 19.

22. Aufricht (1964), 58–59.

23. The Fund Agreement states that "A member may not make net use of the Fund's resources to meet a large or sustained outflow of capital." Article VI, Section I(a), quoted from Aufricht (1964), 56. The Fund Agreement states that "The Fund is not intended to provide facilities for relief and reconstruction" because the UN Relief and Rehabilitation Administration existed for that. Article XIV, Section I, quoted in Aufricht (1964), 55–56. It was also "clearly not the intention to have the Fund 'deal with international indebtedness arising out of the war.'" Article XIV, Section I, quoted in Aufricht (1964), 56. As Aufricht writes, the IMF "was also not directly concerned with questions of economic development" Aufricht (1964), 56.

24. Quoted in Aufricht (1964), 57. Also SM/66/4, January 24, 1966, "From the Acting Secretary to members of the Executive Board, regarding policies on the use of fund resources," 4, IMF Archives.

25. Quoted in Horsefield and Lovasy (1969), 2:392.

26. SM/52/5, January 22, 1952, IMF Archives.

27. OV 38/27, J. W. Beyen, November 20, 1950, quoted in James (1996), 76.

28. Specifically, the Fund's powers over a drawing member ceased after the first of those Fund's were drawn. Horsefield and Lovasy (1969), 2:393.

29. Dell (1981), 7.

30. Horsefield and Lovasy (1969), 1:389. See also Gold (1979), 3, n3. Decision No. 284–84; SM/66/14, January 24, 1966, 4, IMF Archives.

31. SM/66/14, January 24, 1966, 4, IMF Archives.

32. Dell (1981), 4; see also Horsefield and Lovasy (1969), 2:394.

33. SM/66/14, January 24, 1966, 5, IMF Archives. They could only borrow dollars in "exception and unforeseen circumstances."

34. Also in 1948, during the Board's discussion of what possible conditions (general or particular) a country might need to meet in order to draw funds, it was suggested that if a country had high inflation it would be ineligible. Horsefield and

Lovasy (1969), 2:394. James (1996), 78. From April 1947 to April 1948, Fund drawings amounted to $606 million; April 1948 to April 1949, $119.4 million; April 1949 to April 1950, $51.8 million; and April 1950 to April 1951, $28.0 million. SM/66/14, January 24, 1966, 5, IMF Archives.

35. Horsefield and Lovasy (1969), 2:398–99.

36. Ibid., 399.

37. Ibid.

38. Ibid., 400.

39. Ibid.

40. According to Horsefield (1969a, 276), "there were no drawings from the Fund during the calendar year 1950." Between April and September 1946, $209 million of Fund resources were used, over 97% in U.S. dollars. In the 1947–1948 fiscal year, the figure was $430.83 million, of which over 97% was drawn in U.S. dollars. In 1948–1949, drawings dropped off sharply to $88.61 million, partially as a result of the European Recovery Program, which reduced European demand for drawings from the Fund (Horsefield 1969a, 192, 226, 242).

41. Quote of Gold (1969), 524, quoted in Dell (1981), 10; and quote of Camille Gutt in Horsefield (1969, 281), quoted in Dell (1981), 9.

42. Horsefield and Lovasy (1969), 1:400.

43. Ibid., 401.

44. Quoted in Memo from Joseph Gold, July 31, 1953, 3, IMF Archives.

45. Horsefield and Lovasy (1969), 2:401. SM/66/14, January 24, 1966, 5, IMF Archives.

46. SM/52/5, January 22, 1952, IMF Archives.

47. Ibid.; EBM/52/11, February 13, 1952, IMF Archives.

48. SM/52/5, January 22, 1952, IMF Archives; James (1996), 81.

49. As earlier stated, the gold, or reserve, tranche is generally the first 25% of quota drawn. At certain points in the Fund's history, the tranches have been expanded to larger percentages, e.g., 37.5%.

50. SM/52/5, January 22, 1952, IMF Archives.

51. Horsefield and Lovasy (1969), 1:402–3.

52. The French ED abstained. SM/52/8, February 5, 1952; SM/52/5, Suppl. 4, IMF Archives.

53. EBS/52/47, August 6, 1952, IMF Archives.

54. SM/52/49, July 31, 1952, IMF Archives.

55. See also Aufricht (1964); Horsefield and Lovasy (1969), 2:403.

56. EBS/52/54, August 27, 1952, IMF Archives; EBS/52/57, October 1, 1952, IMF Archives. It included Southard's request for the language to be changed to specify that stand-bys be limited to six months in length and that the charges to initiate a stand-by be raised. However, evaluation criteria were not specified, as Southard requested and many other EDs opposed. The concerns of the U.S. ED, although not

completely fulfilled, were clearly in the forefront of the staff's mind in drafting revisions. See Memo from Joseph Gold, July 31, 1953, IMF Archives.

57. Memo from Joseph Gold, March 22, 1957, IMF Archives.

58. Spitzer (1969), 475.

59. For instance, Belgium's ED stated, "The request for the stand-by credit should help give the authorities the confidence they needed to help maintain a liberal economic policy." Quoted in Spitzer (1969), 469–70.

60. Memo from Joseph Gold, March 22, 1957, IMF Archives.

61. EBM/52/54, August 27, 1954, IMF Archives.

62. Memo from Andre van Campenhout, August 20, 1953, IMF Archives.

63. Aufricht (1964), 64.

64. EBM/53/90, December 9, 1953, IMF Archives.

65. See Memo from General Counsel, March 22, 1957, IMF Archives; memo from Joseph Gold, October 14, 1960, 2, IMF Archives. A January 1958 letter from G. A. Constanzo to Herbert Zassenhaus is instructive. He writes that there has been a "hardening of attitude" whereby countries—he mentions France—have committed to more ambitious economic reforms or targets in order to receive a Fund stand-by arrangement. However, "this hardening is also accompanied by an increasing concern that sovereignty be unimpaired. It is felt that principles [general principles like exchange rate flexibility] should be insisted on, but implementation left free." In other words, countries committed to more ambitious reforms or targets, but Fund resources were not conditional on adherence to those reforms or targets. Letter from G. A. Constanzo, January 29, 1958, IMF Archives.

66. Memo from Joseph Gold, May 29, 1958, IMF Archives.

67. Prior notice clauses may have been an innovation of the Western Hemisphere Area Department, which covers these countries and is responsible for drafting their arrangements. See Memo from Lachman, October 16, 1960, IMF Archives; memo from Joseph Gold, May 29, 1958, IMF Archives; memo from Joseph Gold, September 14, 1959, IMF Archives; memo from Joseph Gold, October 14, 1960, 2–3, IMF Archives.

68. EBM/61/6, February 20, 1961, IMF Archives. They could not agree to universally apply the prior notice clause. For instance, Mr. MacGillvray "favored the clause in appropriate cases . . . but would want it made absolutely clear that this would not mean that the United Kingdom would ever accept the clause . . . in any arrangement which it might negotiate in the future." Memo from Joseph Gold, October 14, 1960, 3, IMF Archives.

69. SM/68/28, July 23, 1968, 12, IMF Archives.

70. Memo from Joseph Gold, October 14, 1960, 6, IMF Archives.

71. Dell (1981), 11; memo from Joseph Gold, April 12, 1963, IMF Archives.

72. Memo from Joseph Gold, April 12, 1963, IMF Archives; memo from Rose Skalak, November 7, 1962, IMF Archives.

73. Memo from Joseph Gold, April 12, 1963, 1, IMF Archives.

74. Memo from Frank Southard Jr., April 11, 1963, IMF Archives.

75. For instance, they specified one special circumstance when phasing would not be required: when the stand-by is intended to restore market confidence and stem capital flight (e.g., the then-recent UK stand-by arrangements). Memo from Frank Southard Jr., April 24, 1963, IMF Archives; memo from John Woodley, April 16, 1963, IMF Archives.

76. SM/66/14, January 24, 1966, 1–2, IMF Archives.

77. Gold tranche drawings are drawings that do not "cause the Fund's holding of the purchasing member's currency to increase by more than twenty-five percent of its quota" (Gold 1969b, 70).

78. Executive Board Report of April 1968, quoted in Gold (1979, 9). New practices or facilities "would not permit other unconditional uses of the Fund's resources" (Gold 1969b, 27).

79. EBM/68/122–123, August 14, 1968, IMF Archives; EBM/68/128, September 6, 1968, IMF Archives; EBM/68/131–132, September 20, 1968, IMF Archives.

80. SM/68/128, Suppl. 4, September 13, 1968, IMF Archives.

81. Documents in the IMF Archives that relate to prior discussions and the eventual decision include: SM/78/103 + corr. 1, April 19, 1978; SM/78/296, Revision 1, January 8, 1979; EBM/79/35–36, February 28, 1979; EBM/79/38, March 2, 1979; EBD/79/58, March 1, 1979; Final decision in SM/78/296 Revision 1, Suppl. 3, March 5, 1979; EBM/78/79–80, June 2, 1978; EBM/78/81–82, June 5, 1978; SM/78/263 + corr. 1, October 26, 1978; SM/78/296, December 15, 1978; EBM/78/202, December 20, 1978; EBM/79/29, February 16, 1979.

82. Dell (1981), 25. The Group of 24 was a group that represented "developing country members of the IMF" and was an offspring of the political Group of 77.

83. Polak (1991), 12.

84. Gold (1979), 28.

85. SM/78/296, revision 1, Suppl. 3, March 5, 1979, IMF Archives; Gold (1979), 17.

86. In other words, this is not the actual length of the arrangements, but rather the length specified in the conditionality agreement. Many arrangements were subsequently terminated early or extended. Here I focus on the terms of the arrangement—the contract—not the follow-through, what was actually implemented, how long the arrangement actually was, etc.

87. Memo from Whittome, July 21, 1970, IMF Archives.

88. Gold (1979), 30.

89. SM/78/296, rev. 1, Suppl. 3, March 5, 1979, IMF Archives.

90. Before this study, Polak (1991, 14) provided averages in the number of performance criteria for several time periods that indicated that performance criteria have proliferated from an average of 6 performance criteria from 1968 to 1977, to 7 from 1974 to 1984, to 9.5 from 1984 to 1987. These data have been widely cited (e.g., Killick 1992; Bird 1996, 484).

91. IMF (1975), 52.

92. Polak (1991), 8–9; Horsefield and Lovasy (1969), 2:421.

93. IMF (1975), 52.

94. Gold (1979), 4. According to Polak (1991, 9–10), the CFF "has ceased to exist as a special facility in the Fund." The general wisdom is that even balance of payments problems that are proximately caused by export falls still may need some policy changes; therefore, now countries need a conditional arrangement or equivalent policies even in the case of export shortfalls. Also see Horsefield and Lovasy (1969), 2:424.

95. Horsefield and Lovasy (1969), 2:422.

96. Fifty-five members received SDR 7 billion in loans. Guitián (1981).

97. IMF (1975), 53.

98. de Vries (1986), 141. IMF (1975), 54; Guitián (1981), 18.

99. IMF (1975), 54, emphasis added.

100. Executive Board Decision 4377–(74/114) in IMF (1975), 88.

101. IMF (1975), 89–90. See also Guitián (1981), 20.

102. IMF (1975), 89.

103. It is comparable, according to Hooke (1982, 54), to the standard of conditionality required by upper-credit tranche stand-by arrangements, although Gold (1979, 12) states that "extended arrangements" were "forms of less rigorous conditionality and perhaps implied less rigor in other respects."

104. IMF (1978).

105. Between 1976 and April 30, 1981, the Trust Fund loaned approximately SDR 3 billion from resources from IMF gold sales at a 0.5% interest rate.

106. The Second Amendment was approved by the Board of Governors in Resolution 31–4 on April 30, 1976.

107. Gold (1978), 22–34; Gold (1979), 11–13.

108. Gold (1979), 11–13. The supplementary financing facility was established on August 29, 1977. I will not be discussing it here. It was established from borrowings from surplus countries, and it doubled the assistance available under regular stand-by from 100% to 200% of quota and under extended arrangement from 140% to 280% of quota. Even more assistance was available under "special circumstances." In 1979, SDR 8 billion was made available, and by 1981, all the resources had been committed.

109. "From January 1979 until December 1981, 88 arrangements were approved for a total of SDR 24.4 billion, compared with 54 arrangements totaling SDR 8.1 billion in the previous three years" (Crockett 1982). IMF archival documents that relate to prior discussions and the eventual decision include the following: SM/78/103 + corr. 1, April 19, 1978; SM/78/296 Revision 1, January 8, 1979; EBM/79/35–6, February 28, 1979; EBM/79/38, March 2, 1979; EBD/79/58, March 1, 1979; Final decision in SM/78/296 Revision 1, Suppl. 3, March 5, 1979; EBM/78/79–80, June 2, 1978; EBM/78/81–82, June 5, 1978; SM/78/263 + corr. 1, October 26, 1978;

SM/78/296, December 15, 1978; EBM/78/202, December 20, 1978; EBM/79/29, February 16, 1979.

110. Guitián (1981).

111. IMF (1981a), 87.

112. IMF 1981b, 35 quoted in Dell (1981), 31.

113. James (1996), 337–39; IMF (2001b).

114. Guitián (1981); IMF (1985).

115. IMF (1987), 42.

116. Ibid.

117. Ibid., 34.

118. IMF (1988), 76.

119. Ibid., 50; IMF (1989), 35.

120. IMF (2001d).

121. IMF (2001c).

122. IMF (2000c), 67.

123. The development of economic growth as a goal of Fund programs can be traced back to the establishment of the Extended Fund Facility in 1974. This was a notable deviation from prior practices when slow growth was the exclusive domain of the World Bank. The SAF, established in 1986, and the ESAF, established in 1987, both included fostering growth even more explicitly as their second goal, after balance of payments adjustment. This adoption of economic growth was finalized in 1988 with the third comprehensive review of conditionality which "accepted that Fund-supported adjustment programs should foster sustainable economic growth in a medium-term perspective." IMF (1988), 48. Poverty alleviation became incorporated as a goal of Fund programs in the early 1990s, after two generations of criticism that Fund policies aggravated income inequalities and two generations of commitment on the part of the Fund to leave tax and spending decisions to the countries. Polak (1991), 24–26; Gupta et al. (1998).

124. Goldstein (2000, 37, tables 5 and 6) reports somewhat different patterns using the Fund's MONA database for 1993 to 1999. According to that data (and their definitions), EFFs and stand-bys tend to require fewer performance criteria and structural performance criteria than ESAF/PRGF programs. According to his tables, the average number of quantitative performance criteria is generally similar; the difference arises from the inclusion of structural conditions. By contrast, the Conditionality Data Set (Appendix 1) suggests that stand-by arrangements and EFF arrangements, at least during the earlier 1986 to 1995 period, have also contributed to the change in the type of binding condition required.

125. For example, Dell (1981); Killick (1992); Williamson (1983); Gold (1979); de Vries (1986); Schadler et al. (1995); Pauly (1997); Spitzer (1969); Horsefield and Lovasy 2: (1969); Polak (1991); Guitián (1981).

126. IMF (1988), 48.

127. See Polak (1991) on the change in goals. The official explanation for why the IMF programs and foci have changed so dramatically is that the objective conditions in the international system, and hence the objective problems facing member countries, have changed. See, e.g., Gold (1979), 3; Guitián (1981).

128. The first description was in Horsefield (1969a) and the second from Schadler et al. (1995, 14–15). Securing external financing, which often includes "rescheduling or restructuring debt and debt-service payments," is an altogether new activity for the Fund. Another comparison with Horsefield (1969a) is the two main factors of structural adjustment delineated in the 1990 Annual Report. It writes that there are two "broad categories of structural measures": "(1) Measures that eliminate the inefficient use of resources and allow more rapid adjustment to technological innovation and changes in relative prices. . . . (2) Measures that increase output potential by adding to productive resources (such as capital and labor) or by raising overall productivity." IMF (1990), 13.

129. Spitzer (1969), 492. Polak (1991), 40–41.

130. The groups that are not included in the table appeared less frequently in Fund arrangements.

131. IMF (1988), 48.

132. Ibid., emphasis added.

133. Ibid.

134. Ibid.

135. The fact that the 1979 Review stipulated that performance criteria should be limited to macroeconomic targets indicates that they had already begun to extend beyond that limit. Polak (1991), 39.

136. The third and final (thus far) amendment was approved by the Board of Governors in Resolution 45–3 adopted July 28, 1990, and effective November 11, 1992.

CHAPTER FOUR

1. On observable implications, see King et al. (1994), 28–29.

2. See, e.g., Thacker (1999); Williamson (1982).

3. An internal Fund memo stated, "For these reasons, and since he did not think that it was in the Fund's interests to prejudice close and amicable relations with India for the sake of $70 million, Mr. Jacobsson [the managing director] was prepared to recommend approval of a stand-by for $200 million, and had so informed Mr. Southard [the U.S. ED]." Memo from G. L. L. de Moubray, January 17, 1957, IMF Archives.

4. James (1996, 333–34): "In general, at this point, the United States was increasingly explicit about its desire to use multilateral financial institutions primarily for the ends of U.S. policy."

5. Interview 4 with author, February 2000.

6. Interview 2 with author, February 2000; Interview 4 with author, February 2000; Southard (1979).

7. One notable example was the proposed 1979 Sierra Leone stand-by arrangement, which was reduced, but not denied. I learned about the Sierra Leone case from an e-mail correspondence with James Boughton, the Fund's historian, around December 1998 and a conversation with Jacques J. Polak. It is also mentioned in Kapur et al. (1997), 496.

8. I conducted interviews with EDs, or members of the EDs' staff, from 10 of the 24 ED offices in February 2000.

9. In particular, one ED discussed the Asian crisis programs and mentioned strong disagreement between EDs and staff regarding the fiscal elements of those programs. The staff ended up being successful in pushing through the type of program they wanted, but this ED thinks that the Board turned out to be correct about the negative consequences of such severe fiscal tightening. Interview 2 with author, February 2000.

10. See Chapter 3; Horsefield and Lovasy (1969), 1:398–99; SM/52/5, January 22, 1952, IMF Archives.

11. Southard (1979), 19–20.

12. EBM/68/122–3, August 14, 1968, IMF Archives. The exceptions were one elected ED—Patrick Reid from Canada (with 4.1% of the vote as of April 30, 1968)—and one appointed ED—Guenther Schleiminger from Germany (with 5.21% of the vote as of April 30, 1968).

13. EM/68/128, Suppl. 3, September 1968, IMF Archives.

14. EBM/66/13, February 23, 1966, 5, IMF Archives.

15. EBM/68/122, August 14, 1968, 27, IMF Archives.

16. EBM/68/122–123, August 14, 1968, IMF Archives; EBM/68/128, September 6, 1968, IMF Archives; EBM/68/131, September 20, 1968, IMF Archives.

17. SM/68/128, Suppl. 4, September 13, 1968, IMF Archives; see also Horsefield (1969), 534.

18. SM/68/128, Suppl. 4, September 13, 1968, IMF Archives.

19. For example, EBM/68/122–123, August 14, 1968, IMF Archives; EBM/68/128, September 6, 1968, IMF Archives; EBM/68/131–132, September 20, 1968, IMF Archives. Kafka has in many ways spearheaded this discussion, demanding uniform criteria to be applied to stand-by arrangements; this debate seems to have been triggered to some extend by the UK 1967 stand-by arrangement.

20. SM/77/128, June 6, 1977, table 1–6, IMF Archives.

21. According to the Conditionality Data Set (Appendix 1).

22. The use of fiscal binding conditions relating to "specific revenue or expenditure measures" did decrease in the 1969–1978 period. Seven stand-by arrangements between 1969 and 1978 included binding conditions relating to specific revenue or expenditure measures, according to an internal Fund staff report. DM/80/7, January 23, 1980, 2, 5, IMF Archives.

23. EBM/78/82, June 5, 1978, 16–17, IMF Archives, emphasis added.

24. Another useful quote is from Samuel Nana-Sinkam from Cameroon (who represented 18 African countries, mainly former French colonies, with 2.56% of the vote as of June 30, 1978): "normally it may be desirable not to include the fulfillment of any of the fiscal targets in a performance clause. Budgetary operations as well as the operations of public agencies reflect the social and economic priorities of the member; they represent compromises often arrived at after difficult negotiations among interested economic and social groups or geographic subdivisions. If they are included in a performance clause, the impression may be created that the Fund is making a judgment on the priorities of the member." EBM/78/82, June 5, 1978, 9, IMF Archives.

25. EBM/78/82, June 5, 1978, 4, IMF Archives.

26. Ibid., 17.

27. EBM/78/79, June 2, 1978, 21, IMF Archives.

28. EBM/78/82, June 5, 1978, 15, IMF Archives. Also see de Vries (1986), 504; IMF (1983), 20–23.

29. Documents held in the IMF Archives that relate to prior discussions and the eventual decision include: SM/78/103 plus correction 1, April 19, 1978; SM/78/296 Revision 1, January 8, 1979; EBM/79/35–36, February 28, 1979; EBM/79/38, March 2, 1979; EBD/79/58, March 1, 1979; Final decision in SM/78/296 Revision 1, Suppl. 3, March 5, 1979; EBM/78/79–80, June 2, 1978; EBM/78/81–82, June 5, 1978; SM/78/263 plus corr. 1, October 26, 1978; SM/78/296, December 15, 1978; EBM/78/202, December 20, 1978; EBM/79/29, February 16, 1979.

30. SM/78/296, revision 1, Suppl. 3, March 5, 1979, IMF Archives; Gold (1979), 17.

31. This is the average of the sampled stand-by arrangements in the Conditionality Data Set (Appendix 1). This is not the actual length of the arrangements, but rather the length specified in the conditionality agreement itself. Many arrangements were subsequently terminated early or extended.

32. Gold (1979), 30.

33. SM/78/296 Rev 1, Supp3, March 5, 1979, IMF Archives.

34. Polak (1991), 53–54.

35. Polak (1991), 14; see chap. 3, note xc.

36. See Chapter 3. Part of those changes have been linked to the creation of new lending facilities with new purposes.

37. Krasner (1999).

38. I would argue that this is an instance of coercion (Krasner 1999, 25–27). Countries are not necessarily better off if they comply with the Fund's dictates, but they are certainly worse off—from losing Fund and other financing—if they violate Fund conditions.

39. These are all examples of binding conditions coded as "economic policy reform" conditions by the Conditionality Data Set (Appendix 1).

40. As a result, the standard history of Fund conditionality, which contends that most arrangements required broad economic targets until the early 1970s and then shifted to microconditionality does not appear to be accurate.

41. Although both the Clinton and Reagan administrations broadly pushed for weaker conditionality policy, in individual cases—including the Asian financial crisis country cases for Clinton and Grenada and Pakistan for Reagan—these administrations were believed to have pushed for stricter conditionality.

42. Lipson (1986), 229. The United States also opposed certain high-profile cases under the Reagan administration, most notably the 1981 India EFF program. This was the "largest single transaction in the history of the Fund" to date, and the United States initially opposed it and then abstained from the vote, rather than block the program. James (1996), 333.

43. Joseph Kahn, "Treasury secretary offers a new vision for the IMF: Less long-term lending and more candor," *New York Times*, December 15, 1999, C3. Other U.S. government, academic, and media leaders—including the *New York Times*, the IFIAC Commission, and the Joint Economic Committee of the U.S. Congress—rallied around the Clinton administration's proposal that the Fund restrict its lending to short-term emergency financing, rather than longer-term developmental loans focused on poverty reduction and economic growth, which make up the bulk of its current activities. The IFIAC Commission advocated this unanimously (3 of 59) "A focused role for the IMF," *New York Times*, December 20, 1999, A38).

44. For two comparisons of these literatures, see Moe (1991) and Barnett and Finnemore (1999).

45. Moe (1984), Niskanen (1971, 1975). Martin (2000) argues that states strategically delegate authority to the bureaucracy when it serves their interests.

46. Vaubel (1986, 1991, 1996).

47. This point is well stated in Barnett and Finnemore (1999), 707. See also Meyer and Rowan (1977), 341, 348, 354; Finnemore (1996), 330; Ascher (1983).

48. Finnemore (2000); Barnett and Finnemore (2004).

49. On "most likely" observations, see Eckstein (1975) and King et al. (1994), 209.

50. Paper from the Secretary, July 23, 1968, 23, IMF Archives; SM/68/141, August 29, 1968, IMF Archives.

51. SM/68/141, August 29, 1968, 1–2, IMF Archives.

52. SM/68/141, August 29, 1968, 5, IMF Archives.

53. Ibid., 4. They note that this ceiling on domestic bank credit will not be effective if the government has wide access to foreign credit markets; a ceiling on domestic bank credit will not limit public expansion in this case, and a separate ceiling, e.g., on the fiscal deficit, may be necessary.

54. EBM/78/82, June 5, 1978, 16–17, IMF Archives.

55. Interview 4 with author, February 2000.

56. IMF (2001), cited in Goldstein (2000), 86.

57. Barnett and Finnemore (1999), 707; see also Finnemore (2000); Barnett and Finnemore (2004).

58. For example, Dell (1981), 31. Guitián (1981, 15) wrote that binding conditions through the 1970s continued to be broad, concerned not only with the expansion of domestic credit, management of net international reserve, and avoidance of exchange restrictions, but also reliance on bank credit and foreign borrowing.

59. Spitzer (1969), 492.

60. As John Woodley wrote, "Comparisons have been made frequently among countries within a given area but comparisons among areas are made, if at all, on a completely informal basis." He continues, "While a common legal practice has been developed for stand-by arrangements, the economic policy prescriptions have varied quite widely" (draft memo from Woodley, April 16, 1963, IMF Archives). In a later memo debating general policy and restrictions concerning the use of binding conditions in the first credit tranche, the head of the Western Hemisphere Area Department, Jorge Del Canto, wrote, "Over the past seven years, *principally in the operation of my Department*, the policy of requiring legally binding conditions limiting the availability of resources under stand-by arrangements has evolved." Memo from Jorge Del Canto, December 2, 1963, IMF Archives, emphasis added.

61. For instance, Irving Friedman, one staff member, requested including a new conditions—that there be no new restrictions on new payments and transfers and no multiple currency practices—be included as a standard binding condition for Article VIII countries. Memo from Irving Friedman, May 31, 1962, IMF Archives. Also see memo from Herbert Zassenhaus for the files, August 9, 1963, IMF Archives, which concerns the inclusion of a foreign debt repayment ceiling in the Indonesian 1963 stand-by.

62. Memo, November 21, 1963, IMF Archives.

63. Ibid.

64. Memo from Jorge Del Canto, December 2, 1963, IMF Archives.

65. Memo from Mr. Wai, November 26, 1963, IMF Archives.

66. Memo, February 28, 1964, IMF Archives.

67. Fund staff documents that detail conditions include SM/68/128, Suppl. 2, August 12, 1968, IMF Archives, which lists arrangements and their binding conditions individually; SM/66/128, July 23, 1968, IMF Archives.

68. Haiti 1760 file. EBS/59/82, September 18, 1959, IMF Archives.

69. Haiti 1760 file. EBS/66/218, Suppl. 1, September 21, 1966, IMF Archives.

70. The Western Hemisphere Division covers Latin American and Caribbean countries.

71. On the four basic requirements, see Chapter 3. Most post-1990 arrangements sampled also required binding conditions stipulating balance of payments conditions and relating to the country's relations with the Fund.

72. Memo from Robichek to Brand, February 17, 1960, IMF Archives.

73. Ibid. The one very interesting point is that in this memo, the only two cases discussed regarding parallel credits are Haiti and Peru, which just happen to be the two cases where the prior notice clauses originated. The linked arrangement for Haiti began in March 1959, while the prior notice clause started in 1958. For Peru, the prior notice clause started in 1954, and so did parallel stabilization credits from the U.S. Treasury.

74. Quoted from Memo from James G. Evans Jr., September 12, 1960, IMF Archives. Venezuela quotes are from EBS/60/32, March 29, 1960, IMF Archives; Spain quotes are from EBS/59/50, Suppl. 1, July 15, 1959, IMF Archives.

75. Argentina 1760 file. EBS/58/76, Suppl. 2, December 18, 1958, IMF Archives.

76. Memo from Joseph Gold, April 12, 1963, IMF Archives.

77. Ibid., p. 4.

78. Draft memo, "Policy on stand-by arrangements," December 19, 1967, 4–5, IMF Archives.

79. Ibid.

80. Memo from Jorge Del Canto, December 2, 1963, 3, IMF Archives.

81. SM/66/14, January 24, 1966, 21, IMF Archives.

82. Memo from John R. Woodley, April 16, 1963, 4, IMF Archives.

CHAPTER FIVE

1. For a comprehensive review of the literature on the determinants of foreign aid, see Neumayer (2003, 20–29).

2. See Chapter 2, n38.

3. See Chapter 2, n39.

4. See, e.g., Kahler (1990).

5. Kahler (1990), 104.

6. Boughton (2001), 564.

7. Boughton (2001, 565–66) cites the sharp words of Donald Syvrud, then the alternate ED for the United States, who stated, in reaction to a 1981 stand-by arrangement for Grenada, that "while Executive Directors talk a great deal about the need for adjustment and financing to go hand in hand, in practice he saw more and more financing and less and less adjustment." The United States took action in 1981, "withholding support for that small arrangement . . . [and] abstaining from very large requests from India and Pakistan on similar grounds." Minutes, EBM/81/79, May 11, 1981, 5, cited in Boughton (2001), 566.

8. Boughton (2001), 560–61, quotes from France and the UK at the annual meeting in Belgrade in 1979.

9. Boughton (2001), 565.

10. Clyde H. Farnsworth, "U.S. proposals hearten IMF and World Bank," *New York Times*, May 16, 1987, D1.

11. Krueger (1993), 80–81.

12. Ibid., 98.

13. Ibid., 99–100.

14. Kahler (1990), 105.

15. Williamson (1982).

16. Boughton (2001), 563.

17. Williamson (1982), 48–52.

18. E-mail from Miles Kahler, April or May 2003.

19. Krueger (1993), 39.

20. Ibid., 42; Sewell and Contee (1985), 104.

21. Krueger (1993), 40.

22. AID, *Congressional Presentation FY1985* (Washington, DC, 1985), 4, cited in Contee and Sewell, 106. On the rhetoric to support reform, see Krueger (1993, 91); Krueger (1993, 95) on Treasury Secretary James Baker's address to the IMF–World Bank meetings; and Nicolas Brady's announcement of Brady Plan.

23. Sewell and Contee (1985), 105; Herbst (1992), 12–13.

24. Sewell and Contee (1985), 106; see also Krueger (1993, 41), who notes that "when, in the aftermath of the early 1980s debt crisis, worldwide attention centered on the overall economic policy framework of developing countries, USAID was unable to plan an effective role, having lost its capacities for macroeconomic analysis."

25. General Accounting Office, *AID's assistance to Jamaica* (Washington, DC: GAO, April 19, 1983, 8), cited in Sewell and Contee (1985), 102.

26. Sewell and Contee (1985), 97–98.

27. Radelet (2003), 5.

28. Aid has also served certain domestic political interests. For instance, Congress has included various restrictions in foreign aid appropriation bills in order to influence the administration of aid. For instance, "tied aid," which "requires that foreign aid funds be spent on goods and services" from the United States, accounted for 82% of U.S. bilateral aid in 1976 and 57% in 1985–1986 (Krueger 1993, 56–57). See Krueger (1993), 60, table 4–7, for various metrics of increasing congressional restrictions of U.S. aid.

29. Sewell and Contee (1985), 103.

30. Nelson with Eglinton (1992).

31. Quoted in Nelson with Eglinton (1992), 15–16. For an empirical study of whether bilateral and multilateral aid is actually more likely to be given to countries with "good governance," see Neumayer (2003).

32. Radelet (2003), 5.

33. In fact at one point, the U.S. Congress passed an amendment to the appropriations bill that explicitly tried to delink U.S. aid from Fund conditionality and its requirements, which suggests (again) that changes in Fund conditionality did not reflect U.S. (or at least Congress') preferences for its own aid policy. Sewell and Contee (1985), 107, n19.

34. Krueger (1993), 55–56.
35. Boughton (2001), 1046–47.
36. Ibid.
37. Nancy Dunne and Lionel Barber, "IMF silent on resignation," *Financial Times*, March 21, 1987, 2: Boughton (2001, 1047, n125) clarifies that "Finch also cited pressure from French and German officials in his memoirs," which remain unpublished.
38. Finch (1988), 126.
39. Clyde H. Farnsworth, "$327 million loan set for Egypt by IMF," *New York Times*, May 16, 1987, 37.
40. Finch (1988), 127.
41. Farnsworth, "$327 million loan."
42. Krueger (1993), 100.
43. Finch (1988), 127.
44. Farnsworth, "$327 million loan."
45. Krueger (1993).
46. John Barham, "IMF likely to approve standby for Argentina," *Financial Times* (London), July 2, 1991, 5.
47. Finch (1989), 13.
48. Ibid., 13, 19.
49. Stone (2002), 18.
50. Stone (2002, 57) uses foreign aid as his indicator of international influence.
51. Ibid., 119–20.
52. Stone (2002, 124), citing *New York Times*, March 27, 1993, I, 1.
53. Stone (2002, 124), citing *New York Times*, April 10, 1993, I, 5.
54. Fishlow (1986), 44, 75.
55. Stallings (1987), 83.
56. Killick (1997, 90–91) writes, "However, at a time of high demand and rapid expansion, it was soon decided that America should provide Europe with critical goods in short supply rather than with money, grants or credits."
57. Ibid., 102.
58. Ibid., 96.
59. World Bank data do not include certain categories of Fund lending to developing countries in their multilateral PPG external debt data. In order to remedy this problem, I have added IMF purchases to the multilateral PPG disbursement data.
60. Country group labels are taken from the OECD. In OECD DAC language, the series is "total official net" which "represents the total net disbursements by the official sector at large to the recipient country" to all developing countries, specifically Part I and Part II developing countries. It includes the concessional official development assistance and the nonconcessional other official financing. Organisation for Economic Co-operation and Development (2000).
61. The DAC flow data from EC/EU countries "cover the fifteen countries that were members in 1998."

62. United States Agency for International Development (1998). This variable equals U.S. military aid plus U.S. economic aid plus the amount pledged from the Economic Stabilization Fund plus the larger of the quantity of Export-Import Bank loans or loans listed under "Other Loans" in the above-mentioned publication, all divided by the amount of the Fund loan agreement in that year. All numbers are in current millions of U.S. dollars but are normalized by the division. The source for the Exchange Stabilization Fund (ESF) is Henning (1999). The ESF and the Fund loan amounts were not necessarily drawn upon or fully drawn down.

63. Kapur (2001, 27) offers an opposing interpretation that the "less the size of foreign aid programs of major shareholders, the less the agency of the IMF" and the more the influence of powerful states over the Fund. He views foreign aid and multilateral financing as substitutes. My argument and evidence suggest that they are complements.

64. World Development Indicators, supplemented with World Bank annual report and archive values.

65. These proxies are used because they fit the logic of the supplementary financier argument: U.S. or creditor state influence is expected to be related to the relative amount of financing given to a particular borrowing country. Other scholars have chosen alternative proxies to test U.S. or powerful state influence—for instance, the country's IMF quote (Stone 2002, 57); Stone also uses various measures of U.S. aid, which is similar to the U.S. influence measure used here (Stone 2002, 248), or to a country's United Nations voting record in relation to the United States' United Nations voting record (Thacker 1999, 52–55).

66. Quotes from Vaubel (1996), 195; see also Vaubel (1986, 1991).

67. Data from 1952 to 1970 are derived from Vaubel (1991), 223. Data from 1971 and 1995 are presented in Boughton (2001, 1051), and were obtained through correspondence with the author.

68. Vaubel uses both staff size and average salaries as proxies for bureaucratic power and autonomy. However, staff and year are almost perfectly correlated, suggesting that this is a flawed proxy (see below).

69. Vaubel (1996), 195.

70. Boughton (2001).

71. Vreeland (2001); Conway (1994).

72. This is language describing the Fund's ESAF, revamped in 1999 to be the Poverty Reduction and Growth Facility.

73. Polak (1999); Guitián (1981), 24.

74. World Bank (2000).

75. For instance, Polak (1994, 8) contends that the Fund's changing "clientele" led "the Fund in the 1970s [to begin] to tailor its credit facilities to the specific needs of developing countries." Kapur (2001) argues that the shift in clientele reduced the risk to creditor countries of pushing for increases in conditionality.

76. World Bank (2000). GNP per capita is constant in 1995 U.S. dollars.

77. Vreeland (2001) is concerned with borrower demand for Fund programs. He argues that governments with more veto players (which also tend to be more democratic by his measure) are more likely to enter Fund programs because they need conditionality to help them overcome domestic opposition and enact their preferred policies. If we accept that Fund conditionality is variable, an extension to this argument is that democracies may demand higher conditionality programs than authoritarian governments with fewer veto players.

78. Marshall and Jaggers (2000). The Polity IV score for the borrowing countries in the first year of their Fund loan arrangement.

79. SM/66/14, January 24, 1966, 1–2, IMF Archives.

80. For example, Meltzer (1998).

81. World Bank (2000).

82. King (1989), 163.

83. Ibid.

84. In Chapters 5 and 7, I use the Lagged Y, whereas in Chapter 6 I use a linear time trend to control for unexplained over-time change. This choice is discussed more in Chapter 6.

85. On poisson and negative binomial distribution models, see King (1989), 48–53; Greene (1990), 707–9; King (1998).

86. For a clear discussion, see Long (1997), chap. 8. For the models in Table 5.2 (as well later tables that have a positive count dependent variable), I first ran the model using a Poisson distribution regression model and then tested whether the Poisson distribution was appropriate using a goodness-of-fit test in Stata, "poisgof." Poisgof is a function in Stata that tests whether or not the Poisson regression model is appropriate. When the test is significant, it indicates that the Poisson model is not appropriate and that the negative binomial model may be preferable. No models in Table 5.2 had significant "poisgof" results. StataCorp (1999), 25.

87. Certain economic data, including reserves, is only available after 1970.

88. On log likelihood ratio tests, see King (1989), 87–92. The mean log likelihood ratio allows you to compare across nested models with different Ns.

89. Kahler (1990) discussed how the United States had influenced appointments of Fund upper management; De Gregorio et al. (1999, 82) also discuss the relationship between the U.S. Treasury and management.

90. On the Paris Club, see Reiffel (1985).

91. Boughton (2001), 1010–13; Finch (1989), 12.

92. Finch (1989, 12–13) describes that by the 1970s, the Paris Club creditors still demanded a Fund program to reschedule debts, but they "were no longer willing to wait for policies that would keep the use of IMF resources temporary, and pressured mounted on the IMF to act on inadequate programs."

93. Letter from Per Jacobbson, June 5, 1959, IMF Archives.

94. "Brazil to ask aid direct from U.S.," *New York Times*, June 11, 1959, 15.

95. "Extract from a letter by Mr. S., dated Rio de Janeiro 5.6.1959," June 5, 1959, IMF Archives.

96. EBM/61/55, page 7, May 17, 1961, IMF Archives.

97. Memo from Jorge Del Canto, November 3, 1961, "Summary of Brazil's Financial Arrangements with the Fund," IMF Archives.

98. Memo from Jorge Del Canto to the Managing Director and Deputy Managing Director, November 3, 1961, IMF Archives.

99. Memo from Jorge Del Canto, November 3, 1961, IMF Archives.

100. Cardoso and Dornbusch (1989), 299.

101. Coes (1995), 12.

102. Smith (2002), 169; Cardoso and Fishlow (1990, 273).

103. Cardoso and Fishlow (1990), 2:273.

104. See Marshall et al. (1983), 277; Coes (1995), 3, 13.

105. Memo for the files, Frank Southard Jr., "U.S. attitudes on Brazil," June 5, 1964, IMF Archives.

106. Memo from Jorge Del Canto, October 14, 1964, IMF Archives.

107. Burns (1980), 503.

108. Burns (1980), 504. On the 1984 Hague Club agreement, which repudiated many of Brazil's outstanding official arrears and restructured existing debt, see Odell (1979), 261–62, and Bitterman (1973), 124–25.

109. Memo for the files by Frank Southard Jr., November 20, 1964, IMF Archives.

110. Ibid.

111. Ibid.

112. Ibid, emphasis in original.

113. Memo from Jorge Del Canto, December 9, 1964, IMF Archives.

114. Marshall et al. (1983), 300.

115. *O Estado de Sao Paulo*. "Help given to Brazil is an office to other countries," December 8, 1964, 7 (translated), IMF Archives.

116. Memo from William B. Dale, December 17, 1964, IMF Archives.

117. The liabilities include PL 40 and "Agencia para Desenvolvimento Internacional." See EBS/64/210, Suppl. 2, Brazil Stand-by Arrangement, January 13, 1965, 11–12, IMF Archives.

118. Memo from Jorge Del Canto, December 30, 1964, IMF Archives.

119. EBM/65/3, January 13, 1965, 8, IMF Archives.

120. Ibid., 10–11.

121. Ibid., 14–15.

122. Ibid., 9.

123. Memo, February 16, 1966, IMF Archives.

124. EBM/65/3, January 13, 1965, 11–12, IMF Archives.

CHAPTER SIX

Parts of this chapter have been previously published as Erica R. Gould, "Money talks: Supplementary financiers and International Monetary Fund conditionality," *International Organization* 57:551–86, © the IO Foundation. Reprinted with the permission of Cambridge University Press.

1. It is useful to distinguish between the three because each has a different interest in providing financing, and hence different preferences over the design of Fund conditionality programs. As a result, states, private financial institutions, and multilateral organizations try to influence the Fund's activities in systematically different ways.

2. For Wellons (1987), banks act according to state interests. For Oatley (2002) and Broz and Hawes (2003), states act according to banks' interests.

3. For a concurrent perspective from someone who worked at the Fund, Citibank, and First Boston Corporation, see Friedman (1983), 120–21. Although this profit motive may seem obvious, others have argued that PFIs' loans and investments reflect their country's political interests, rather than a profit motive. See, e.g., Feis (1974); Krasner (1999); Wellons (1987).

4. Their own attempts to impose conditionality were not successful; see, e.g., Gersovitz (1985), 72.

5. Alternatively, scholars have considered the signing of a Fund conditionality agreement itself as a "signal" of a country's type or commitment to reform. See, e.g., Marchesi and Thomas (1999) and Dhonte (1997). According to this account, private financial institutions may be less interested in influencing the contents of a Fund agreement and more reliant on the Fund's expertise. Some interesting empirical research lends support for the idea that Fund programs—regardless of design—decrease the probability of loan default. See, e.g., Easton and Rockerbie (1999).

6. Boot and Kanatas (1995); Cohen and Sachs (1986); Diwan (1990).

7. Boot and Kanatas (1995), 364.

8. Claessens and Diwan (1990), 21.

9. See Lipson (1985) on the different incentives of small and large banks.

10. Olson (1971).

11. Lipson (1981, 1985); see also Aggarwal (1987).

12. North and Weingast (1989), 806.

13. Oatley (2002); Broz and Hawes (2003).

14. Oatley (2002), 10.

15. Broz and Hawes (2003).

16. Broz and Hawes (2003) depict this causal story with more force than does Oatley (2002). However, they simply provide evidence that commercial banks appear to influence Congressional votes on IMF quota increases, and then replicate Oatley's finding that commercial bank indebtedness is positively related to the size of the Fund loan with a larger sample. No evidence of this circuitous mechanism of influence is provided.

17. Fishlow (1986), 42–43, table 1. His estimates of European net assets are from the UK, France, Germany, and the Netherlands. "Changes in the stock of assets before 1914 approximate flows of foreign investment."

18. Fishlow (1986), 70.

19. Fishlow (1986, 53–55) argues that their investment were often more explicitly political than UK investing.

20. Ibid., 48.

21. Ibid., 38.

22. Simon (1968), 23.

23. Jenks (1963), 426.

24. Fishlow (1986), 44, 75.

25. Ibid., 44, 75.

26. Pauly (1997), 53; James (1996), 21. Pauly (1997), 53, writes, "Unlike the IMF, the League had no funds of its own and with intergovernmental lending frowned on in principle, any significant external financing had to come from the private capital markets."

27. Fishlow (1986), 72–73.

28. Ibid., 44.

29. Ibid., 78.

30. Ibid., 81–82.

31. See Cohen with Basagni (1981), 23, table 1.14.

32. Letter from A. Mohammed, April 2, 1983; IMF Official Interfund Message from J. B. Zulu, May 3, 1983; IMF Official Cable from Masihur Rahman, July 1, 1983; IMF Official Interfund Message from J. B. Zulu, July 1, 1983. IMF Archives.

33. Press release 92/27, March 31, 1992; EBS/92/46, Suppl. 1, April 13, 1992.

34. In addition, data problems make this an unwieldy metric. Financing data are generally not available before 1970. Post-1970 private financing data continue to be spotty.

35. And in fact there is basically no relationship between the two. The presence of bank-friendly conditions and the proportion of aggregate net flows that come from private sources (portfolio flows plus debt flows) is only correlated at 0.02.

36. Hardy (1982), 4–5; OECD (1981), tables 12, 13; World Bank (1997), 72–78; Frank (1970), 27.

37. Lipson (1985); Aggarwal (1987).

38. Thacker (1999). Kapur (2001) offers a more nuanced version of this argument.

39. See Chapter 5 for a complete description of this and other variables.

40. Data from 1952 to 1970 are derived from Vaubel (1991), 223. Data from 1971 and 1995 are presented in Boughton (2001, 1051) and were obtained through correspondence with the author.

41. Vaubel (1996), 195.

42. World Bank (2000).

43. Ibid. GNP per capita is constant in 1995 U.S. dollars.

44. The Polity IV score for the borrowing countries in the first year of their Fund loan arrangement.

45. Vreeland (2001) is concerned with borrower demand for Fund programs. He argues that governments with more veto players (which also tend to be more democratic by his measure) are more likely to enter Fund programs because they need conditionality to help them overcome domestic opposition and enact their preferred policies. If we accept that Fund conditionality is variable, an extension to this argument is that democracies may demand higher conditionality programs than authoritarian governments with fewer veto players.

46. SM/66/14, January 24, 1966, 1–2, IMF Archives.

47. World Bank (2000).

48. For example, Meltzer (1998).

49. The data set is not a traditional "rectangular" cross-sectional, time-series panel data set, which includes observations for each cross-sectional unit during each unit of time; therefore, the analysis does not use typical panel data techniques (e.g., Beck and Katz 1995).

50. Efforts to impute the missing data (e.g., via *Amelia*)—the preferred way to deal with missing data problems—have been unsuccessful.

51. Long (1997), 49.

52. Stone (2002) reports similar results that powerful states push for weaker Fund treatment of borrowers.

53. I also tried a specification with only the reserves-to-imports ratio omitted, but Model 3's specification was a better fit by all three metrics.

54. Jackman (2001), 15. The null model predicts that 100% of the cases are equal to 1 if more than 50% of the cases are equal to 1, and predicts 100% of the cases are equal to 0 if less than 50% of the cases are equal to 1. As a result, it correctly predicts the largest of the actual distribution of Y.

55. Lipson (1985), 202.

56. EBM/99/64, June 14, 1999, IMF Archives. On the external arrears policy, see de Vries (1976), 2:214–15; see also 1:531–32. This decision was first revised in 1980 (see EBS/80/190, reprinted in Boughton 2001, 531–32), then in 1983 (see EBS/83/58, reprinted in Boughton 2001, 532–33).

57. Boughton (2001), 477, 498–99. See also Polak (1991), 15.

58. EBD 3153–(70/95), October 26, 1970, reprinted in de Vries (1976), 2:214–15. See also de Vries (1976), 1:531–32. This decision was first revised in 1980; see EBS/80/190, August 27, 1980, reprinted in Boughton (2001), 531–32.

59. EBS/83/58, April 6, 1983, 36–37, reprinted in Boughton (2001), 532–33.

60. Boughton (2001), 477. See also Polak (1991), 15.

61. EBM/89/61, May 23, 1989 reprinted in Boughton (2001), 533–35. It stated that the "Fund's policy of nontoleration of arrears to official creditors remains unchanged."

62. Boughton (2001), 498–99.

63. The influence of private actors has arguably continued to increase in recent years, as portfolio investment has increased relative to the bank financing of the 1980s. Clearly the Fund staff and Executive Board perceive a continued influence of PFIs. Two more formal revisions of the Fund's arrears policy were passed in 1998 and 1999, both intended to reduce PFI influence further. The 1998 decision extended the 1989 policy of sanctioned lending into private arrears to nonbank private creditors (e.g., bondholders) and nonsovereign arrears. The 1999 decision relaxed the criteria when the Fund could lend into private arrears in order to prevent "creditors—particularly bondholders—[from exercising] a de facto veto over Fund lending." EBM/99/64, June 14, 1999, reprinted in IMF (1999d), 5.

64. The private influence variable is positively correlated with a time period dummy coded 1 if the program began in 1983 to 1989, and 0 otherwise. However, the significance of the private influence variable is not reducible to the time period. I reran Models 1 through 3 using the time period dummy instead of the private influence variable, and it was not significant in any of the specifications.

65. EBM/99/64, June 14, 1999 reprinted in IMF (1999d).

66. Boughton (2001), 304.

67. Most notably, Kraft (1984); see also Boughton (2001).

68. Kraft (1984), 1. Both Lipson (1986, 229) and Boughton (2001, 299) discuss these negotiations as a turning point in the Fund's relationship with commercial banks.

69. The banks represented at this meeting included Bank of America, Bank of Montreal, Bank of Tokyo, Bankers Trust, Chase, Chemical, Citibank, Deutsche Bank, Lloyds, Manufacturers Hanover, Morgan, Société Générale, and Swiss Bank Corporation. Another meeting on November 21 in London also included Paribas. The Fund's EFF loan was eventually $3.75 billion. Kraft (1984), 48.

70. Boughton (2001), 307.

71. Lipson (1986), 229.

72. Kraft (1984), 9; Aggarwal (1987), 336–44.

73. Boughton (2001), 308; Aggarwal (1987), 342.

74. EBS/82/208, Suppl. 3, December 21, 1982, 2, IMF Archives.

75. EBS/82/208, Suppl. 4, December 30, 1982, IMF Archives.

76. Bleakley (1978), 50; Celâsun and Rodrik (1989), 3:639.

77. World Bank (2000). This is the total amount of private, public, or publicly guaranteed debt commitments in that year, divided by the total amount of public or publicly guaranteed debt commitments in that year (private or official). Because of lack of availability of data, this ratio omits private nonguaranteed debt.

78. Celâsun and Rodrik (1989), 3:638.

79. Ibid., 630–31.

80. Memo from Woodward, September 20, 1977; Briefing Paper, September 1977, IMF Archives.

81. Bleakley (1978), 48.

82. Ibid., 50.

83. Celâsun and Rodrik (1989), 3:754. Swiss Bank Corporation dropped out of the coordinating committee midway through; thus it ended up being a group of seven banks; see Bleakley (1978), 58.

84. Memo from L. A. Whittome, November 16, 1977, IMF Archives.

85. Emphasis added. Memo from L. A. Whittome, November 9, 1977, IMF Archives.

86. Emphasis added. Memo for the files, November 10, 1977, IMF Archives; memo for the files, November 16, 1977, IMF Archives.

87. Memo from U. Baumgartner, December 9, 1977, IMF Archives.

88. EBM/78/65, April 24, 1978, IMF Archives.

89. EBS/78/154, Suppl. 4, April 25, 1978, 7, IMF Archives.

90. Memo from L. A. Whittome, November 20, 1977, IMF Archives.

91. EBM/78/151, September 20, 1978, IMF Archives.

92. Memo from L. A. Whittome, November 3, 1978, IMF Archives; memo for the files from L. A. Whittome, December 6, 1978, IMF Archives.

93. Memo from L. A. Whittome, December 1978, IMF Archives.

94. Memo from A. C. Woodward, March 30, 1979, 3, IMF Archives. In 1978 PPG debt disbursements from commercial banks only totaled US$305.7 million, whereas in 1979 PPG debt disbursements from commercial banks totaled US$3 billion. World Bank (1999).

95. Celâsun and Rodrik (1989), 3:757; memo for the files, February 16, 1979, IMF Archives; memo for the files, February 22, 1979, IMF Archives.

96. Turkey—Staff Visit Under Stand-by Arrangement, April 20, 1979, 8, IMF Archives.

97. Celâsun and Rodrik (1989), 3:755, n1.

98. World Bank (2000).

CHAPTER SEVEN

1. World Bank (2000). These percentages are IDA PPG debt disbursements and IBRD PPG debt disbursements divided by multilateral PPG debt disbursements. The multilateral PPG series excludes most IMF disbursements, which makes this an appropriate metric of *supplementary* (to the Fund's loan) multilateral financing.

2. There are ample reasons to believe that multilateral organizations actions are not perfectly controlled by states. For a few different takes, see Chapter 5; and Upton (2000), 39–45; Barnett and Finnemore (1999); Nielson and Tierney (2003).

3. For the language of their purposes as stated in their respective Articles of Agreement, see Shihata (2000), 772–75, and Appendix 2. By contrast, others have suggested that World Bank staff are rewarded for granting loans and thus their interest is in lending as much as possible; hence, they are interested simply in loan pushing. See, e.g., Treakle (1998), 20, quoted in Upton (2000), 23. Others interpret the organizational culture differently. For instance, Miller-Adams (1997, 8) argues

that certain informal rules define the Bank's organizational culture and its receptivity to change, including "the Bank's insistence that its work is apolitical and its belief in technical approaches to development." Ascher (1983) considers the World Bank staff's professional identities—as development specialists—as the defining attribute of the World Bank's organizational culture. Still others have argued that the World Bank represents U.S interests and ideology and uses certain institutional mechanisms to maintain organizational conformity. See Wade (1996), esp. 31–35; Wade (2002).

4. On these two separate missions and their subsequent evolution, see Polak (1994), Krueger (1997), and Shihata (2000, chap. 31).

5. Krueger (1997), 8; in fact, development was only "an incidental purpose of the Fund," according to Shihata (2000, 776).

6. Kapur et al. (1997), 2.

7. Shihata (1991), 10. The IFC was created in 1952 and provides financing to public enterprises. The IDA was created in 1960, the ICSIP in 1966, and the MIGA in 1988.

8. Shihata (1991), 14.

9. Kapur et al. (1997), 5–6. Finnemore (1996, chap. 4) argues that poverty alleviation was not an integral part of mainstream understanding of "development" before the 1970s and that the World Bank (and its president in the late 1960s and early 1970s, Robert McNamara) was a key agent in popularizing the idea that development also involved poverty alleviation (not just GNP growth and infrastructure building).

10. For an extended discussion of their similarities and differences, see Polak (1994) and Krueger (1997).

11. Shihata (1991), 25; see also table in Kapur et al. (1997), 6.

12. Kapur et al. (1997), 8. However, this expansion in sector-specific development specialists was, according to Kapur et al., "not just a demand-driven phenomenon. It was facilitated by the growing availability of field-seasoned sector specialists previously employed by the colonial regimes of Asia and Africa."

13. Ibid., 457, table 9–1; see also Stern (1983), 102.

14. Ibid., 42.

15. Shihata (1991), 26; Stern (1983).

16. Kapur et al. (1997), 29.

17. Ibid., 534.

18. Ibid., 455.

19. Krueger (1997), 17.

20. Polak (1994), 21.

21. Krueger (1997), 13. On the regional development banks, see White (1972).

22. The bureaucratic proxy is meant to test the bureaucratic argument articulated by Roland Vaubel and others that the Fund bureaucrats are trying to "maximize their budget, their staff and their independence" and that Fund conditionality is a mechanism to pursue those interests. This variable was also used in the quantitative

analyses of Chapters 5 and 6. A more detailed discussion of this variable is available in these chapters. Vaubel (1996), 195; see also Vaubel (1986, 1991).

23. Data on debt disbursements and reserves to imports are only available after 1970.

24. On Poisson and negative binomial distribution models, see King (1989), 48–53; Greene (1990), 707–9.

25. For Model 2, the p value equals 0.249; for Model 3, the p value equals 0.124.

26. Boughton (2001).

27. See discussion in Chapters 5 and 6.

28. On log likelihood ratio tests, see King (1989), 87–92. The mean log likelihood ratio allows you to compare across nested models with different Ns.

29. Negative binomial distribution regression analyses are used, not Poisson, because of Poisson's more restrictive assumptions.

30. Polak (1994), 4–5; see also the "appropriate specialization" of the two institutions specified in a 1949 Fund memo. Shihata (2000), 780.

31. de Vries (1985), 3:611, quoted in Polak (1994), 5; see also Boughton (2001), 997; Shihata (2000), 780–81.

32. Shihata (2000), 782.

33. Polak (1994), 8–9; Krueger (1997).

34. Polak (1994), 10.

35. Ibid., 26–27.

36. "Fund-bank collaboration—Developments in 1985," IMF Board document SM/86/40, February 25, 1986, 19, cited in Polak (1994), 26.

37. Polak (1991), 7.

38. Minutes of EBM/85/141, September 13, 1985, 36–39, quoted in Boughton (2001), 647.

39. Boughton (2001), 652.

40. Polak (1994), 28–29; Boughton (2001), 649–52. World Bank programs, by contrast, are not similarly influenced by the Fund staff and Board in such a formal, institutionalized manner.

41. According to Polak (1991, 7), the ESAF is "'more ambitious' in terms of both magnitude and timing" than the SAF.

42. See Schadler et al. (1995, 29–31) and Boughton (2001, 685) regarding the role of ESAF in "catalyzing" official flows, including from the African Development Bank and the European Economic Community.

43. Boughton (2001), 700.

44. Polak (1994), 37; see also Clyde H. Farnsworth, "World Bank and IMF in a conflict over roles," *New York Times*, February 28, 1989, D1.

45. Farnsworth, "World Bank and IMF"; see text of Concordat on Fund-Bank Collaboration (SM/89/54, Rev. 1, March 31, 1989), reprinted in Boughton (2001), 1056–62.

46. Polak (1994), 13.

47. Letter from S. Shahid Husain to Richard Webb, October 2, 1992, 7, quoted in Kapur et al. (1997), 531.

48. For instance, the IFIAC (or Meltzer) Commission report and Larry Summers's comments when he was U.S. Treasury secretary mentioned in Chapters 1 and 4.

49. Boughton (2001), 1000.

50. Polak (1994), 14–15, 22.

51. Ibid., 17.

52. Lancaster (1997), 181–82.

53. Interview 4 with author, February 9, 2000.

54. Kapur et al. (1997, 521) include a table that reports the frequency of types of conditions in World Bank adjustment lending from 1980 to 1991 and gives a sense of World Bank policy preferences.

55. Kapur et al. (1997), 579–87; Boughton (2001), 673–79; Herbst (1993), esp. 27–37.

56. Martin (1993), 134; Roe and Schneider (1992), 16–17.

57. See, e.g., Nowak et al. (1999); Kapur et al. (1991).

58. For instance, Kapur et al. (1997, 584) state, "In Ghana, as it had in most of, at least non-Francophone, Sub-Saharan Africa, the World Bank had become the ringleader among aid donors. Its own credits were a minority fraction of total concessional transfers to the region, but they were the largest fraction, and the Bank was the influential pattern setter."

59. Boughton (2001), 701.

60. In a press release (no. 84/31, August 29, 1984, in the IMF Archives), the IMF states explicitly, "The current economic and financial program . . . has been formulated in cooperation with the World Bank."

61. IMF lending is not considered aid and is thus not included in these numbers. As a result, these numbers are a good reflection of official supplementary financing. Government of Ghana (1984), Annex Table 13, IMF Archives.

62. EBS/83/140, Suppl. 1, August 4, 1983, 2, IMF Archives.

63. IMF Press Release No. 87/36, November 9, 1987, IMF Archives.

64. Boughton (2001), 678.

65. EBM/88/165, November 9, 1988, 6–9, IMF Archives.

66. Ibid, 8.

67. EBS/88/207, Suppl. 2, November 14, 1988, IMF Archives.

68. Kapur et al. (1997), 794; Boughton (2001), 679; Martin (1993), 162–63; Roe and Schneider (1992), 117–18; on the implementation, see Brydon and Legge (1996), chap. 5.

69. Ghana Briefing Paper, November 13, 1995, IMF Archives.

70. Boughton (2001), 661.

71. Sobhan (1982), esp. chap. 7; Parkinson (1981).

72. Guhan (1997).

73. For an assessment of the effects of this program, see Bhattacharya (1995).

74. EBS/87/7, Suppl. 3, February 11, 1987, IMF Archives, 33.

75. Boughton (2001), 661–62, emphasis added. For the poverty alleviation program, see EBS/87/7, January 15, 1987, 44–45, IMF Archives.

CHAPTER EIGHT

1. Interview 16 with author, May 28, 2002.

2. Vreeland (2003) finds that Fund programs hurt growth and have negative distributional consequences.

3. See, e.g., Cortell and Peterson (2004), Alter (1998), Nielson and Tierney (2003).

APPENDICES

1. These labels and classifications correspond to those used by the International Monetary Fund. The Fund is organized in Area Departments, which are responsible for countries in their particular area. The Western Hemisphere includes Latin American and Caribbean countries.

2. The data set does not code preconditions, which are required before the program goes into effect. Preconditions are often agreed upon by the Fund staff and borrowing countries and often are a key element of conditionality, but they were not possible to code because they are not consistently mentioned in the actual agreement.

3. This is not a comprehensive list; it excludes the buffer stock financing facility and other facilities that were less important. Information was taken from a variety of sources, including Polak (1991); IMF (1990), 36; IMF (2000), 67.

4. "Tranches" equal 25% of quota. The term *first credit tranche* is somewhat misleading because actually the first 25% that a country draws is often called the gold or reserve tranche, if the country has paid 25% of its quota in gold and 75% in its home currency. The gold tranche is not subject to conditionality. IMF (1990), 36.

5. IMF (1990), 36.

6. Bird (1995), 59.

7. IMF (1990), 36; Polak (1991), 7.

Bibliography

Abbott, Kenneth W., and Duncan Snidal. 1998. Why states act through formal international organizations. *Journal of Conflict Resolution* 42: 3–32.

Adams, C., D. J. Mathieson, D. Schinasi, and B. Chadha. 1998. *International capital markets: Developments, prospects and key policy issues*. Washington, DC: International Monetary Fund.

Aggarwal, Vinod K. 1987. *International debt threat: Bargaining among creditors and debtors in the 1980s*. Berkeley: Institute for International Studies, University of California.

———. 1996. *Debt games: Strategic interaction in international debt rescheduling*. New York: Cambridge University Press.

Ahmed, Masood, Timothy Lane, and Marianne Schultze-Ghattas. 2001. Refocusing IMF conditionality. *Finance and Development* (December).

Alter, Karen J. 1998. Who are the masters of the treaty? European governments and the European Court of Justice. *International Organization* 52: 125.

Ascher, William. 1983. New development approaches and the adaptability of international agencies: The case of the World Bank. *International Organization* 37: 415–39.

Aufricht, Hans. 1964. *The International Monetary Fund: Legal bases, structure, functions*. London: Steven & Sonds.

Barnett, Michael N., and Martha Finnemore. 1999. The politics, power, and pathologies of international organizations. *International Organization* 53: 699–732.

———. 2004. *Rules for the world: International organizations in global politics*. New York: Cornell University Press.

Barro, Robert J., and Jong-Wha Lee. 2001. IMF programs: Who is chosen and what are the effects? Draft manuscript. November.

Beck, Nathaniel, and Jonathan N. Katz. 1995. Nuisance vs. substance: Specifying and estimating time-series-cross-sectional models. *Political Analysis* 6: 1–36.

Bhattacharya, Debapriya. 1995. Bangladesh's experience with the structural adjustment and enhanced structural adjustment facilities. In *Bangladesh strategies for development*, ed. Roy H. Grieve and M. Mozammel Huq, 63–70. Dhaka, Bangladesh: University Press Limited.

Bird, Graham. 1995. *IMF lending to developing countries: Issues and evidence*. New York: Routledge.

———. 1996. The International Monetary Fund and developing countries: A review of the evidence and policy options. *International Organization* 50: 477–511.

Bird, Graham, and Dale Rowlands. 1997. The catalytic effect of lending by international financial institutions. *World Economy* 20: 967–91.

Bitterman, Henry J. 1973. *The refunding of international debt*. Durham, NC: Duke University Press.

Bleakley, Fred T. 1978. The rush to rescue Turkey. *Institutional Investor*, international edition, November, 47–64.

Boot, Arnoud W. A., and George Kanatas. 1995. Rescheduling of sovereign debt: Forgiveness, precommitment and new money. *Journal of Money, Credit and Banking* 27: 363–77.

Boughton, James. 2001. *Silent revolution: The International Monetary Fund, 1979–1989*. Washington, DC: International Monetary Fund.

Broz, J. Lawrence, and Michael Hawes. 2003. Domestic politics of International Monetary Fund policy. Draft manuscript. September.

Brydon, Lynne, and Karen Legge. 1996. *Adjusting society: The World Bank, the IMF and Ghana*. London: I. B. Tauris.

Burns, E. Bradford. 1980. *A history of Brazil*. 2nd ed. New York: Columbia University Press.

Cardoso, Eliana A., and Rudiger Dornbusch. 1989. Brazilian debt: A requiem for muddling through. In *Debt, adjustment and recovery: Latin America's prospects for growth and development*, ed. Sebastian Edwards and Felipe Larraín, 294–318. Cambridge, MA: Basil Blackwell.

Cardoso, Eliana A., and Albert Fishlow. 1990. The macroeconomics of the Brazilian external debt. In *Developing country debt and economic performance*, ed. Jeffrey D. Sachs, 2:271–391. Chicago: University of Chicago Press.

Celâsun, Merih, and Dani Rodrik. 1989. Debt, adjustment, and growth: Turkey. In *Developing country debt and economic performance*, ed. Jeffrey D. Sachs, 3:615–808. Chicago: University of Chicago Press.

Chwieroth, Jeffrey M. 2003. Neoliberal norms and capital account liberalization in emerging markets: The role of domestic-level knowledge-based experts. Presented at the Annual Meeting of the American Political Science Association, Philadelphia, Pennsylvania, August 28–31.

Claessens, Stijn, and Ishac Diwan. 1990. Investment incentives: New money, debt relief, and the critical role of conditionality in the debt crisis. *World Bank Economic Review* 41: 21–41.

Clark, I. D. 1996. Should the IMF become more adaptive? IMF Working Paper WP/96/17.

Clark, Ian D. 1998. Inside the IMF: Comparisons with policy-making organizations in Canadian governments. *Canadian Public Administration* 39: 157–91.

Coes, Donald V. 1995. *Macroeconomic crises, policies, and growth in Brazil, 1964–90.* Washington, DC: World Bank.

Cohen, Benjamin J. 1983. Balance of payments financing: Evolution of a regime. In *International regimes*, ed. Stephen D. Krasner, 315–36. Ithaca, NY: Cornell University Press.

Cohen, Benjamin J., with Fabio Basagni. 1981. *Bank and the balance of payments: Private lending in the international adjustment process.* Montclair, NJ: Allanheld, Osmun.

Cohen, Daniel, and Jeffrey Sachs. 1986. Growth and external debt under risk of debt repudiation. *European Economic Review* 30: 529–60.

Conway, Patrick J. 1994. IMF lending programs: Participation and impact. *Journal of Development Economics* 45: 365–91.

Cortell, Andrew P., and Susan Peterson. 2004. Historical institutionalism and IO design: A synthetic approach to IO independence. Presented at the Conference on Theoretical Synthesis and the Study of International Organization, February 6–7.

Council on Foreign Relations. 1999. *Task Force report on safeguarding prosperity in a global financial system: The future international financial architecture.* Washington DC: Institute for International Economics.

Crawford, Vincent P. 1987. *International lending, long-term credit relationships, and dynamic contract theory.* Essays in International Finance 59. Princeton, NJ: Princeton University Press.

Crockett, Andrew. 1982. Issues in the use of Fund resources. *Finance and Development* (June).

De Gregorio, Jose, Barry Eichengreen, Takatoshi Ito, and Charles Wyplosz. 1999. *An independent and accountable IMF.* Geneva Reports on the World Economy 1. London: Cenre for Economic Policy Research.

de Vries, Margaret Garritsen. 1976. *The International Monetary Fund, 1966–1971: The system under stress.* 2 vols. Vol. 1, *Narrative.* Vol. 2, *Documents.* Washington, DC: International Monetary Fund.

———. 1985. *The International Monetary Fund, 1972–78: Cooperation on trial.* Vol. 1, *Narrative and analysis.* Washington, DC: International Monetary Fund.

———. 1986. *The IMF in a changing world, 1945–85.* Washington DC: International Monetary Fund.

Dell, Sidney. 1981. *On being grandmotherly: The evolution of IMF conditionality.* Essays in International Finance 144. Princeton, NJ: Princeton University Press.

Dhonte, Pierre. 1997. *Conditionality as an instrument of borrower credibility.* IMF Paper on Policy Analysis and Assessment 97/2. Washington, DC: International Monetary Fund.

Diwan, Ishac. 1990. Linking trade and external debt strategies. *Journal of International Economics* 29: 293–310.

Diwan, Ishac, and Dani Rodrik. 1992. *External debt, adjustment, and burden sharing: A unified framework*. Essays in International Finance 73. Princeton, NJ: Princeton University Press.

Dorfman, Paul M. 1994. *Credit at BankAmerica*. San Francisco: Bank of America.

Drake, Paul W., ed. 1994. *Money doctors, foreign debts, and economic reforms in Latin America from the 1890s to the present*. Wilmington, DE: Scholarly Resources.

Dreher, Axel, and Nathan Jensen. 2003. Independent actor or agent? An empirical analysis of the impact of U.S. interests on IMF conditions. Draft manuscript.

Easton, Stephen T., and Duane W. Rockerbie. 1999. Does IMF conditionality benefit lenders? *Weltwirtschaftliches Archiv* 135: 347–57.

Eckstein, Harry. 1975. Case study and theory in political science. In *Handbook of political science*, vol. 1, *Political science: Scope and theory*, ed. Fred I. Greenstein and Nelson W. Polsby. Reading, MA: Addison-Wesley.

Edwards, Martin S. 2000. Reevaluating the "catalytic" effect of IMF Programs. Columbia International Affairs Online. http://www.ciaonet.org/wps/edm01/edm01.html.

Eichengreen, Barry, and Richard Portes. 1989. Dealing with debt: The 1930s and 1980s. In *Dealing with the debt crisis: A World Bank symposium*, ed. I. Husain and I. Diwan, 69–86. Washington DC: World Bank.

Einhorn, Jessica P. 1979. Cooperation between public and private lenders to the Third World. *World Economy* 2: 229–41.

Faini, Riccardo, Jaime de Melo, Abdel Senhadji-Semlali, and Julie Stanton. 1991. Macro performance under adjustment lending. In *Restructuring economies in distress*, ed. Vinod Thomas, Ajay Chhibber, Mansoor Dailami, and Jaime de Melo, 222–42. New York: Oxford University Press.

Fearon, James D. 1997. Tying hands versus sinking costs. *Journal of Conflict Resolution* 41: 68–90.

Feis, Herbert. 1974. *Europe, the world's banker, 1870–1914: An account of European foreign investment and the connection of world finance with diplomacy before the war*. Clifton, NJ: Augustus M. Kelley.

Finch, C. David. 1988. Let the IMF be the IMF. *International Economy* 1: 126–28.

———. 1989. *The IMF: The record and prospect*. Essays in International Finance 175. Princeton, NJ: Princeton University Press.

Finnemore, Martha. 1996. *National interests in international society*. Ithaca, NY: Cornell University Press.

———. 2000. Expertise and bureaucratic power at the International Monetary Fund. Draft manuscript.

Fishlow, Albert. 1986. Lessons from the past: capital markets during the 19th century and the interwar period. In *The politics of international debt*, ed. Miles Kahler, 37–96. Ithaca, NY: Cornell University Press.

Frank, Charles R., Jr. 1970. *Debt and terms of aid.* Washington, DC: Overseas Development Council.

Friedman, Irving S. 1983. Private bank conditionality: Comparison with the IMF and the World Bank. In *IMF conditionality,* ed. John Williamson, 109–24. Washington, DC: Institute for International Economics.

Gersovitz, Mark. 1985. Banks' international lending decisions: What we know and the implications for future research. In *International debt and the developing countries,* ed. Gordon W. Smith and John T. Cuddington, 61–78. Washington, DC: World Bank.

Gold, Joseph. 1969. Use of Fund's resources. In *The International Monetary Fund: 1945–65,* ed. J. Keith Horsefield, 2:522–46. Washington, DC: International Monetary Fund.

Gold, Joseph. 1969b. *The reform of the Fund.* Pamphlet Series No. 12. Washington, DC: International Monetary Fund.

———. 1972. *Voting and decisions in the International Monetary Fund.* Washington, DC: International Monetary Fund.

———. 1978. *The second amendment of the Fund's Articles of Agreement.* Washington, DC: International Monetary Fund.

———. *Conditionality.* 1979. Washington, DC: International Monetary Fund.

———. 1982. *Order in international finance, the promotion of IMF stand-by arrangements, and the drafting of private loan agreements.* Washington, DC: International Monetary Fund.

Goldstein, Judith. 1996. International law and domestic institutions. *International Organizations* (Autumn): 541–64.

Goldstein, Morris. 2000. IMF structural conditionality: How much is too much? Institute for International Economics, April. Columbia International Affairs Online. http://iic.com/publications/wp/01 4.pdf.

Goreux, Louis M. 1989. The fund and the low-income countries. In Gwin and Feinberg, *International Monetary Fund in a multipolar world,* 141–64.

Gould, Erica R. 2003. Money talks: Supplementary financiers and International Monetary Fund conditionality. *International Organization* 573: 551–86.

Gourevitch, Peter. 1978. The second image reversed: The international sources of domestic politics. *International Organization* 32: 881–912.

Government of Ghana 1985 *Economic recovery programme, 1984–6.* Accra: The Government.

Greene, William H. 1990. *Econometric analysis.* New York: Macmillan.

Guhan, S. 1997. The World Bank's lending in South Asia. In Kapur et al., *World Bank,* 2:317–83.

Guitián, Manuel. 1975. *Fund conditionality: Evolution of principles and practices.* Pamphlet Series No. 38. Washington DC: International Monetary Fund.

———. 1981. *Fund conditionality: Evolution of principles and practices.* Washington, DC: International Monetary Fund.

Gupta, Sanjeev, Benedict Clements, Calvin McDonald, and Christian Schiller. 1998. *The IMF and the poor*. Washington DC: International Monetary Fund.

Hardy, Chandra S. 1982. *Rescheduling developing-country debts, 1956–1981: Lessons and recommendations*. Washington, DC: Overseas Development Council.

Henning, C. Randall. 1999. *The exchange stabilization fund: Slush money or war chest?* Washington, DC: Institute for International Economics.

Herbst, Jeffrey. 1992. *U.S. economic policy toward Africa*. New York: Council of Foreign Relations Press.

———. 1993. *The politics of reform in Ghana, 1982–1991*. Berkeley: University of California Press.

Hooke, A. W. 1982. *The International Monetary Fund: Its evolution, organization and activities*. Pamplet Series No. 37. Washington, DC: International Monetary Fund.

Horsefield, J. Keith, ed. 1969a. *The International Monetary Fund, 1945–65: Twenty years of international monetary cooperation*. Vol. 1. Washington, DC: International Monetary Fund.

———. 1969b. *The International Monetary Fund, 1945–65: Twenty years of international monetary cooperation*. Vol. 3. Washington, DC: International Monetary Fund.

Horsefield, J. Keith, and Gertrud Lovasy. 1969. Evolution of the Fund's policy on drawings. In *The International Monetary Fund, 1945–65: Twenty years of international monetary cooperation*, vol. 2, ed. J. Keith Horsefield, 381–427. Washington, DC: International Monetary Fund.

International Financial Institution Advisory Commission. 2000. Final report of the International Financial Institution Advisory Commission IFIAC or Meltzer Commission. http://www.house.gov/jec/imf/meltzer.htm.

International Monetary Fund (IMF). 1975. *Annual report of the Executive Board for the financial year ended April 30, 1975*. Washington, DC: International Monetary Fund.

———. 1978. *Annual report of the Executive Board for the financial year ended April 30, 1978*. Washington, DC: International Monetary Fund.

———. 1981a. *Annual report of the Executive Board for the financial year ended April 30, 1981*. Washington, DC: International Monetary Fund.

———. 1981b. *IMF survey*. February 9. Washington, DC: International Monetary Fund.

———. 1983. *Selected decisions of the International Monetary Fund and selected documents*. 10th issue. April 30. Washington, DC: International Monetary Fund.

———. 1987. *Annual report of the Executive Board for the financial year ended April 30, 1987*. Washington, DC: International Monetary Fund.

———. 1988. *Annual report of the Executive Board for the financial year ended April 30, 1988*. Washington, DC: International Monetary Fund.

————. 1989. *Annual report of the Executive Board for the financial year ended April 30,*
1989. Washington, DC: International Monetary Fund.

————. 1990. *Annual report of the Executive Board for the financial year ended April 30,*
1990. Washington, DC: International Monetary Fund.

————. 1999a. IMF expanding public access to archives. Press release 99/8. March
19. http://www.imf.org/external/np/sec/pr/1999/PR9908.HTM.

————. 1999b. *Annual report of the Executive Board for the financial year ended April 30,*
1999. Washington DC: International Monetary Fund.

————. 1999c. *External evaluation of IMF surveillance: Report by a group of indepen-*
dent experts. Washington, DC: International Monetary Fund.

————. 1999d. IMF policy on lending into arrears to private creditors. Policy
Development and Review and Legal Departments. http://www.international
monetaryfund.com/external/pubs/ft/privcred/index.htm.

————. 2000c. *Annual report of the Executive Board for the financial year ended April*
30, 2000. Washington, DC: International Monetary Fund.

————. 2000a. IMF board agrees to changes to fund financial facilities. Public
Information Notice 00/79. September 18.

————. 2000b. Streamlining structural conditionality. 18 September.
http:/www.imf.org/external/np/pdr/cond/2001/eng/091800.pdf.

————. 2001a. Structural conditionality in fund-supported programs. Prepared
by the Policy Development and Review Department. February 16.

————. 2001b. Conditionality in fund-supported programs—Overview.
February 20. Prepared by the Policy Development and Review Department.
http://www.imf.org/external/np/pdr/cond/2001/eng/overview/index.htm.

————. 2001c. How we lend: A fact sheet. http://www.imf.org/external/np/exr/
facts/howlend.htm.

. 2001d. Debt relief under the Heavily Indebted Poor Countries (HIPC)
initiative: A fact sheet. http://www.imf.org/external/np/hipc/hipc.htm.

————. 2002a. IMF Board discusses the real-time assessments of conditionality.
Public Information Notice 02/42. April 19. http://www.imf.org/external/np/
sec/pn/2002/pn0242.htm.

————. 2002b. IMF Executive Board approves new conditionality guidelines.
Press release 02/43. September 26. http://www.imf.org/external/np/sec/pr/
2002/pr0243.htm.

————. 2002c. *Annual report of the Executive Board for the financial year ended April 30,*
2002. Washington DC: International Monetary Fund.

Ivanova, Anna, Wolfgang Mayer, Alex Mourmouras, and George Anayiotas. 2003.
What determines the implementation of IMF-supported programs? IMF
Working Paper WP/03/8.

Jackman, Simon. 2001. Binary outcomes and proportions. Unpublished manuscript, Stanford University, Stanford, CA.

James, Harold. 1996. *International monetary cooperation since Bretton Woods*. Washington DC: International Monetary Fund.

JEC. IMF reform effort joined by Treasury press release by Joint Economic Committee and Vice Chairman Saxton. December 14, 1999.

Jenks, Leland Hamilton. 1963. *The migration of British capital to 1875*. London: Thomas Nelson and Sons.

Kahler, Miles. 1990. The United States and the International Monetary Fund: Declining influence or declining interest? In *The United States and multilateral institutions: Patterns of changing instrumentality and influence*, ed. Margaret P. Karns and Karen A. Mingst, 91–114. Boston: Unwin Hyman.

———. 1992. External influence, conditionality and the politics of adjustment. In *The politics of economic adjustment*, ed. Stephan Haggard and Robert R. Kaufman. Princeton, NJ: Princeton University Press.

———. 1995. *International institutions and the political economy of integration*. Washington, DC: Brookings Institution.

Kapstein, Ethan B. 1994. *Governing the global economy: International finance and the state*. Cambridge, MA: Harvard University Press.

Kapur, Devesh. 2001. Expansive agenda and weak instruments: Governance related conditionalities of international financial institutions. *Policy Reform* 4: 207–41.

Kapur, Devesh, John P. Lewis, and Richard Webb. 1997. *The World Bank: Its first half century*. Vol. 1, *History*. Washington, DC: Brookings Institution.

Kapur, Ishan, Michael T. Hadjimichael, Paul Hilbers, Jerald Schiff, and Philippe Szymcsak. 1991. *Ghana: Adjustment and growth, 1983–91*. Washington, DC: International Monetary Fund.

Kenen, Peter B. 1989. The use of Fund credit. In Gwin and Feinberg, *International Monetary Fund in a multipolar world*, 69–92.

Keohane, Robert O. 1984. *After hegemony*. Princeton, NJ: Princeton University Press.

Keohane, Robert O., and Joseph Nye, eds. 1972. Transnational relations and world politics: An introduction. In *Transnational relations and world politics*, ix–xxix. Cambridge, MA: Harvard University Press.

———. 1977. *Power and interdependence: World politics in transition*. Boston: Little, Brown.

Killick, John. 1997. *The United States and European reconstruction, 1945–1960*. Edinburgh: Keele University Press.

Killick, Tony. 1992. *Continuity and change in IMF programme design, 1982–1992*. Overseas Development Institute.

King, Gary. 1989. *Unifying political methodology: The likelihood theory of statistical inference*. New York: Cambridge University Press.

———. 1998. Statistical models for political science event counts: Bias in conventional procedures and evidence for the exponential Poisson regression model. *American Journal of Political Science* 32: 838–63.

King, Gary, Robert O. Keohane, and Sidney Verba. 1994. *Designing social inquiry: Scientific inference in qualitative research*. Princeton, NJ: Princeton University Press.

Kraft, Joseph. 1984. *The Mexican rescue*. New York: Group of Thirty.

Krasner, Stephen D. 1993. Global communications and national power: Life on the Pareto frontier. *World Politics* 43: 336–66.

———. 1999. *Sovereignty: Organized hypocrisy*. Princeton, NJ: Princeton University Press.

Krueger, Anne O. 1993. *Economic policies at cross-purposes: The United States and developing countries*. Washington, DC: Brookings Institution.

———. 1997. Whither the World Bank and IMF? National Bureau of Economic Research Working Paper 6327.

Kuhn, Thomas S. 1996. *The structure of scientific revolutions*. 3rd ed. Chicago: University of Chicago Press.

Lancaster, Carol. 1997. The World Bank in Africa since 1980: The politics of structural adjustment. In Kapur et al., *World Bank*, 2: 161–89.

Lindert, Peter H., and Peter J. Morton. 1989. How sovereighn debt has worked. In *Developing country debt and economic performance*, vol. 1, *The international financial system*, ed. Jeffrey Sachs, 39–106. Chicago: University of Chicago Press.

Lipson, Charles. 1981. The international organization of Third World debt. *International Organization* 35: 603–31.

———. 1985. Bankers' dilemmas: Private cooperation in rescheduling sovereign debts. *World Politics* 38: 200–225.

———. 1986. International debt and international institutions. In *The politics of international debt*, ed. Miles Kahler, 219–43. Ithaca, NY: Cornell University Press.

Long, J. Scott. 1997. *Regression models for categorical and limited dependent variables*. Thousand Oaks, CA: Sage.

Luard, Evan. 1982. IMF loan conditions: The case for income redistribution. *Financial Times*, January 6.

Lumsdaine, David Halloran. 1993. *Moral vision in international politics: The foreign aid regime, 1949–89*. Princeton, NJ: Princeton University Press.

Marchesi, Silvia, and Jonathan P. Thomas. 1999. IMF conditionality as a screening device. *Economic Journal* 109: 111–25.

Marshall, Jorge, José Luis Mardones, and Isabell Marshall. 1983. IMF conditionality: The experiences of Argentina, Brazil and Chile. In Williamson, *IMF conditionality*.

Marshall, Monty G., and Keith Jaggers. 2000. *Polity IV Project: Political regime characteristics and transitions, 1800–1999*. Polity IV data set version 2000 <p4v2000>.

Martin, Lisa L. 2000. Agency and delegation in IMF conditionality. Unpublished manuscript.

Martin, Matthew. 1993. Neither phoenix nor Icarus: Negotiating economic reform in Ghana and Zambia, 1983–92. In *Hemmed in: Responses to Africa's economic decline*, ed. Thomas M. Callaghy and John Ravenhill, 130–79. New York: Columbia University Press.

Masson, Paul R., and Michael Mussa. 1995. *The role of the IMF: Financing and its interactions with adjustment and surveillance*. Washington, DC: International Monetary Fund.

McCauley, Robert N. 1986. IMF: Managed lending. In *World debt crisis: International lending on trial*, ed. Michael P. Claudon, 123–45. Cambridge, MA: Ballinger.

Mearsheimer, John J. 1994–1995. The false promise of international institutions. *International Security* 19: 5–49.

Meltzer, Allan H. 1998. Asian problems and the IMF. *CATO Journal* 17(3).

Meyer, John W., and Brian Rowan. 1977. Institutionalized organizations: Formal structure as myth and ceremony. *American Journal of Sociology* 83: 340–63.

Milgrom, Paul R., Douglass C. North, and Barry R. Weingast. 1990. The role of institutions in the revival of trade: The law merchant, private judges, and the champagne fairs. *Economics and Politics* 2: 1–26.

Miller-Adams, Michelle Beth. 1997. The World Bank in the 1990s: Understanding institutional change. PhD diss. Columbia University.

Milner, Helen. 1997. *Interests, institutions and information: Domestic politics and international relations*. Princeton, NJ: Princeton University Press.

Moe, Terry M. 1984. The new economics of organization. *American Journal of Political Science* (November): 739–77.

———. 1991. Politics and the theory of organizations. *Journal of Law, Economics and Organization* 7: 106–29.

Moggridge, Donald, ed. 1980. *The collected writing of John Maynard Keynes*. Vol. 25. Cambridge: Cambridge University Press.

Moravcsik, Andrew. 1997. Taking preferences seriously: A liberal theory of international politics. *International Organization* 51: 513–53.

Nelson, Joan, with Stephanie J. Eglinton. 1992. *Encouraging democracy: What role for conditioned aid?* Washington, DC: Overseas Development Council.

Neumayer, Eric. 2003. *The pattern of aid giving: The impact of good governance on development assistance*. London: Routledge.

Nielson, Daniel L., and Michael J. Tierney. 2003. Delegation to international organizations: Agency theory and World Bank environmental reform. *International Organization* 57: 241–76.

Niskanen, William A. 1971. *Bureaucracy and representative government*. Chicago: Rand McNally.

———. 1975. Bureaucrats and politicians. *Journal of Law and Economics* 18: 617–43.

North, Douglass, and Barry R. Weingast. 1989. Constitutions and credible commitments: The evolution of the institutions of public choice in 17th century England. *Journal of Economic History* 49: 803–32.

Nowak, Michael, Rifaat Basanti, Balazs Horvath, Kalpana Kochar, and Roohi Prem. 1999. Ghana, 1983–91. In *Adjustment for growth: The African experience*, ed. Michael T. Hadjimichael, Michael Nowak, Robert Sharer, Amor Tahari, and a staff team from the African Department. Washington, DC: International Monetary Fund.

Oatley, Thomas. 2002. Commercial banks and the International Monetary Fund: An empirical analysis. Draft manuscript. July.

Odell, John. 1979. The politics of debt relief: Official creditors and Brazil, Ghana and Chile. In *Debt and the less developed countries*, ed. Jonathan David Aronson, 253–28. Boulder, CO: Westview Press.

Olson, Mancur. 1971. Increasing the incentives for international cooperation. *International Organization*, 866–74.

Organization for Economic Cooperation and Development. 1981. *External debt of developing countries*. October. Paris: OECD.

———. 2000. *International Development Statistics*. CD-ROM. Paris: OECD.

Parkinson, Jack. 1981. The role of the World Bank. In *Aid and influence: The case of Bangladesh*, ed. Just Faaland, 147–64. Hong Kong: Macmillan.

Pauly, Louis. 1997. *Who elected the bankers? Surveillance and control in the world economy*. Ithaca, NY: Cornell University Press.

Polak, Jacques J. 1991. *The changing nature of IMF conditionality*. Essays in International Finance 184. Princeton, NJ: Princeton University Press.

———. 1994. *The World Bank and the IMF: A changing relationship*. Washington, DC: Brookings Institution.

———. Streamlining the financial structure of the International Monetary Fund. Essay in International Finance No. 216. Princeton, NJ: Princeton University.

Prezworski, Adam, and James Raymond Vreeland. 2000. The effect of IMF programs on economic growth. *Journal of Development Economics* 62: 385–421.

Radelet, Steven. 2003. *Challenging foreign aid: A policymaker's guide to the millennium challenge account*. Washington, DC: Center for Global Development.

Reiffel, Alexis. 1985. *The role of the Paris Club in managing debt problems*. Essays in International Finance 161. Princeton, NJ: Princeton University Press.

Risse, Thomas. 2002. Transnational actors and world politics. In *Handbook of International Relations*, ed. Walter Carlsnaes, Thomas Risse, and Beth Simmons, 255–74. London: Sage.

Rodrik, Dani. 1995. Why is there multilateral lending? National Bureau of Economic Research Working Paper 5160.

Roe, Alan, and Hartmut Schneider. 1992. *Adjustment and equity in Ghana*. Paris: Organisation for Economic Co-operation and Development.

Romer, Thomas, and Howard Rosenthal. 1978. Political resource allocation, controlled agendas, and the status quo. *Public Choice* 33:27–43.

Root, Hilton L. 1989. Tying the king's hands: Credible commitments and royal fiscal policy during the old regime. *Rationality and Society* 1: 240–58.

Rowlands, Dane. 2001. The response of other lenders to the IMF. *Review of International Economics* 9: 531–46.

Sachs, Jeffrey D. 1989. Strengthening IMF programs in highly indebted countries. In Gwin and Feinberg, *International Monetary Fund in a multipolar world*, 101–22.

Santaella, Julio. 1995. Four decades of fund arrangements: Macroeconomic stylized facts before the adjustment process. IMF Working Paper 74. Washington, DC: International Monetary Fund.

Schadler, Susan, Adam Bennett, Maria Carkovic, Louis Dicks-Mireaux, Mauro Mecagni, James H. J. Morsink, and Miguel Savastano. 1995. *IMF conditionality: Experience under stand-by and extended arrangements*. Part 1, *Key issues and findings*. Washington, DC: International Monetary Fund.

Schraeder, Peter J., Steven W. Hook, and Bruce Taylor. 1998. Clarifying the foreign aid puzzle: A comparison of American, Japanese, French and Swedish aid flows. *World Politics* 50: 294–323.

Sewell, John W., and Christine E. Contee. 1985. U.S. foreign aid in the 1980s: Reordering priorities. In *U.S. foreign policy and the Third World: Agenda 1985–86*, ed. John W. Sewell, Richard E. Feinberg, and Valeriana Kallab, 95–118. New Brunswick, NJ: Transaction Books.

Shanks, Cheryl, Harold K. Jacobson, and Jeffrey H. Kaplan. 1996. Inertia and change in the constellation of international governmental organizations, 1981–1992. *International Organization* 50: 593–627.

Shihata, Ibrahim F. I. 1991. *The World Bank in a changing world*. Dordrecht, The Netherlands: Martinus Nijhoff.

———. 2000. *The World Bank legal papers*. The Hague: Kluwer Law International.

Shultz, George. 1995. Economics in action: ideas, institutions, policies. *American Economic Review* 85: 1–8.

Simon, Matthew. 1968. The pattern of New British portfolio investment, 1865–1914. In *The export of capital from Britain, 1870–1914*, ed. A. R. Hall. London: Methuen.

Smith, Joseph. 2002. *A history of Brazil*. London: Pearson Education Limited.

Sobhan, Rehman. 1982. *The crisis of external dependence: The political economy of foreign aid to Bangladesh*. Dhaka, Bangladesh: University Press Limited.

Southard, Frank A. 1979. *The evolution of the International Monetary Fund*. Princeton, NJ: International Finance Section, Department of Economics, Princeton University.

Spiro, David E. 1999. *The hidden hand of American hegemony: Petrodollar recycling and international markets*. Ithaca, NY: Cornell University Press.

Spitzer, Emil G. 1969. Factors in stabilization programs. In *The International Monetary Fund, 1945–1965: Twenty years of international monetary cooperation*, ed. J. Keith Horsefield, 492–510. Washington DC: International Monetary Fund.

Stallings, Barbara. 1987. *Banker to the Third World: U.S. Portfolio Investment in Latin America, 1900–1986*. Berkeley: University of California Press.

StataCorp. 1999. *Stata Reference Manual, Release 6*. Vol. 3, *P-St*. College Station, TX: Stata Press.

Stern, Ernest. 1983. World Bank financing of structural adjustment. In Williamson, *IMF conditionality*, 87–107.

Stiglitz, Joseph. 2003. *Globalization and its discontents*. New York: W. W. Norton.

Stone, Randall W. 2002. *Lending credibility: The international monetary fund and the post-communist transition*. Princeton, NJ: Princeton University Press.

Thacker, Strom. 1999. The high politics of IMF lending. *World Politics* 52: 38–75.

Treakle, Kay. 1998. Accountability at the World Bank: What does it take? Presented at the meeting of the Latin American Studies Association, Chicago, Illinois, September 24–25.

United States Agency for International Development. 1998. *U.S. overseas loans and grants and assistance from international organizations*. Washington, DC: Office of Planning and Budgeting, Bureau for Program Policy and Coordination, Agency for International Development.

Vaubel, Roland. 1983. The moral hazard of IMF lending. *World Economy* 6: 291–304.

———. 1986. A public choice approach to international organization. *Public Choice* 51: 39–57.

———. 1991. The political economy of the International Monetary Fund: A public choice analysis. In *The political economy of international organizations: A public choice approach*, ed. Roland Vaubel and Thomas D. Willett, 204–44. Boulder, CO: Westview Press.

———. 1996. Bureaucracy at the IMF and the World Bank. *World Economy* 19: 195–210.

Vreeland, James Raymond. 2001. Institutional determinants of IMF programs. Draft manuscript. http://www.isanet.org/noarchive/Vreeland_ISA02.pdf.

———. 2002. The effect of IMF programs on labor. *World Development* 30: 121–39.

———. 2003. *The IMF and economic development*. New York: Cambridge University Press.

von Furstenberg<B8> George. 1987. The IMF as market-maker for official business between nations. In *The political morality of the IMF*, ed. Robert J. Meyers, 111–26. New Brunswick, NJ: Transaction Books.

Wade, Robert Hunter. 1996. Japan, the World Bank, and the art of paradigm maintenance: The East Asian miracle. *New Left Review* 217 (May–June): 3–37.

———. 2002. U.S. hegemony and the World Bank: The fight over people and ideas. *Review of International Political Economy* 9: 215–43.

Waltz, Kenneth N. Political structures. In *Neorealism and its critics*, ed. Robert O. Keohane, 70–97. New York: Columbia University Press.

Wellons, Philip A. 1985. International debt: The behavior of banks in a politicized environment. *International Organization* 39: 441–71.

———. 1987. *Passing the buck: Banks, governments and Third World debt*. Boston, MA: Harvard Business School Press.

White, John. 1972. *Regional development banks: The Asian, African and Inter-American development banks*. New York: Praeger.

Willett, Thomas D. 2001. Understanding the IMF debate. *Independent Review* 5: 593–610.

Williamson, John. 1982. *The lending policies of the International Monetary Fund*. Washington, DC: Institute for International Economics.

———. 1990. The design and implementation of IMF conditionality. In *The international monetary system and its reform: Papers prepared for the Group of Twenty-four by a United Nations project directed by Sidney Dell, 1979–1986*, ed. D. W. Jorgenson and J. Waelbroeck, 601–29. North-Holland, The Netherlands: Elsevier.

Williamson, John, ed. 1983. *IMF conditionality*. Washington, DC: Institute for International Economics.

World Bank. 1997. *Global development finance*. Vol. 1. Washington, DC: World Bank.

———. 1999. *Global development finance*. CD-ROM. Washington DC: World Bank.

———. 2000. *Global development finance*. CD-ROM. Washington DC: World Bank.

Index

Page numbers in italics refer to illustrative material.